W9-ADN-119

MONEY MISCHIEF

MILTON FRIEDMAN

MONEY MISCHIEF

Episodes in Monetary History

HARCOURT BRACE JOVANOVICH, PUBLISHERS
New York San Diego London

Some material previously appeared in *Free to Choose* by Milton Friedman and Rose D. Friedman, copyright © 1980, 1979 by Milton Friedman and Rose D. Friedman.
Some chapters first published by *Journal of Political Economy,* 1990; *Journal of Economic Perspectives,* 1990; and *Monetary and Economic Studies* (Bank of Japan), 1985.

Library of Congress Cataloging-in-Publication Data
Friedman, Milton, 1912–
Money mischief : episodes in monetary history/Milton Friedman.—1st ed.
p. cm.
Includes bibliographical references.
ISBN 0-15-162042-3
1. Monetary policy—History. 2. Monetary policy—United States—History. 3. Money—History. I. Title.
HG230.3.F75 1992
332.4′6—dc20 91-23760

Designed by G. B. D. Smith

Printed in the United States of America

First edition
ABCDE

To RDF
and more than half a century
of loving collaboration

Contents

Preface

In the course of decades of studying monetary phenomena, I have been impressed repeatedly with the ubiquitous and often unanticipated effects of what seem like trivial changes in monetary institutions.

In the Preface to an earlier book, *The Optimum Quantity of Money*, I wrote: "Monetary theory is like a Japanese garden. It has esthetic unity born of variety; an apparent simplicity that conceals a sophisticated reality; a surface view that dissolves in ever deeper perspectives. Both can be fully appreciated only if examined from many different angles, only if studied leisurely but in depth. Both have elements that can be enjoyed independently of the whole, yet attain their full realization only as part of the whole."

What is true of monetary theory is equally true of monetary history. Monetary structures that, looked at from one angle, appear bizarre, when looked at from another are seen to be simply unfamiliar versions of structures we take for granted, almost as if they were part of the natural world. The first chapter of this book is a striking example: stone money and gold money are so alike that they might be found in the same quarry.

That brief chapter having, I hope, intrigued you by illustrating how misleading surface appearances can be in dealing with monetary phenomena, the second chapter sketches the essence of monetary theory in simple terms. It provides a background for appreciating the historical episodes that follow.

The next three chapters tell true stories of seemingly minor events that have had far-reaching and utterly unanticipated effects in history. Chapter 3 tells how the seemingly innocent omission of one line from a coinage law came to have major effects on both the politics and the economics of the United States over several decades; chapter 4 provides the empirical underpinning for those conclusions; and chapter 5 tells how the work of two obscure Scottish chemists destroyed the presidential prospects of William Jennings Bryan, one of the most colorful and least appreciated politicians of the past century.

Following this examination of historical episodes, chapter 6 examines a great issue—bimetallism—that played a major role in the events described in chapters 3, 4, and 5. A recent writer describes bimetallism as giving rise "from the mid-1860s to the mid-1890s [to] the liveliest theoretical disputes among economists and the sharpest economic policy debates in the 'civilized world' " (Roccas 1987, p. 1).

Chapter 6 contends that conventional wisdom about the merits and demerits of bimetallism as a monetary system is seriously mistaken. My focus is narrow: it is to compare bimetallism as a system with monometallism. It is *not* to maintain that the United States, or any other country, should seek under current conditions to institute a bimetallic system. Indeed, to try to do so would conflict completely with my belief that (as Walter Bagehot pointed out more than a century ago) monetary systems, like Topsy, just grow. They are not and cannot be constructed *de novo*. However, as is exemplified by "the crime of 1873," they *can* be altered and affected in all sorts of ways by deliberate action—which is why an understanding of monetary phenomena is of much potential value.

These four chapters, then, all deal with many of the same events looked at from different points of view.

Chapter 7 returns to a particular historical episode, the effects of the U.S. silver purchase program of the 1930s. It seems fantastic that the decision of President Franklin Delano Roosevelt to placate a few senators from western states could have contributed in any detectable way to the triumph of communism in far-off China. Yet the sequence of events by which it did is clear and unmistakable, and the early steps were clear even to those contemporary observers who had some understanding of basic monetary theory.

The final step in the sequence to which the U.S. silver policy contributed was hyperinflation, an extreme form of a disease that has stricken many countries over the course of millennia. Chapter 8 examines the cause and cure of inflation, using recent and historical data for a number of countries to illustrate its central thesis: that inflation is always and everywhere a *monetary* phenomenon.

Chapter 9 is a testament to the role of chance on the effect of monetary changes. What happened in the United States—and it was completely outside the range of influence of the policymakers in Chile and Israel—had the effect of rendering one set of policymakers in one of those countries villains, while another set of policymakers in the other country became heroes.

Chapter 10 explores the probable consequences of the

monetary system that now prevails throughout the world—a system that has no historical precedent. Since the time when President Richard Nixon broke the final tenuous link between the dollar and gold in 1971, no major currency, for the first time in history, has any connection to a commodity. Every currency is now a fiat currency, resting solely on the authorization or sanction of the government.

The final chapter is an epilogue that draws a few general lessons from the episodes examined in the preceding chapters.

This book provides only small glimpses at the endlessly fascinating monetary gardens that have flourished and decayed in the course of the several millennia since the day when mankind found it useful to separate the act of sale from the act of purchase, when someone decided it was safe to sell a product or service for something—a something that he had no intention of consuming or employing in production but, rather, intended to use as a means to purchase another product or service to be consumed or employed in production. The "something" that connects the two transactions is called money, and it has taken innumerable physical forms—from stones to feathers to tobacco to shells to copper, silver, and gold to pieces of paper and entries in ledger books. Who knows what will be the future incarnations of money? Computer bytes?

Earlier versions of some chapters of this book have been published separately: chapters 3 and 4 in the *Journal of Political Economy* (December 1990), chapter 6 in the *Journal of Economic Perspectives* (Fall 1990), chapter 7 in the *Journal of Political Economy* (February 1992), and Chapter 10 in *Bank of Japan Monetary and Economic Studies*

(September 1985). I am indebted to these journals for permission to reprint. Chapter 8 is a revised version of chapter 9 of Milton Friedman and Rose D. Friedman, *Free to Choose* (1980). I have made minor revisions of the earlier versions in order to avoid repetition between chapters and to provide greater continuity, as well as to take account of reactions to the published versions.

I have benefited greatly from the knowledge and advice of many friends. Their contributions to particular chapters are acknowledged in the notes to those chapters. I owe a more general acknowledgment to Anna Jacobson Schwartz, my longtime collaborator on monetary studies, who has as always been there when I needed some help. Also, to my longtime secretary and assistant, Gloria Valentine, who did invaluable background research in basic sources, patiently typed, retyped, and revised version after version of the text, made sure that all references were accurate, and was available when I needed her in and out of office hours.

William Jovanovich, who contributed so much to two previous books by my wife and myself, *Free to Choose* and *The Tyranny of the Status Quo,* has made an important contribution to this one as well. And the readers and I owe a debt to Marianna Lee, who served as executive editor of this book, and to the skilled copy editor who corrected many an infelicity in the original text.

The Hoover Institution, under two successive directors, W. Glenn Campbell and John Raisian, provided ideal working arrangements, giving me maximum freedom to pursue my interests and providing nearly ideal resources for doing so.

I have left the best to last. I have been fortunate beyond my dreams in my mate, Rose Director Friedman, who has enriched my life since we first met fifty-nine years ago. I cannot count the many ways she has contributed to this book, as she has to all of my other personal and intellectual activities.

Milton Friedman
Stanford, California
July 5, 1991

MONEY MISCHIEF

CHAPTER I

The Island of Stone Money

From 1899 to 1919 the Caroline Islands, in Micronesia, were a German colony. The most westerly of the group is the island of Uap, or Yap, which at the time had a population of between five thousand and six thousand.

In 1903 an American anthropologist named William Henry Furness III spent several months on the island and wrote a fascinating book about the habits and customs of its inhabitants. He was particularly impressed by the islanders' monetary system, and accordingly he gave his book the title I have given this chapter: *The Island of Stone Money* (1910).

> [A]s their island yields no metal, they have had recourse to stone; stone, on which labour in fetching and fashioning has been expended, is as truly a representation of labour as the mined and minted coins of civilisation.
>
> Their medium of exchange they call *fei,* and it consists of large, solid, thick, stone wheels, ranging in diameter from a foot to twelve feet, having in the centre a hole varying in size with the diameter of the stone, wherein a pole may be inserted sufficiently large and strong to bear the weight and facilitate transportation. These stone "coins" [were made

from limestone found on an island some four hundred miles distant. They] were originally quarried and shaped [on that island and the product] brought to Uap by some venturesome native navigators, in canoes and on rafts. . . .

[A] noteworthy feature of this stone currency . . . is that it is not necessary for its owner to reduce it to possession. After concluding a bargain which involves the price of a *fei* too large to be conveniently moved, its new owner is quite content to accept the bare acknowledgment of ownership and without so much as a mark to indicate the exchange, the coin remains undisturbed on the former owner's premises.

My faithful old friend, Fatumak, assured me that there was in the village near-by a family whose wealth was unquestioned—acknowledged by every one—and yet no one, not even the family itself, had ever laid eye or hand on this wealth; it consisted of an enormous *fei,* whereof the size is known only by tradition; for the past two or three generations it had been, and at that very time it was lying at the bottom of the sea! Many years ago an ancestor of this family, on an expedition after *fei,* secured this remarkably large and exceedingly valuable stone, which was placed on a raft to be towed homeward. A violent storm arose, and the party, to save their lives, were obliged to cut the raft adrift, and the stone sank out of sight. When they reached home, they all testified that the *fei* was of magnificent proportions and of extraordinary quality, and that it was lost through no fault of the owner. Thereupon it was universally conceded in their simple faith that the mere accident of its loss overboard was too trifling to mention, and that a few hundred feet of water off shore ought not to affect its marketable value, since it was all chipped out in proper form. The purchasing power of that stone remains, therefore, as valid as if it were leaning visibly against the side of the owner's house. . . .

There are no wheeled vehicles on Uap and, conse-

> quently, no cart roads; but there have always been clearly defined paths communicating with the different settlements. When the German Government assumed the ownership of The Caroline Islands, after the purchase of them from Spain in 1898, many of these paths or highways were in bad condition, and the chiefs of the several districts were told that they must have them repaired and put in good order. The roughly dressed blocks of coral were, however, quite good enough for the bare feet of the natives; and many were the repetitions of the command, which still remained unheeded. At last it was decided to impose a fine for disobedience on the chiefs of the districts. In what shape was the fine to be levied? . . . At last, by a happy thought, the fine was exacted by sending a man to every *failu* and *pabai* throughout the disobedient districts, where he simply marked a certain number of the most valuable *fei* with a cross in black paint to show that the stones were claimed by the government. This instantly worked like a charm; the people, thus dolefully impoverished, turned to and repaired the highways to such good effect from one end of the island to the other, that they are now like park drives. Then the government dispatched its agents and erased the crosses. Presto! the fine was paid, the happy *failus* resumed possession of their capital stock, and rolled in wealth. (pp. 93, 96–100)

The ordinary reader's reaction, like my own, will be: "How silly. How can people be so illogical?" However, before we criticize too severely the innocent people of Yap, it is worth contemplating an episode in the United States to which the islanders might well have that same reaction. In 1932–33, the Bank of France feared that the United States was not going to stick to the gold standard at the traditional price of $20.67 an ounce of gold. Accordingly, the French bank asked the Federal Reserve Bank of New York to convert into gold a major part of the dollar assets that it had in the United States. To avoid the necessity of shipping the gold across the ocean, the Federal Reserve Bank was requested simply to store the gold on the Bank of France's account. In response, officials of the Federal Reserve Bank went to their gold vault, put in separate drawers the correct amount of gold ingots, and put a label, or mark, on those drawers indicating that the contents were the property of the French. For all it matters, the drawers could have been marked "with a cross in black paint," just as the Germans had marked the stones.

The result was headlines in the financial newspapers about "the loss of gold," the threat to the American financial system, and the like. U.S. gold reserves were down, French gold reserves up. The markets regarded the U.S. dollar as weaker, the French franc as stronger. The so-called drain of gold by France from the United States was one of the factors that ultimately led to the banking panic of 1933.

Is there really a difference between the Federal Reserve Bank's believing that it was in a weaker monetary position because of some marks on drawers in its basement and the Yap islanders' belief that they were poorer because of some marks on their stone money? Or between the Bank of France's belief that it was in a stronger monetary position because of some marks on drawers in a basement more than three thousand miles away and the Yap family's conviction that it was rich because of a stone under the water some hundred or so miles away? For that matter, how many of us have literal personal direct assurance of the existence of most of the items we regard as constituting our wealth? What we more likely have are entries in a bank account, property certified by pieces of paper called shares of stocks, and so on and on.

The Yap islanders regarded as a concrete manifestation of their wealth stones quarried and shaped on a distant island and brought to their own. For a century and more, the civilized world regarded as a concrete manifestation of its wealth a metal dug from deep in the ground, refined at great labor, transported great distances, and buried again in elaborate vaults deep in the ground. Is the one practice really more rational than the other?

What both examples—and numerous additional ones that could be listed—illustrate is how important appearance or illusion or "myth," given unquestioned belief, becomes in monetary matters. Our own money, the money we have grown up with, the system under which it is controlled, these appear "real" and "rational" to us. Yet the money of other countries often seems to us like paper or worthless metal, even when the purchasing power of individual units is high.

CHAPTER 2

The Mystery of Money

The term *money* has two very different meanings in popular discourse. We often speak of someone "making money," when we really mean that he or she is receiving an income. We do not mean that he or she has a printing press in the basement churning out greenbacked pieces of paper. In this use, money is a synonym for income or receipts; it refers to a flow, to income or receipts per week or per year. We also speak of someone's having money in his or her pocket or in a safe-deposit box or on deposit at a bank. In that use, money refers to an asset, a component of one's total wealth. Put differently, the first use refers to an item on a profit-and-loss statement, the second to an item on a balance sheet.

In this book I shall try to use the term *money* exclusively in the second sense, as referring to an item on a balance sheet. I say "try" because, with use of the term as a synonym for income or receipts so ubiquitous, I cannot guarantee that even I, who have been aware for decades of the importance of distinguishing between the two uses, will not occasionally slip and use the term in the first sense.

One reason why money is a mystery to so many is the

role of myth or fiction or convention. I started this book with the chapter on stone money precisely in order to illustrate that point. To make the same point in a way that is perhaps more relevant to the everyday experience of most of us, consider two rectangles of paper of about the same size. One rectangle is mostly green on the back side and has a picture of Abraham Lincoln on the front side, which also has the number 5 in each corner and contains some printing. One can exchange pieces of this paper for a certain quantity of food, clothing, or other goods. People willingly make such trades.

The second piece of paper, perhaps cut from a glossy magazine, may also have a picture, some numbers, and a bit of printing on its face. It may also be colored green on the back. Yet it is fit only for lighting the fire.

Whence the difference? The printing on the five-dollar bill gives no answer. It simply says, "FEDERAL RESERVE NOTE / THE UNITED STATES OF AMERICA / FIVE DOLLARS" and, in smaller print, "THIS NOTE IS LEGAL TENDER FOR ALL DEBTS, PUBLIC AND PRIVATE." Not very many years ago, the words "WILL PROMISE TO PAY" were included between "THE UNITED STATES OF AMERICA" and "FIVE DOLLARS." Did that mean the government would give you something tangible for the paper? No, it meant only that if you had gone to a Federal Reserve bank and asked a teller to redeem the promise, the teller would have given you five identical pieces of paper having the number 1 in place of the number 5 and George Washington's picture in place of Abraham Lincoln's. If you had then asked the teller to pay the $1.00 promised by one of these pieces of paper, he would have given you coins, which, if you had melted them down (despite its being illegal to do so), would have sold for less than $1.00 as metal. The present wording—no longer with a "promise to pay"—is at least more candid, if equally unrevealing.

The "legal tender" quality means that the government will accept the pieces of paper in discharge of debts and taxes due to itself and that the courts will regard them as discharging any debts stated in dollars. Why should they also be accepted by private persons in private transactions in exchange for goods and services?

The short answer—and the right answer—is that private persons accept these pieces of paper because they are confident that others will. The pieces of green paper have value because everybody thinks they have value. Everybody thinks they have value because in everybody's experience they have had value—as is equally true for the stone money of chapter 1. The United States could barely operate without a common and widely accepted medium of exchange (or at most a small number of such media); yet the existence of a common and widely accepted medium of exchange rests on a convention: our whole monetary system owes its existence to the mutual acceptance of what, from one point of view, is no more than a fiction.

That fiction is no fragile thing. On the contrary, the value of having a common money is so great that people will stick to the fiction even under extreme provocation. But neither is the fiction indestructible: the phrase "not worth a Continental" is a reminder of how the fiction was destroyed by the excessive amount of Continental currency the Continental Congress issued to finance the American Revolution.

The numerous inflations throughout history—whether the recent moderate inflations in the United States, Britain, and other advanced countries, or the very large recent inflations in South and Central American countries, or the hyperinflations after World Wars I and II, or the more ancient inflations going back to Roman times—have demonstrated the strength of the fiction and, indirectly, its usefulness. It takes very high rates of inflation—rates well up in double digits that persist for years—before people will stop using the money that is so obviously inflating. And when they do lose faith in the fiction, they do not revert to straight barter. No, they adopt substitute currencies. The substitute currencies in most inflations in history have been gold, silver, or copper specie, often, as during the American Revolution, in the form of coins of foreign countries. What's more, people may not abandon paper altogether: they may turn instead to paper money that has not been overissued.

Two particularly revealing examples are provided by the American Revolution, more than two centuries ago, and the Russian Revolution of 1918. The Continental currency was overissued. The result was that the promise of redemption in specie was not honored, and Continental currency came to be accepted only at the point of a gun. On the other hand, some of the original thirteen colonies issued their own paper money, which remained limited in amount, and this paper money continued to be used, along with coins of foreign countries. An even more striking example is that provided by the Russian Revolution of 1918, which was followed by a hyperinflation of far greater magnitude than the American revolutionary inflation. When, in 1924, the inflation was ended and a new currency established, one of the new chervonets rubles was exchanged for 50 billion old rubles! *These old rubles were the ones that had been issued by the new Soviet government.* There also still existed old czarist paper rubles. Since there was small prospect that a czar would return to redeem the promise printed on the czarist rubles, it is remarkable that they were still being accepted as substitute currency and had retained their purchasing power. They retained their value precisely because no new czarist rubles could be created, and hence the quantity available to circulate was fixed.

During the German hyperinflation after World War I, currencies of foreign countries served as a substitute currency. After World War II, the Allied occupational authorities exercised sufficiently rigid control over monetary matters, in the course of trying to enforce price and wage controls, that it was difficult to use foreign currency. Nonetheless, the pressure for a substitute currency was so great that cigarettes and cognac emerged as substitute currencies and attained an economic value far in excess of their value purely as goods to be consumed.

I personally experienced a remnant of the use of cigarettes as money in 1950, by which time monetary stability had been restored to Germany and the paper German mark was again the common medium of circulation. Driving from Paris, where I was spending a few months as a consultant to the U.S. agency administering the Marshall Plan, to Frankfurt, the newly established temporary capital of Germany and also the base of U.S. occupation authorities, I had to refill the gasoline tank of the "Quatre Chevaux" (a small Renault car) that I was driving. As it happened, I had no marks with me, because I was to get an allotment of them when I arrived in Frankfurt. But I did have dollars, French francs, and British pounds. The German *frau* who filled my tank would accept none of these in payment—that was illegal, she said. *"Haben sie keine wäre* ["Have you any goods"]?" was her next remark. We settled amicably when I gave her a carton of cigarettes (for which I had paid $1.00 at the Paris PX—remember, this was a long time ago) for gasoline that she valued at $4.00 at the official exchange rate for marks but that I could purchase at a U.S. PX for $1.00. As she viewed it, she got $4.00 worth of cigarettes in return for $4.00 worth of gasoline. As I viewed it, I got $1.00 worth of gasoline in return for $1.00 worth of cigarettes. And both of us were happy. But, as I used to ask my students, what became of the missing $3.00?

I should add that a few years earlier, before Ludwig Erhard's 1948 monetary reform—the first step in the remarkable postwar recovery of Germany—a carton of cigarettes would have been valued as the equivalent of a far larger number of marks than the number that, at the then official exchange rate, could have been purchased for $4.00. As currency, cigarettes were typically traded by the pack, or even the single cigarette, not by the carton—that would have been far too high a denomination for most purchases. Foreigners often expressed surprise that Germans were so addicted to American cigarettes that they would pay a fantastic price for them. The usual reply was: "Those aren't for smoking; they're for trading."

As the example of cigarettes (or cognac) suggests, an amazing variety of items have been used as money at one time or another. The word "pecuniary" comes from the Latin *pecus,* meaning "cattle," one of the many things that have been used as money. Others include salt, silk, furs, dried fish, tobacco, even feathers and, as we saw in chapter 1, stones. Beads and cowrie and other shells, such as the American Indians' wampum, have been the most widely used forms of primitive money. Metals—gold, silver, copper, iron, tin—have been the most widely used forms among advanced countries before the victory of paper and the bookkeeper's pen (although a temporary use of paper as money occurred in China more than a millennium ago).

What determines the particular item that will be used as money? We have no satisfactory general answer to that simple question. We do know that, however the habit of using one item or another as money arises, the habit takes on a life of its own and, like Topsy, just grows. As Walter Bagehot, a nineteenth-century editor of the English periodical *The Economist* puts it in his masterpiece, *Lombard Street:* "Credit is a power which may grow, but cannot be constructed" (1873, p. 69). Substitute "unit of account" or "money" for "credit" to translate that statement into the terms we have been using.

We can come closer to giving a reasonably general answer to a different, and basically more important, question: What determines the value in terms of goods and services of whatever item has come to be accepted as money?

When most money consisted of silver or gold or some other item that had a nonmonetary use, or of an enforceable promise to pay a specified amount of such an item, the "metallist" fallacy arose that "it is logically essential for money to consist of, or be 'covered' by, some commodity so that the logical source of the exchange value or purchasing power of money is the exchange value or purchasing power of that commodity, considered independently of its monetary role" (Schumpeter 1954, p. 288). The examples of the stone money of Yap, of cigarettes in Germany after World War II, and of paper money currently make clear that this "metallist" view is a fallacy. The usefulness of items for consumption or other nonmonetary purposes may have played a role in their acquiring the status of money (though the example of the stone money of Yap indicates that this has not always been the case). But once they acquired the status of money, other factors clearly affected their exchange value. The nonmonetary value of an item is never a fixed magnitude. The number of bushels of wheat or pairs of shoes or hours of labor that an ounce of gold can be exchanged for is not a constant fact. It depends on tastes and preferences and on relative quantities. The use of, say, gold as money tends to alter the quantity of gold available for other purposes and in that way to alter the amount of goods that an ounce of gold can be exchanged for. As we shall see in chapter 3, in which we analyze the effect of the demonetization of silver in the United States in 1873, the nonmonetary demand for an item used as money has an important effect on its monetary value, but, similarly, the monetary demand affects its nonmonetary value.

For present purposes, we can simplify our attempt to demystify money by concentrating on the monetary arrangement that, while historically a very special case, is currently the general rule: a pure paper money that has practically no value as a commodity in itself. Such an arrangement has been the general rule only since President Richard M. Nixon "closed the gold window" on August 15, 1971—that is, terminated the obligation that the United States had assumed at Bretton Woods to convert dollars held by foreign monetary authorities into gold at the fixed price of $35 an ounce.

Before 1971, every major currency from time immemorial had been linked directly or indirectly to a commodity. Occasional departures from a fixed link did occur but, generally, only at times of crisis. As Irving Fisher wrote in 1911, in evaluating past experience with such episodes: "Irredeemable paper money has almost invariably proved a curse to the country employing it" (1929, p. 131). As a result, such episodes were both expected to be and were temporary. The link was successively weakened, however, until it was finally eliminated by President Nixon's action. Since then, no major currency has had any link to a commodity. Central banks, including the U.S. Federal Reserve System, still carry an entry on their balance sheets for gold, valued at a fixed nominal price, but that is simply the smile of a vanished Cheshire cat.

What, then, determines how much one can buy with the greenbacked five-dollar paper bill we started with? As with every price, the determinant is supply and demand. But that only begs the question. For a full answer, we must ask: What determines the supply of money? And what determines the demand for money? And what, concretely, is "money"?

The abstract concept of money is clear: money is whatever is generally accepted in exchange for goods and services—accepted not as an object to be consumed but as an object that represents a temporary abode of purchasing power to be used for buying still other goods and services. The empirical counterpart of this abstract concept is far less clear. For centuries, when gold and silver were the major mediums of exchange, economists and others regarded only coins as money. Later they added bank notes redeemable on demand for gold or silver specie. Still later, a little over a century ago, they accepted bank deposits payable on demand and transferable by check. Currently, in the United States, a number of monetary aggregates are regularly compiled, each of which may be regarded as the empirical counterpart of money. These range from currency, the narrowest total, to the total of specified liquid assets, the aggregate designated "L" by the Federal Reserve.*

We can bypass this highly technical issue by considering a hypothetical world in which the only medium of circulation is paper money like our five-dollar bill. For consistency with the present situation, we shall assume that the number of dollars of such money in circulation is determined by a governmental monetary authority (in the United States, the Federal Reserve System).

The Supply of Money

Analysis of the supply of money, and in particular of changes in the supply of money, is simple in principle but extremely complex in practice, both in our hypothetical world and in the current real world. Simple in principle, because the supply of money is whatever the monetary authorities make it; complex in practice, because the decisions of the monetary authorities depend on numerous factors. These include the bureaucratic needs of the authorities, the personal beliefs and values of the persons in charge, current or presumed developments in the economy, the political pressures to which the authorities are subject, and so on in endless detail. Such is the situation that prevails today. Historically, of course, the situation was very different because the commitment to redeem government- or bank-issued money in specie meant that the physical conditions of production played a significant role. Later chapters explore the consequences of the commitment to redeem in considerable detail.

*For a full discussion of the definition of money, see Friedman and Schwartz (1970, part 1).

It's simple to state how the money supply is so centrally controlled. It's hard to believe. I have observed that noneconomists find it almost impossible to believe that twelve people out of nineteen—none of whom have been elected by the public—sitting around a table in a magnificent Greek temple on Constitution Avenue in Washington have the awesome legal power to double or to halve the total quantity of money in the country. How they use that power depends on all the complex pressures listed in the previous paragraph. But that does not alter the fact that they and they alone have the arbitrary power to determine the quantity of what economists call base or high-powered money—currency plus the deposits of banks at the Federal Reserve banks, or currency plus bank reserves. And the entire structure of liquid assets, including bank deposits, money-market funds, bonds, and so on, constitutes an inverted pyramid resting on the quantity of high-powered money at the apex and dependent on it.

Who are these nineteen people? They are seven members of the Board of Governors of the Federal Reserve System, appointed by the president of the United States for fourteen-year nonrenewable terms, and the presidents of the twelve Federal Reserve banks, appointed by their separate boards of directors, subject to the veto of the Board of Governors. These nineteen constitute the Open Market Committee of the Federal Reserve System, though only five of the bank presidents have a vote at any one time (in order to assure that the seven members of the central board have ultimate authority).

The exercise of this arbitrary power has sometimes been beneficial. However, in my view, it has more often been harmful. The Federal Reserve System, authorized by the Congress in 1913 and beginning operations in 1914, presided over the more than doubling of prices that occurred during and after World War I. Its overreaction produced the subsequent sharp depression of 1920–21. After a brief interval of relative stability in the 1920s, its actions significantly intensified and lengthened the great contraction of 1929–33. More recently, the Fed was responsible for the accelerating inflation of the 1970s—to cite just a few examples of how its powers have in fact been used.*

The Demand for Money

The Federal Reserve can determine the quantity of money—the number of dollars in the hands of the public. But what makes the public willing to hold just that amount, neither more nor less? For an answer, it is crucial to distinguish between the nominal quantity of money—the number of dollars—and the real quantity of money—the amount of goods and services that the nominal quantity will purchase. The Fed can determine the first; the public determines the second, via its demand for money.

*For a full discussion, see Friedman and Schwartz (1963).

A somewhat amusing example of the kind of petty personal concerns that can enter into the activities of such an august body is the renaming of the ruling body in Washington in 1935. The name was changed from "Federal Reserve Board" to "Board of Governors of the Federal Reserve System." Why substitute the more cumbersome name for the more compact? The reason was entirely considerations of prestige. In central bank history, the head of a central bank has been called the governor. That is the prestigious title. Before 1929, the heads of the twelve separate Federal Reserve banks were designated as governors, in line with the desire of the founders to have a truly regional, decentralized system. On the Federal Reserve Board, only the chairman was designated governor; the other six members were simply that—members of the Federal Reserve Board. As part of the Banking Act of 1935, the heads of the separate Federal Reserve banks were redesignated presidents, and the central body was renamed the Board of Governors of the Federal Reserve System so that each member of it could be a governor! Petty, but also a symbol of a real transfer of power from the separate banks to Washington.

There are many ways to express the real quantity of money. One particularly meaningful way is in terms of the flow of income to which the cash balances correspond. Consider an individual receiving an income of, say, \$20,000 a year. If that individual on the average holds \$2,000 in cash, his cash balances are the equivalent of one-tenth of a year's income, or 5.2 weeks of income: his cash balances give him command over the quantity of goods and services that he can buy with 5.2 weeks' income.

Income is a flow; it is measured as dollars per unit of time. The quantity of money is a stock, not in the sense of equity traded on an exchange but in the sense of a store of goods or inventory, by contrast with a flow. Nominal cash balances are measured as dollars at a point in time—\$2,000 at 4:00 P.M. on July 31, 1990. Real cash balances, as just defined, are measured in units of time, like 5.2 weeks; "dollars" do not enter in.*

It is natural for you, as a holder of money, to believe that what matters is the number of dollars you hold—your nominal cash balances. But that is only because you take dollar prices for granted, both the prices that determine your income and the prices of the things you buy. I believe that on reflection you will agree that what *really* matters is your real cash balances—what the nominal balances will buy. For example, if we expressed nominal magnitudes in cents instead of dollars, both nominal income and nominal

*The more usual practice is to define real cash balances by dividing nominal balances by a price index. The price index itself typically represents the estimated cost at various dates of a standard basket of goods (so many loaves of bread, pounds of butter, pairs of shoes, and so on, to encompass, for a consumer price index, the typical budget of a consumer). Under this definition, real cash balances have the dimension of the number of baskets of goods the nominal balances could purchase.

cash balances would be multiplied by 100, but real balances would be unaffected, and it would make no difference to anyone (except those who had to write down the larger numbers).

Similarly, try to conceive of every price, including those that determine your income, being multiplied by 100 overnight—or divided by 100—and, correspondingly, your cash balances, nominal debts, and nominal assets being simultaneously multiplied or divided by 100. Nothing would be really changed. Of course, that is not the way changes in the quantity of money or in prices generally come about, which is what raises all the difficulties in monetary analysis. But it is what happens when a government, typically during or after a major inflation, announces a so-called monetary reform that substitutes one monetary unit for another. It is what, for example, General Charles de Gaulle did in France on January 1, 1960, when he replaced the then franc with the *nouveau franc,* or new franc, by simply striking two zeros from all calculations in the old franc. In other words, 1 new franc equaled 100 old francs. De Gaulle made this change as part of an extensive monetary and fiscal reform that did have significant effects, though the mere change of units did not. However, the episode is another instance of how deeply embedded are public attitudes to money. For decades thereafter, many French residents continued to express prices and perform monetary calculations in old francs, striking off the final two zeros only when offered payment in *nouveau francs.*

When such alterations of monetary units are combined with superficial monetary and fiscal changes, as when Argentina in 1985 replaced the peseta with the austral, they have at most had highly temporary and minor effects, because they do not by themselves alter real magnitudes.

Given that it is the real quantity of money, not the nominal quantity, that matters, what determines whether people will want to hold cash balances averaging about five weeks' income—as in practice they have done in many countries over long periods of time—or only about three or four days' income—as they did, for example, in Chile in 1975?*

Two major forces determine how much cash people will want to hold: (1) the usefulness of cash balances as a temporary abode of purchasing power; (2) the cost of holding cash balances.

(1) *Usefulness.* Cash balances are useful as a means of enabling an individual to separate the act of purchase from the act of sale. In a world without money, transactions would have to take the form of barter. You have A to sell and want to acquire B. To do so you must find someone who has B to sell and wants A and must then make a mutually acceptable deal—what the textbooks dub "the double coincidence of barter." In a money economy, you can sell A for money, or generalized purchasing power, to anyone who wants A and has the purchasing power. You can in turn buy B for money from anyone who has B for sale, regardless of what the seller of B in turn wants to buy. This separation of the act of sale from the act of purchase is the fundamental productive function of money.

A related reason for holding money is as a reserve for future emergencies. Money is only one of many assets that can serve this function, but for some people at some times it may be the preferred asset.

*These illustrative numbers are chosen to correspond with the identification of money as currency and are realistic for currency. For broader aggregates, such as the U.S. M2, cash balance holdings are much larger. In the United States currently, they are about nine months of national income.

How useful money is for these purposes depends on many factors. For example, in an underdeveloped economy consisting of largely self-sufficient households, each producing mostly for its own consumption, monetary transactions are relatively unimportant. As such societies develop and the range of monetary transactions increases, cash balances rise much faster than income, so that real cash balances, expressed as weeks of income, increase. Such development generally occurs along with urbanization, which has much the same effect, because it means that a larger fraction of transactions are impersonal. Credit at the local grocery store is not likely to be as readily available to smooth over discrepancies between receipts and expenditures.

At the other extreme, in financially advanced and complex societies, such as the United States today, a wide array of assets is available that can serve as more or less convenient temporary abodes of purchasing power. These range from cash in pocket, to deposits in banks transferable by generally accepted check, to money-market funds, credit-card accounts, short-term securities, and so on, in bewildering variety. They reduce the demand for real cash balances narrowly defined, such as currency, but they may increase the demand for real cash balances more broadly defined by making temporary abodes of purchasing power useful in facilitating shifts between various assets and liabilities.*

(2) *Cost*. Cash balances are an asset and, as such, an alternative to other kinds of assets, ranging from other

*As it happens, for most of the post–World War II period these further effects have roughly balanced in the United States, so that M2, as currently defined, has ranged around nine months, mostly in response to changes in the cost of holding cash balances.

nominal assets, such as mortgages, savings accounts, short-term securities, and bonds, to physical assets, such as land, houses, machines, or inventories of goods, which may be owned either directly or indirectly, via equities, or common stocks. Accumulating an asset requires saving, that is, abstaining from consumption. Once the asset is accumulated, it may cost something to maintain, as with physical inventories, or it may yield a return in the form of a flow of income, such as interest on a mortgage or bond or dividends on stock.

As with cash balances, it is important to distinguish between the nominal return on an asset and the real return. For example, if you receive 10 cents per dollar on a bond when prices in general are rising by, say, 6 percent a year, the real yield is only 4 cents per dollar because you must reinvest 6 cents per dollar to have the same purchasing power invested at the end of the year as at the beginning.* The nominal yield is 10 percent, the real yield 4 percent. Similarly, if prices are falling, the real yield will exceed the nominal yield by the rate of the price drop.

What matters ultimately is the real, not the nominal, magnitudes. As a result, the nominal yield on assets such as bonds has tended to adjust *over long periods* in order to keep the real yield roughly the same. However, that has been very far from the case over short periods, because of the time it takes for people to adapt to changed circumstances.

For cash balances, one cost—the cost that has been stressed in monetary literature—is the interest return that is sacrificed by holding cash rather than "safe"

*In practice, the situation is more complex because of the need to allow for tax effects.

interest-earning assets, for example, the interest received per dollar of a U.S. Treasury bill as against the interest, if any, received per dollar of cash balances (zero for currency).

Another cost or return—and one less stressed, though often far more important—is the change in the real value of a dollar. If prices are rising at a rate of 6 percent a year, say, $1.00 will be able to buy only as much at the end of the year as 94 cents would have bought at the beginning. To keep the real value of your cash balances constant, you would have to hold balances of 6 percent more at the end of the year than at the beginning. On the average, it would cost you 6 cents for every dollar that you held during the year. Conversely, if prices were falling at the rate of 6 percent a year, you would in effect receive a return of 6 cents for every dollar you held during the year. Clearly, cash is a less attractive asset when prices are rising than when they are falling.

For a nominal asset, the nominal interest sacrificed and the change in purchasing power cannot be added for the reason already noted—that the nominal interest rate is affected by the rate of price change, and so already includes an allowance for it. For a real asset, the cost of holding a dollar has two parts: the loss (or gain) in purchasing power because of rising (or falling) prices, plus the real return sacrificed on the alternative asset.

Over long periods of time, real returns on various classes of assets do tend toward equality. But at any one point in time, real returns may vary widely for different classes of assets. Moreover, what people who acquire assets *expect* them to yield—the *ex ante* yield—may differ widely from what the holders do in fact receive—the *ex post* yield.

Figure 1 is a striking example. It plots over more than a hundred years the observed nominal yield each year on a collection of long-term securities, the actual *ex post* real yield year by year, and the average real yield for the century 1875–1975. The nominal yield is fairly stable for most of the period, while the *ex post* real yield fluctuates all over the graph. Clearly, the assets were not purchased in anticipation of such widely variable yields. Such assets are typically held for long periods, so that the *ex post* yield for a holder of these assets was actually much less variable than the year-by-year calculations show. Indeed, the relatively stable nominal yield implies that the holders of the securities expected, *on the average,* zero inflation. And, until World War II, they were right: the price level in the United States in 1939 was roughly the same as in 1839.

The lines on the graph gradually change character after World War II, as the public came to recognize that inflation was more than a passing phenomenon. The nominal

Figure 1

Nominal and Real Bond Interest Rate, Annually, 1875–1989

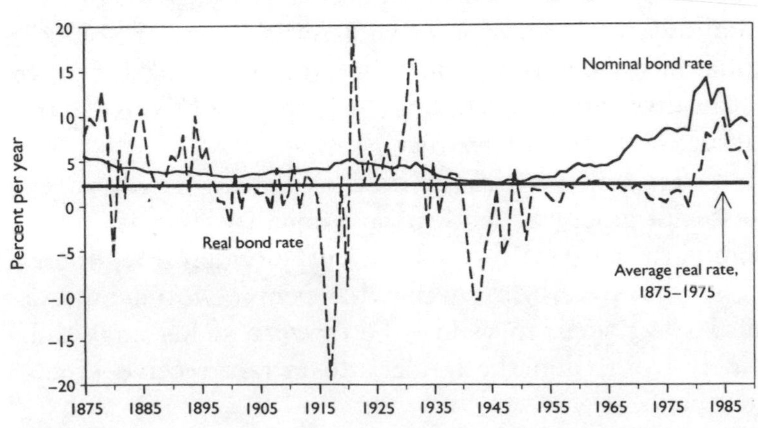

yield rose to incorporate that recognition, and the real yield became more stable, started rising toward the long-term average, and then overshot it in the 1980s.

Given the wide range of assets that are alternatives to holding money, it is a great simplification to speak of *the* cost of holding money. There is in fact a vector of costs, depending on the particular alternative considered. And that is still an oversimplification. Even for a single asset, there is a range of possible yields, both nominal and real. Uncertainty about the nominal yield of alternative assets is one reason for holding money—there is little uncertainty about its nominal yield. But there remains uncertainty about the real yield of money. Empirically, high rates of inflation tend to be more unstable than low rates of inflation. As a result, both the level and the instability of inflation discourage the holding of money. That is why during periods of high and uncertain inflation, as in Chile in 1975, real cash balances are reduced so low, even though that greatly increases the costs of transactions.

Reconciling Supply and Demand

We have come a long way from our initial simple question: what determines how much we can buy with the greenbacked five-dollar bill we started with? We are ready to return to that question by putting together the two blades of the monetary scissors, supply and demand.

In our hypothetical world in which paper money is the only medium of circulation, consider first a stationary situation in which the quantity of money has been constant for a long time, and so have other conditions. Individual members of the community are subject to enough uncertainty that they find cash balances useful to cope with unanticipated discrepancies between receipts and expenditures. But these uncertainties average out, so that the community as a whole wishes to hold as cash balances an amount equal to one-tenth of a year's income.

Under those circumstances, it is clear that the price level is determined by how much money there is—how many pieces of paper of various denominations. If the quantity of money had settled at half the assumed level, every dollar price would be halved; at double the assumed level, every price would be doubled. Relative prices would be unchanged.

This very hypothetical and unreal situation, from which we shall shortly depart, brings out sharply one special feature of money: its usefulness to the community as a whole does not depend on how much money there is. For almost all goods and services, the utility derived from them depends on their physical quantity, on the number of units. For money, it does not. Doubling or halving the number of dollars simply means that the numbers written on price tags are doubled or halved. When gold ruled the monetary roost, there was much talk about whether there would be enough gold to serve as monetary reserves. That was the wrong question. In principle, one ounce would be enough. It would not physically circulate, as most gold did not, but claims to it could be issued in any fractional denominations—for example, one-billionth of an ounce—that were convenient.

The reason it was the wrong question is that no important or interesting issues of monetary theory arise in the hypothetical situation of constant demand and supply. As David Hume wrote more than two centuries ago, "it is of no manner of consequence, with regard to the domestic happiness of a state, whether money be in a greater or less quantity" ([1742] 1804b, p. 305). As he also said, what matters is changes in the quantity of money and in the conditions of demand for money.

Let us suppose, then, that one day a helicopter flies over our hypothetical long-stationary community and drops additional money from the sky equal to the amount already in circulation—say, $2,000 per representative individual who earns $20,000 a year in income.* The money will, of course, be hastily collected by members of the community. Let us suppose further that everyone is convinced that the event is unique and will never be repeated.

To begin with, suppose further that each individual happens to pick up an amount of money equal to the amount he or she already holds, so that all find themselves with twice the cash balances they had before.

If everyone simply decided to hold on to the extra cash, nothing more would happen. Prices would remain what they were before, and individual incomes would remain at $20,000 per year. The community's cash balances would be 10.4 weeks' income instead of 5.2.

But people do not behave in that way. Nothing has occurred to make it more attractive for them to hold cash than it was before, given our assumption that everyone is convinced the helicopter miracle will not be repeated. (In the absence of that assumption, the appearance of the helicopter might increase the degree of uncertainty anticipated by the members of the community, which in turn might change the demand for real cash balances.)

Consider the representative individual who formerly held 5.2 weeks' income in cash and now holds 10.4 weeks'

*The helicopter example, and the rest of this section, is based on Friedman (1969, chap. 1).

income. He could have held 10.4 weeks' income before, if he had wanted to, by spending less than he received for a sufficiently long period. When he held 5.2 weeks' income in cash, he did not regard the gain from having $1.00 extra in cash balances as worth the sacrifice of consuming at the rate of $1.00 per year less for one year, or at the rate of 10 cents less per year for ten years. Why should he think it worth the sacrifice now, when he holds 10.4 weeks' income in cash? The assumption that he was in a position of stable equilibrium before means that he will now want to raise his consumption and reduce his cash balances until they are back at the former level. Only at that level is the sacrifice of consuming at a lower rate just balanced by the gain from holding correspondingly higher cash balances.

Note that the individual has two decisions to make:

1. To what level does he want to reduce his temporarily enlarged cash balances? Since the appearance of the helicopter did not change his real income or any other basic condition, we can answer unambiguously: to the former level.

2. How rapidly does he want to return to the former level? To this question we have no answer. The answer depends on characteristics of his preferences that are not reflected in the stationary equilibrium position.

We know only that each individual will seek to reduce his cash balances at some rate. He will do so by trying to spend more than he receives. However, one person's expenditure is another's receipt. The members of the community as a whole cannot spend more than the community as a whole receives. The sum of individual cash balances is equal to the amount of cash available to be held. Individuals as a whole cannot "spend" balances; they can only transfer them. One person can spend more than he receives only by inducing another to receive more than he spends. They are, in effect, playing a game of musical chairs.

It is easy to see what the final position will be. People's attempts to spend more than they receive will be frustrated, but in the process these attempts will bid up the nominal value of goods and services. The additional pieces of paper do not alter the basic conditions of the community. They make no additional productive capacity available. They alter no tastes. They alter neither the apparent nor the actual rates at which consumers wish to substitute one commodity for another or at which producers can substitute one commodity for another in production. Hence, the final equilibrium will be a nominal income of $40,000 per representative individual instead of $20,000, with precisely the same flow of real goods and services as before.

It is much harder to say anything about the transition. To begin with, some producers may be slow to adjust their prices and may produce more for the market at the expense of nonmarket uses of resources. Others may try to make spending exceed receipts by taking a vacation from production for the market. Hence, measured income at initial nominal prices may either rise or fall during the transition. Similarly, some prices may adjust more rapidly than others, so that relative prices and quantities will be affected. There might be overshooting and, as a result, a cyclical adjustment pattern. In short, without a much more detailed specification of reaction patterns, we can predict little about the transition. It might vary all the way from an instantaneous adjustment, with all prices doubling overnight, to a long-drawn-out adjustment, with many ups and downs in prices and output for the market.

We can now drop the assumption that each individual happened to pick up an amount of cash equal to the amount he had to begin with. Let the amount each individual picks up be purely a matter of chance. This will introduce initial distribution effects. During the transition, some people will consume more, others less. But the ultimate position will be the same.

The existence of initial distributional effects has, however, one substantive implication: the transition can no longer, even as a conceptual possibility, be instantaneous, since it involves more than a mere bidding up of prices. Let prices double overnight. The result will still be a disequilibrium position. Those individuals who have picked up more than their pro rata share of cash will now have larger real balances than they want to maintain. They will want to spend the excess, but over a period of time, not immediately. On the other hand, those individuals who have picked up less than their pro rata share will have lower real balances than they want to maintain. But they cannot restore their cash balances instantaneously, since their stream of receipts flows at a finite time rate.

This analysis carries over immediately from a change in the nominal quantity of cash to a once-and-for-all change in preferences with respect to cash. Let individuals on the average decide to hold half as much cash, and the ultimate result will be a doubling of the price level, a nominal income of $40,000 a year with the initial $2,000 of cash.

This simple example embodies most of the basic principles of monetary theory:

1. The central role of the distinction between the *nominal* and the *real* quantity of money.

2. The equally crucial role of the distinction between

the alternatives open to the individual and to the community as a whole.

3. The importance of attempts, as summarized in the distinction between *ex ante* and *ex post.* At the moment when the additional cash has been picked up, desired spending exceeds anticipated receipts (*ex ante*, spending exceeds receipts). *Ex post,* the two must be equal. But the *attempt* of individuals to spend more than they receive, even though doomed to be frustrated, has the effect of raising total nominal expenditures (and receipts).

Let us now complicate our example by supposing that the dropping of money, instead of being a unique, miraculous event, becomes a continuous process, which, perhaps after a lag, is fully anticipated by everyone. Money rains down from heaven at a rate that produces a steady increase in the quantity of money, let us say of 10 percent a year.

Individuals could respond to this steady monetary downpour as they ultimately did to the once-and-for-all doubling of the quantity of money, namely, by keeping their real balances unchanged. If they did this, and responded instantaneously and without friction, all the real magnitudes would remain unchanged. Prices would behave in precisely the same manner as the nominal money stock, rising from their initial level at the rate of 10 percent a year.

Again, while people could behave that way, they would not. Before the helicopter arrives, our representative individual could spend all his income and add nothing to his cash balances, yet the cash balances would remain equal to 5.2 weeks' income. They remained constant in real as well as nominal terms because prices were stable. Storage costs and depreciation costs were zero, as it were.

Now that the representative individual is getting cash

from the helicopter, he can keep his *real* cash balances at 5.2 weeks' income from the sale of services only by adding all the extra cash to his *nominal* balances to offset rising prices. However, the money from heaven seems to be a bonanza enabling him to do better. If he reduces his cash balances by $1.00 over a year, he can now increase his consumption at the rate of $1.10 per year, whereas before he could have increased his consumption at the rate of only $1.00 a year. Since he was just on the margin before, he will now be over the margin. Storage and depreciation costs are now 10 cents per dollar per year, instead of zero, so he will try to hold a smaller real quantity of money. Suppose, to be specific, that when prices are rising at 10 percent a year, he wants to hold one-twelfth instead of one-tenth of a year's proceeds from the sale of services in cash balances, that is, 4⅓ weeks' income instead of 5.2.

We are now back to our earlier problem. To each individual separately, it looks as if he can consume more by reducing his cash balances, but the community as a whole cannot do so. Once again, the helicopter has changed no real magnitude, added no real resources to the community, changed none of the physical opportunities available. The attempt of individuals to reduce their cash balances will simply mean a further bidding up of prices and income, so as to make the nominal stock of money equal to one-twelfth instead of one-tenth of a year's nominal income. Once that happens, prices will rise by 10 percent a year, in line with the increasing amount of money. Since both prices and nominal income will be rising at 10 percent a year, real income will be constant. Since the nominal quantity of money is also rising at 10 percent a year, it stays in a constant ratio to income—equal to 4⅓ weeks of income from the sale of services.

Attaining this path requires two kinds of price increase: (1) a once-and-for-all rise of 20 percent, to reduce real balances to the level desired when it costs 10 cents per dollar per year to hold cash; (2) an indefinitely continued inflation at the rate of 10 percent per year, to keep real balances constant at the new level.

Something definite can be said about the transition process this time. During the transition, the rate of inflation must average more than 10 percent. Hence, inflation must overshoot its long-term equilibrium level. It must display a cyclical reaction pattern. In Figure 2, the horizontal solid line is the ultimate equilibrium path of inflation. The three broken curves after t_0, the date at which the quantity of money starts to rise, illustrate alternative possible transitional paths: curve A shows a single overshooting and then a gradual return to the permanent position; curves B and C show an initial undershooting, then an overshooting, followed by either a gradual return (curve B) or a damped cyclical adjustment (curve C).

The necessity for overshooting in the rate of price change and in the rate of income change (though not

Figure 2

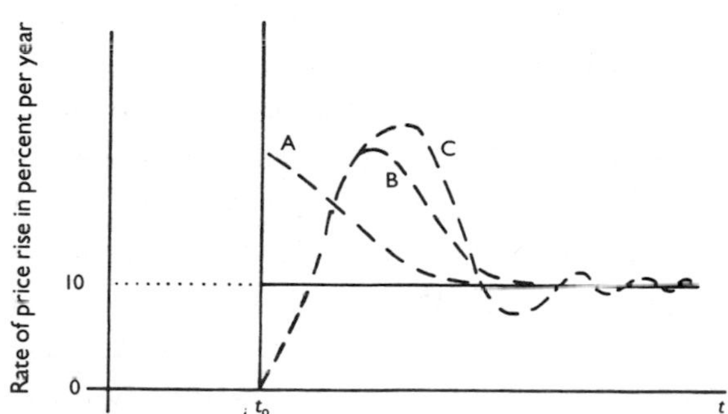

necessarily in the level of either prices or income) is, I believe, the key element in monetary theories of business cycles. In practice, the need to overshoot is reinforced by an initial undershooting (as in curves B and C). When the helicopter starts dropping money in a steady stream—or, more generally, when the quantity of money starts unexpectedly to rise more rapidly—it takes time for people to catch on to what is happening. Initially, they let actual balances exceed long-run desired balances, partly out of inertia; partly because they may take initial price rises as a harbinger of subsequent price declines, an anticipation that raises desired balances; and partly because the initial impact of increased money balances may be on output rather than on prices, which further raises desired balances. Then, as people catch on, prices must for a time rise even more rapidly, to undo an initial increase in real balances as well as to produce a long-run decline.

While this one feature of the transition is clear, little can be said about the details without much more precise specification of the reaction patterns of the members of the community and of the process by which they form their anticipations of price movements.

One final important detail. Implicitly, we have been treating the real flow of services as if it were the same on the final equilibrium path as it was initially. That is wrong, for two reasons. First, and less important for our purposes, there may be permanent distributional effects. Second, and more important, real cash balances are at least in part a factor of production. To take a trivial example, a retailer can economize on his average cash balances by hiring an errand boy to go to the bank on the corner to get change for large bills tendered by customers. When it costs the retailer 10 cents per dollar per year, rather than nothing, to hold an extra dollar of cash, there will be a greater incentive to hire the errand boy, that is, to substitute other productive resources for cash. This will mean both a lower real flow of services from the given productive resources and a change in the structure of production, since different productive activities may differ in cash-intensity, just as they differ in labor- or land-intensity.

Our simple hypothetical helicopter example brings out clearly a phenomenon—some might call it a paradox—that is of the utmost importance in the actual course of events. To each individual separately, the money from the sky seems like a bonanza, a true windfall gain. Yet when the community has adjusted to it everyone is worse off in two respects: (1) the representative individual is poorer because he now has a reserve for emergencies equal to 4⅓ weeks' income rather than 5.2 weeks'; (2) he has a lower real income because productive resources have been substituted for cash balances, raising the price of consumption services relative to the price of productive services. This contrast between appearance to the individual and the reality for the community is the basic source of most monetary mischief.

The Famous Quantity Equation of Money

The preceding discussion can be summarized in a simple equation—an equation that was envisaged by scholars centuries ago, was stated carefully and precisely in the late nineteenth century by Simon Newcomb, a world-famous American astronomer who, on the side, was also a great economist, and was further developed and popularized by Irving Fisher, the greatest economist the United States has ever produced. In Fisher notation, the equation is

$$MV = PT .$$

M is the *nominal quantity of money*. As we have seen, it is currently determined in the United States by the Federal Reserve System. *V* is the *velocity of circulation*, the number of times each dollar is used on the average to make a purchase during a specified period of time. If we restrict purchases to final goods and services, and if the public holds 5.2 weeks of income in cash, as in our example, then the velocity is 10 times per year, since a year's income (equal to a year's purchases of final goods and services, which include savings) is ten times the quantity of money.* *V* is determined, as we have seen, by the public according to how *useful* it finds cash balances and how much it *costs* to hold them. The product of *M* and *V*, the left side of the equation, is total spending or income.

On the right side, *P* is an *average price*, or an index of the average price, of the goods and services purchased. *T* stands for *transactions*, to be interpreted as an index of the total quantity of goods and services purchased. Fisher, in his original version, used *T* to refer to all transactions—purchases of final goods and services (like bread purchased by the final consumer), intermediate transactions (flour purchased by the baker), and capital transactions (the purchase of a house or a share of stock). In current usage, the item has come to be interpreted as referring to purchases of final goods and services only, and the notation has been changed accordingly, *T* being replaced by *y*, as corresponding to real income.

*Again, I should warn that this is a reasonable number only for money defined as currency or base money. In recent years, base money velocity has been around 15 or 20, decidedly higher than earlier. For a definition like the current U.S M2, velocity is much lower, about 1.3 a year.

As written, the equation is an identity, a truism. Every purchase can be viewed in two ways: the amount of money spent and the quantity of a good or service purchased multiplied by the price paid. Entering the amount of money on the left side and quantity times price on the right, and adding up those sums for all purchases, we have a standard case of double-entry bookkeeping. As in double-entry bookkeeping in general, the truism is highly useful.

Consider once more our original question: What determines how much you can buy with the greenbacked five-dollar bill we started with? *Nothing can affect* P *except as it changes one or more of the other items in the equation.* Will a boom in the stock market, for example, change how much you can buy with a five-dollar bill? It will reduce the amount you can buy (raise P) only if it leads the Fed to create more money (increases M), or induces people to hold lower real cash balances, perhaps because they think the alternatives have become more attractive (raises V), or reduces the quantity of goods and services available for purchase, perhaps because workers are paying less attention to their work and more to the stock ticker (lowers T). The stock-market boom can raise the amount you can buy (lower P) only if it has the opposite effect, and clearly there are all sorts of possible combinations.

As this exceedingly simplified example illustrates, the equation is a useful way to organize an analysis of the effect of changes in circumstances. In short, Fisher's equation plays the same foundation-stone role in monetary theory that Einstein's $E = mc^2$ does in physics.

Changes in the Quantity of Money

In the real world, money does not drop from helicopters. When money consisted largely of physical commodities like gold and silver, new discoveries and technological advances were a major source of changes in the quantity of money. Chapter 3 discusses the effects of the nineteenth-century discoveries of gold and silver, the most dramatic of which were the Californian (1849) and Australian (1850s) discoveries; the opening of the Comstock Lode (1859), rich in silver and gold; and, later in the century, the Alaskan and South African finds. Chapter 5 discusses the effect on William Jennings Bryan's political career of the most dramatic technological change, the perfection of the cyanide process for extracting gold from low-grade ore.

Consider, in light of the helicopter fable, the effect of the flood of gold from California and Australia in the 1850s. Like those who were quickest to pick up the helicopter money, the first to extract the gold were clearly enriched. My favorite example comes from a visit to a major Australian gold-mining town, now preserved as a tourist attraction. One antique document on display was an advertisement for ice from Walden Pond. Ice, cut in the winter from Walden Pond in Massachusetts, was loaded in sawdust into the hulls of ships, which then sailed around the tip of South America and across the wide Pacific—about fifteen thousand miles—to Melbourne, where the ice was unloaded onto carts and dragged by horses some hundred and more miles to the gold-mining community, to satisfy the desire for cold drinks of the lucky and newly wealthy gold miners!

The gold from California and Australia, being first spent where it was found, attracted people and goods (like the ice) from all over the world by bidding up prices. As this occurred, the gold came to be distributed around the rest of the world and ended by raising prices in all gold-standard countries. As in the helicopter fable, it took a long time for the effects of the discoveries to work themselves out. As they did, the initial wide discrepancies in prices were reduced.

Also as in the fable, the effect on individuals was very different from the effect on the community at large. The lucky persons who first extracted the gold were clearly enriched. But what about the community at large? At the end of the process, the community was worse off. The appeal of the lottery involved in the several gold rushes meant that the resources spent to extract the gold from the earth, transport it to distant lands, mint it into coins, and bury it in bank vaults were almost surely greater in value than the new gold. Some of the new gold doubtless went into jewelry, gold plate, and the like. This part, at least, provided a continuing source of utility. But the rest of the gold, used as money, mostly meant only that prices were higher than they otherwise would have been. As David Hume wrote in 1742, "augmentation [in the quantity of money] has no other effect than to heighten the price of labour and commodities. . . . In the progress towards these changes, the augmentation may have some influence, by exciting industry, but after the prices are settled . . . it has no manner of influence" (1804a, p. 314). "Exciting industry" may have produced some increase in output, but it is hard to believe that any such increase could have offset more than a trifling part of the cost in resources of the additional money.

While the welfare effects of the gold discoveries were almost surely negative, *it does not follow that the existence of a gold standard—or, more generally, a commodity standard—is a mistake and harmful to society.* True, such a standard does involve the cost of digging the gold out of the ground in one part of the world in order, in effect, to bury it in another. However, we have seen that having a widely accepted medium of exchange is of critical importance for any functioning complex society. No money can serve that function unless its nominal quantity is limited. For millennia, the only effective limit was provided by the link between money and a commodity. That link provided an anchor for the price level. Departures in general were, in Irving Fisher's words, "a curse to the country involved." As noted earlier and discussed in more detail in chapter 10, the world is now engaged in a great experiment to see whether it can fashion a different anchor, one that depends on government restraint rather than on the cost of acquiring a physical commodity. That experiment is less than twenty years old as I write—young even on a personal time scale, let alone on a historical time scale. The verdict is far from in on whether fiat money will involve a lower cost than commodity money (see Friedman 1987 and also 1986).

I turn now to the other major source of changes in the quantity of money throughout history, and since 1971 the only source—action by government. From time immemorial, government has played a major role in the monetary system. One element of that role has been to seek to monopolize the coining of money. The objective was partly to standardize the money. The sovereign's seal on a coined piece of metal was intended to certify its weight and fineness and thus enable such coins to be used in transactions by tale, or number, rather than by weight, thereby reducing the cost of transactions. Another objective was to earn seignorage, the mint's charge for converting bullion into coins.

Payment by tale, or count, rather than by weight greatly facilitated commerce.* But it also encouraged such practices as clipping (shaving off tiny slivers from the sides or edges of coins) and sweating (shaking a bunch of coins together in a leather bag and collecting the dust that was knocked off), whereby a lighter coin could be passed on at its face value. Gresham's law (that "bad money drives out good" when there is a fixed rate of exchange between them) came into operation, and heavy, good coins were held for their metallic value, while light coins were passed on. The coins became lighter and lighter, and prices rose higher and higher. Then payment by weight would be resumed for large transactions, and pressure would develop for recoinage.

Sweating and clipping were effectively ended by the milling of coins (the process of making the serrations around the circumference that we have come to take for granted), first used in 1663, and followed in Britain by the Great Recoinage of 1696 to 1698, which produced a much more homogeneous coinage.

A more serious matter was the attempt by the sovereign to benefit from his monopoly of coinage. In this respect, the Greek and the Roman experiences offer an interesting contrast. Though Solon, on taking office in Athens in 594 B.C., instituted a partial debasement of the currency, for the next four centuries (until the absorption of Greece into the Roman Empire) the Athenian *drachma* had an almost constant silver content (67 grains of fine silver until Alexander, 65 grains thereafter). It became the standard

*Much of the rest of this section is from Friedman (1974).

coin of trade in Greece and in much of Asia and Europe as well, and even after the Roman conquest the *drachma* continued to be minted and widely used.

The Roman experience was very different. Not long after the introduction (in 269 B.C.), of a silver *denarius* patterned after the Greek *drachma,* the prior copper coinage (*aes* or *libra*) began to be debased; by the beginning of the empire, its weight had been reduced from one pound to half an ounce. The silver *denarius* and the gold *aureus* (introduced about 87 B.C.) suffered only minor debasement until the time of Nero (54 A.D.), when almost continuous tampering with the coinage began. The precious-metal content of the gold and silver coins were reduced, and the proportion of alloy was increased to three-fourths or more of the coin's weight. By the end of the three-century-long debasement, the *denarius,* once nearly pure silver, had degenerated to little more than a copper coin with a thin wash at first of silver and then of tin. As an aside, it took less than a century for U.S. dimes, quarters, and half-dollars to go through the same life cycle. We do make progress.

The debasement in Rome (as ever since) was a reflection of the state's inability or unwillingness to finance its expenditures through explicit taxes. But the debasement in turn worsened Rome's economic situation and undoubtedly contributed to the collapse of the empire.

Debasement was necessarily a slow process, involving repeated recoinages and ultimately limited by the real cost of the baser metal. The spread of paper money in the eighteenth and early nineteenth centuries enabled the process to be speeded up. The bulk of the money in use came to consist not of actual gold or silver but of fiduciary money—promises to pay specified amounts of gold or silver. These promises were initially issued by private individuals or companies in the form of bank notes or transferrable book entries that have come to be called deposits. But gradually the state assumed a greater role.

From fiduciary paper money promising to pay gold or silver, it is a short step to fiat paper money—notes that are issued on the fiat of the sovereign, are specified to be so many dollars or francs or yen, and are legal tender, but are not promises to pay something else. The first large-scale fiat issue in a Western country occurred in France in the early eighteenth century (though there are reports of paper money in China a millennium earlier). Later, the French Revolutionary government issued paper money in the form of *assignats* from 1789 to 1796. The American colonies and later the Continental Congress issued bills of credit that could be used in making payments. These early experiments gave fiat money a deservedly bad name. The money was overissued, and prices rose drastically until the money became worthless or was redeemed in metallic money (or promises to pay metallic money) at a small fraction of its initial value.

Subsequent issues of fiat money in the major countries during the nineteenth century were temporary departures from a metallic standard. In Britain, for example, payment in gold for outstanding bank notes was suspended during the Napoleonic Wars (1797–1816). As a result, gold coin and bullion became more expensive in terms of paper. Similarly, in the United States the convertibility of Union currency (greenbacks) into specie was suspended during the Civil War and not resumed until 1879. At the war's peak, in 1864, the price of a twenty-dollar gold coin reached more than $50 in greenbacks.

Changes in the Demand for Money

As pointed out earlier, changes in demand for money can have the same effect as changes in the quantity of money. In speaking about changes in demand, however, it is important to distinguish sharply between those that arise from changes in the usefulness of cash balances, such as the spread of monetization or the increasing range of financial instruments available, and those that arise from changes in the cost of cash balances, such as changes in nominal interest rates and in the rate of price changes. In economic jargon, we must distinguish between shifts in the demand curve and movements along a demand curve for cash balances.

This distinction is important because changes in usefulness tend to proceed slowly and gradually. Many changes in cost conditions also come slowly, but when these changes are sharp, especially in interest rates and the rate of price change, they are generally the result of events put in train by prior changes in the supply of money. One recent example for the United States is the sharp rise in the rate of inflation and in interest rates during the 1970s and the subsequent sharp fall during the 1980s.

The conclusion is that substantial changes in prices or nominal income are almost always the result of changes in the nominal supply of money, rarely the result of changes in demand for money. (Chapter 8 discusses at greater length the key case of inflation.)

Conclusion*

Monetary phenomena have been subject to extensive study over centuries. A summary of some broad empirical find-

*This conclusion is largely from Friedman (1987).

ings from that research may help to focus the discussion of this chapter.

1. For both long and short periods there is a consistent though not precise relation between the rate of growth of the quantity of money and the rate of growth of nominal income. If the quantity of money grows rapidly, so will nominal income, and conversely. The relation is much closer for long than for short periods.

2. Over short periods, the relation between growth in money and growth in nominal income is often hard to see, partly because the relation is less close for short than for long periods, but mostly because it takes time for changes in monetary growth to affect income. And how long a time is itself variable. Today's income growth is not closely related to today's monetary growth; it depends on what has been happening to money in the past. What happens to money today affects what is going to happen to income in the future.

3. For most major Western countries, a change in the rate of monetary growth produces a change in the rate of growth of nominal income about six to nine months later. This is an average that does not hold in every individual case. Sometimes the delay is longer, sometimes shorter. In particular, the delay tends to be shorter under conditions of high and highly variable rates of monetary growth and of inflation.

4. In cyclical episodes, the response of nominal income, allowing for the time delay, is greater in amplitude than is the change in monetary growth.

5. The changed rate of growth of nominal income typically shows up first in output and hardly at all in prices. If the rate of monetary growth increases or decreases, the rate of growth of nominal income and also of physical output tends to increase or decrease about six to

nine months later, but the rate of price rise is affected very little.

6. The effect on prices, like that on income and output, is distributed over time, but it comes some twelve to eighteen months later, so that the total delay between a change in monetary growth and a change in the rate of inflation averages something like two years. That is why it is a long row to hoe to stop an inflation after it has been allowed to start. It cannot be stopped overnight.

7. Even after allowance for the delayed effect of monetary growth, the relation is far from perfect. There's many a slip over short periods 'twixt the monetary change and the income change.

8. In the short run, which may be as long as three to ten years, monetary changes affect primarily output. Over decades, on the other hand, the rate of monetary growth affects primarily prices. What happens to output depends on real factors: the enterprise, ingenuity, and industry of the people; the extent of thrift; the structure of industry and government; the relations among nations; and so on.

9. One major finding has to do with severe depressions. There is strong evidence that a monetary crisis involving a substantial decline in the quantity of money is a necessary and sufficient condition for a major depression. Fluctuations in monetary growth are also systematically related to minor ups and downs in the economy but do not play as dominant a role as other forces. As Anna Schwartz and I put it: "Changes in the money stock are . . . a consequence as well as an independent source of change in money income and prices, though, once they occur, they produce in their turn still further effects on income and prices. Mutual interaction, but with money rather clearly the senior partner in longer-run movements and in major cyclical move-

ments, and more nearly an equal partner with money income and prices in short-run and milder movements—this is the generalization suggested by our evidence" (1963, p. 695).

10. A major unsettled issue is the short-run division of a change in nominal income between output and price. The division has varied widely over space and time, and there exists no satisfactory theory that isolates the factors responsible for the variability.

11. It follows from these propositions that *inflation is always and everywhere a monetary phenomenon* in the sense that it is and can be produced only by a more rapid increase in the quantity of money than in output. Many phenomena can produce temporary fluctuations in the rate of inflation, but they can have lasting effects only insofar as they affect the rate of monetary growth. However, there are many possible reasons for monetary growth, including gold discoveries, the financing of government spending, and the financing of private spending. Hence, these propositions are only the beginning of an answer to the causes and cures for inflation. The deeper question is why excessive monetary growth occurs (see chapter 8).

12. A change in monetary growth affects interest rates in one direction at first but in the opposite direction later on. More rapid monetary growth at first tends to lower interest rates. But later on, the resulting acceleration in spending and still later in inflation produces a rise in the demand for loans, which tends to raise interest rates. In addition, higher inflation widens the difference between real and nominal interest rates. As both lenders and borrowers come to anticipate inflation, lenders demand, and borrowers are willing to offer, higher nominal rates to offset the anticipated inflation. That is why interest rates

are highest in countries that *have had* the most rapid growth in the quantity of money and also in prices—countries like Brazil, Argentina, Chile, Israel, South Korea. In the opposite direction, a slower rate of monetary growth at first raises interest rates but later on, as it decelerates spending and inflation, lowers interest rates. That is why interest rates are lowest in countries that *have had* the slowest rate of growth in the quantity of money—countries like Switzerland, Germany, and Japan.

13. In the major Western countries, the link to gold and the resulting long-term predictability of the price level meant that, until sometime after World War II, interest rates behaved as if prices were expected to be stable and neither inflation nor deflation was anticipated. Nominal returns on nominal assets were relatively stable, while real returns were highly unstable, absorbing almost fully inflation and deflation (as displayed in Figure 1).

14. Beginning in the 1960s, and especially after the end of Bretton Woods in 1971, interest rates started to parallel rates of inflation. Nominal returns on nominal assets became more variable; real returns on nominal assets, less variable.

CHAPTER 3

*The Crime of 1873**

I am persuaded history will write it [the Act of 1873] down as the greatest legislative crime and the most stupendous conspiracy against the welfare of the people of the United States and of Europe which this or any other age has witnessed.

—SENATOR JOHN H. REAGAN (1890)

[The demonetization of silver] . . . was the crime of the nineteenth century.

—SENATOR WILLIAM M. STEWART (1889)

In 1873 we find a simple legal recognition of that [the demonetization of silver] which had been the immediate result of the act of 1853.

—JAMES LAURENCE LAUGHLIN (1886)

You shall not press down upon the brow of labor this

*I am indebted for helpful comments on earlier drafts to Michael D. Bordo, Conrad Braun, Phillip Cagan, Joe Cobb, Harold Hough, David Laidler, Hugh Rockoff, and, as always and especially, Anna J. Schwartz. In addition, David D. Friedman and an anonymous referee on behalf of the *Journal of Political Economy* made a number of very helpful suggestions for revision.

crown of thorns. You shall not crucify mankind upon a cross of gold.

—WILLIAM JENNINGS BRYAN (1896)

The act of 1873 was a piece of good fortune, which saved our financial credit and protected the honor of the State. It is a work of legislation for which we can not now be too thankful.

—JAMES LAURENCE LAUGHLIN (1886)

The Coinage Act of 1873, to which these quotations refer, was passed by a vote of 110 to 13 in the U.S. House of Representatives and 36 to 14 in the Senate, after lengthy, but superficial committee hearings and floor debate. It attracted little attention at the time, even from those members of Congress (including Senator Stewart) who voted for it yet later attacked it in vitriolic terms as a "grave wrong," a "conspiracy" perpetrated by "corrupt bargains," a "blunder which . . . is worse than a crime," a "great legislative fraud," and, finally, "the crime of 1873" (see Barnett 1964, pp. 178–81).*

How did this apparently innocuous legislative measure evoke such strong and contrasting reactions from leading scholars, businessmen, and politicians over so long a period? How did it become a central issue in a presidential campaign conducted more than two decades after its passage? (Chapter 5 tells that story.) Was it a crime, in any sense of the term? What were its actual consequences? To

*According to Paul M. O'Leary (1960, p. 390), "The first person to use the word 'crime' was George M. Weston, the secretary of the U.S. Monetary Commission of 1876 . . . [i]n his special report, attached to the full report of the commission" published in 1877. Barnett (1964, p. 180) attributes the first use of the full phrase "the crime of 1873" to Senator Henry M. Teller of Colorado on July 10, 1890.

answer these questions requires some background in monetary history and theory.

The Background

The U.S. Constitution gives Congress the power "to coin money, regulate the value thereof, and of foreign coin," and prohibits the states from making "anything but gold and silver coin a tender in payment of debts." In initially exercising this power, the Congress, following the recommendation of Alexander Hamilton, passed the Coinage Act of April 2, 1792. That act defined the basic monetary unit of the United States as the dollar and defined subsidiary coinage on a decimal basis—the cent, the "half-disme" (later the nickel), the "disme" (later the dime), the quarter, and so on. It further defined the dollar as equal to 371.25 grains of pure silver or 24.75 grains of pure gold, authorized the *free coinage* of *both* silver and gold at the specified ratio of 15 to 1, and specified the fraction of alloy to be combined with pure metal in striking the coins.*

I have italicized two terms that are critical to understanding "the crime of 1873." *Free coinage* is critical because it gave practical content to a specie standard by providing that the government mint would convert all

*The act stated that "bullion so brought [to be coined at the legal rates] shall be assayed and coined as speedily as may be after the receipt thereof, and that free of expense to the person or persons by whom the same shall have been brought" (Jastram 1981, p. 63). Hence, coinage was free in a dual sense—open to all in unlimited amount, and without charge.

The provision that no charge should be made for coinage is exceptional. Typically, a small charge, called seignorage, is made for the cost of coining. However, the so-called seignorage charge has sometimes been manipulated and used for purposes other than to cover the cost of coinage—as by ancient seignors (lords) for revenue, or by President Franklin Delano Roosevelt as a device for pegging the price of silver (chapter 7).

specie that individuals chose to bring to the mint into legal-tender currency denominated in dollars (initially solely in the form of coins, later in paper certificates as well) at the stated metallic equivalent. *Both* is critical because it effectively established the United States on a bimetallic standard, that is, a monetary standard that authorized the free coinage, and hence the use as money, of either of two metals, silver or gold. These two provisions were equivalent to saying that the U.S. government would buy all silver and gold offered to it at prices of $1.2929 . . . per troy ounce of pure silver and $19.3939 . . . per troy ounce of fine gold—in other words, 15 times as much for an ounce of gold as for an ounce of silver, whence the ratio of 15 to 1.*

Although either silver or gold could legally be used as money, in practice only silver was so used until 1834. The reason was simple. There was and is a market for silver and gold outside the mint—for jewelry, industrial uses, coinage by other countries, and so on. In 1792 the ratio of the market price of gold to the market price of silver was almost exactly 15 to 1, the ratio Hamilton recommended. But shortly afterward the world price ratio went above 15 to 1 and stayed there (see Jastram 1981, pp. 63–69). As a result, anyone who had gold and wanted to convert it to money could do better by first exchanging the gold for silver at the market ratio and then taking the silver to the mint, rather than taking the gold directly to the mint.

To put it another way, look at the mint as if it were a

*The continuing decimals (.2929 . . . , .3939 . . .) arise because one ounce troy equals 480 grains. Given that a dollar was defined as equivalent to 371.25 grains of pure silver or 24.75 grains of fine gold, one ounce of silver was worth 480 divided by 371.25 or $1.2929 . . . , and one ounce of gold was worth 480 divided by 24.75, or $19.3939 . . .

two-way street at a 15 to 1 ratio. An obvious get-rich scheme would be to bring 15 ounces of silver to the mint, get 1 ounce of gold in return, sell the ounce of gold on the market, and with the proceeds buy more than 15 ounces of silver, pocket the profit, and keep going. Clearly, the mint would soon be overflowing with silver and out of gold. That is why the mint's commitment under the bimetallic standard was solely to buy silver and gold (that is, coin freely), although it also could, at its discretion, sell (redeem) one or the other or both metals. The end result was that the United States was effectively on a silver standard from 1792 to 1834. Gold was used for money only at a premium, not at par value. It was too valuable for that. Gresham's law was in full operation: cheap money drove out dear money.*

In 1834 new coinage legislation was introduced, in recognition of the changed gold-silver price ratio, which by then was about 15.625 to 1 on the world market. This ratio was repeatedly recommended by the Select Committee on Coins of the House of Representatives from 1832 to 1834, supposedly in the desire to "do something for gold," which had recently been discovered in Virginia, North Carolina, South Carolina, and Georgia and "had become of genuine importance to the four southern states" (O'Leary 1937, p. 83). However, the Select Committee rather suddenly changed its recommendation to a ratio of 16 to 1, not to do something *for* gold—though it certainly did that—but to do something *against* Nicholas Biddle's Bank of the United States.† This was at the height of the famous "bank war"

*For precision, the "law" must be stated far more specifically, as Rolnick and Weber (1986) point out.

†While the ratio is described as 16 to 1, that is an approximation. In the 1834 act, the weight of the gold dollar was set at 23.2 grains of pure gold, which

between President Andrew Jackson and Nicholas Biddle, which finally resulted in the failure of Biddle's bank to obtain a new charter when its original federal charter expired in 1836. As Paul M. O'Leary (1937, p. 84) put it, the ratio of 16 to 1 was "a golden club . . . used by Jackson and his supporters to belabor their hated enemy, The Bank." The unsatisfactory state of the currency—it was a mixture of U.S. and foreign silver coins, plus paper money issued by state banks, some of doubtful quality—had made the notes issued by Biddle's bank a favored medium of exchange. The act of 1834 was expected to weaken the bank by making gold coins an effective substitute for its notes.

Two points about this episode deserve special mention. First, in 1834, 16 to 1 was a golden club; in the 1890s, 16 to 1 was a silver club. Second, in both cases the club was wielded by much the same political constituency against much the same political constituency—the largely rural, small-business, lower-class southern and western supporters of Andrew Jackson in 1834 and of William Jennings Bryan in 1896, against the bankers, financiers, big-business interests, and urban upper classes of the east and northeast.

In any event, the adoption of the 16 to 1 ratio—making the official price $20.671835. . . (= 480/23.22) per fine ounce of gold—spelled the end of the reign of silver. From then to the Civil War, silver coinage was limited almost entirely to subsidiary coins. They too were overvalued at

gave a gold-silver ratio trivially higher than 16 to 1. The act was amended in 1837 to make the weight equal to 23.22, which gave a ratio trivially below 16 to 1. The reason for the change was to make the percentage of alloy in the minted coin equal to precisely 10 percent. A good source for the early coinage laws of the United States is National Executive Silver Committee (1890). See also U.S. Commission on the Role of Gold (1982, vol. 1, chap. 2).

the new legal ratio until 1853, when Congress voted to reduce their silver content. The difference was so small, however, and so many were underweight, that it was not worthwhile to melt them down (at least until the Civil War greenback inflation) (Carothers 1930, pp. 98–101). From 1834 on, gold coins circulated, and gold was the effective standard. Despite the increased demand for gold for monetary use, the gold-silver market price ratio fell after the California and Australian gold discoveries of the 1840s and 1850s. Gold's status as cheap money seemed secure.

The Civil War temporarily ended the reign of gold. The exigencies of financing the war led to the introduction of paper money—greenbacks—issued without gold or silver backing and without any promise of redemption in either metal.* Paper, as it were, became the cheap money. Gold continued to circulate, however, particularly on the west coast, but of course not on a one-to-one ratio with greenbacks. A free market arose in which the "greenback price of gold" rose above the official legal price—indeed, at the extreme, to more than double the official price. The government required customs duties and certain other obligations to be paid in gold; banks provided separate gold and greenback deposits for their clients. In short, gold and greenbacks circulated side by side at a floating exchange

*A fascinating detail about the greenbacks: Salmon P. Chase was Secretary of the Treasury when the first greenbacks were issued in 1862. Eight years later he was Chief Justice of the Supreme Court when the Court decided the first of the famous greenback cases questioning the constitutionality of their issuance. Not only did Chase not disqualify himself, but, in his capacity as Chief Justice, he joined with the majority of the Court in declaring that what he had done in his capacity as Secretary of the Treasury was unconstitutional! A little over a year later, after the filling of two vacancies on the Court, the decision was reversed in the second of the greenback cases, with Chief Justice Chase this time one of the dissenting justices.

rate determined in the market, although greenbacks were clearly the dominant currency for most purposes and in most areas.

Finally, we come to 1873. A movement was afoot to end the greenback episode and resume a specie standard. It was time for Congress to start tidying up the coinage legislation. The resulting Coinage Act of 1873 listed the coins to be minted. The list included gold coins and subsidiary silver coins, but it omitted the historical standard silver dollar of 371.25 troy grains of pure silver. Further tidying up occurred in 1874.* That was followed by the Resumption Act of 1875 and the successful resumption of a specie standard on the basis of gold on January 1, 1879.†

The events culminating in resumption in 1879 precisely parallel a corresponding sequence in Britain six decades earlier—a bimetallic standard before 1797, followed by the adoption of an inconvertible paper standard, the demonetization of silver in 1816, and resumption in 1821 on a gold basis (whereas, without the 1816 legislation, resumption would have been on silver).‡ The parallelism is not pure coincidence. The initial step, the ending of convertibility

*The 1873 act included provision for coining a heavier silver "trade dollar" to be used in trade with Mexico and the Far East, which were on the silver standard. The trade dollar had legal-tender status, which was removed in June of 1874, when Congress passed the Revised Statutes providing that no silver coin was to be legal tender beyond the amount of $5.00 and that foreign coin was prohibited from being a tender (see Barnett 1964, p. 178).

According to Nugent (1968, pp. 98, 134), the coinage legislation was first introduced by Senator John Sherman in 1868, and the bill that actually passed was initially drafted in 1869 (though clearly with some subsequent changes) and first introduced into the Senate in April 1870.

†For a detailed discussion of the greenback period and resumption, see Friedman and Schwartz (1963, chap. 2).

‡By 1819 the market price of gold had fallen to the legal price, but the Bank of England was not legally required to redeem its notes in gold until 1821.

and the adoption of a paper standard, was a reaction in both countries to the financial pressures of war.* As in the United States, Britain's decision to return to a specie standard reflected the desire to have a sound money, which manifested itself in the outrage of the financial community, holders of government bonds, and some economists at the inflation produced by the departure from a specie standard—though the inflation was exceedingly modest by modern standards, at most about 5 percent to 10 percent a year. While Britain's choice of gold instead of silver was something of an accident, it was a major reason why the United States made the same choice roughly sixty years later.†

If resumption in the United States had occurred under the pre–Civil War coinage legislation, silver would have become the cheap metal whenever the gold-silver ratio rose appreciably above 16 to 1, as happened by 1875. Under those conditions, producers of silver would have found it advantageous to bring their silver to the mint rather than selling it on the market, and owners of gold coins would

*It was not the only possible reaction, despite the tendency of many historians to regard what happened as if it had to happen. France was under even greater financial pressure than Britain was, yet "through twenty years of war, at times against half Europe, [Napoleon] never once allowed a resort to . . . inconvertible paper money" (Walker 1896b, p. 87). Chapter 6 discusses this episode at greater length.

†David Ricardo, one of Britain's most influential proponents of resumption, initially favored silver but not bimetallism ([1816] 1951, p. 63). In subsequent testimony in 1819 before a committee of Parliament, Ricardo shifted to gold because "I have understood that machinery is particularly apposite to the silver mines and may therefore very much conduce to an increased quantity of that metal and an alteration of its value, whilst the same cause is not likely to operate upon the value of gold" ([1819a] 1952, pp. 390–91; see also [1819b] 1952, p. 427). That judgment, like so many based on the opinion of technical "experts," proved to be very wide of the mark. Chapter 6 provides a fuller discussion of this episode.

have found it advantageous to melt their coins down and sell the gold on the market rather than using the coins as money at their nominal face value.*

In practice, neither the conversion of specie into currency at the mint nor the melting down of gold or silver coins is costless. Commonly, a small seignorage charge is made to cover the expenses of the mint, and melting also involves some costs. In addition, interest is lost because of the delays involved in minting, and trading involves costs in selling gold or silver, and conversely. As a result, the tendency to regard the legal ratio as a precise number so that only one metal can circulate at a time is a fallacy. "Gold points" permit the exchange rates of two gold-standard currencies to fluctuate within a range without producing gold shipments; similarly, under a bimetallic standard "gold-silver price ratio points" permit the ratio to fluctuate within a range without producing either a premium on one metal or its complete replacement by the other.†

The omission of any mention of the standard silver dollar in the Coinage Act of 1873 ended the legal status of

*Currently, it pays to bring neither gold nor silver to the mint because both have been replaced by a cheaper money, paper. There still are, however, official prices on the books ($1.2929 for silver, $42.22 for gold). The gold holdings of the U.S. government are still valued on the books at the official price. Yet no one would dream of using a silver coin stamped $1 or a gold coin stamped $20 as money at these nominal values. The coins are numismatic items valued at about $8 and $475, respectively. I am indebted to Conrad J. Braun for the rough estimates of the current market values of the silver and gold coins.

†That was the situation in France from 1803 to 1873. During the whole of that time both gold and silver circulated, despite market ratios that departed from the French legal ratio of 15.5 to 1, although at times silver tended to displace gold and at other times gold tended to replace silver (Walker 1896b, chaps. 4 and 5, esp. p. 121). See chapter 6 for a fuller discussion of a bimetallic standard.

bimetallism in the United States. Had that fateful line not been omitted from the act, resumption in 1879 would almost surely have been on the basis of silver, not gold. That was "the crime of 1873" in the eyes of the proponents of silver.

The events raise two questions. The less important, but easier to answer, is: Was there a "crime," in any meaningful sense? The far more important, but also far harder to answer: What would have been the consequences of including the fateful line?

Was There a "Crime"?

In 1877, "an editorial in *The Nation* . . . read in part as follows: 'Mr. Ernest Seyd, a designing bullionist and secret agent of foreign bondholders, came to this country from London in 1873, and by corrupt bargains with leading members of Congress and officers of the Government brought about the demonetization of silver.' It was said that he brought with him $500,000 to bribe certain members of Congress and the Comptroller of the Currency" (cited in Barnett 1964, p. 178). If that had been true, there would indeed have been a crime in every sense of the term. But no evidence has ever been offered to indicate that the story was truc. In fact, Seyd was anything but a "designing bullionist." He was a British bimetallist who objected strongly to the demonetization of silver by the United States (Nugent 1968, pp. 153, 166). No allegation of bribery has ever been made, let alone documented, against any individual member of Congress or any government official in connection with the passage of the Coinage Act of 1873. The act was discussed at great length both in committee and on the floor of Congress and was openly voted for by large majorities—though later critics claimed that the key provision to which they objected had been barely mentioned and not further discussed on the floor.* In the literal dictionary sense of a crime—"an act punishable by law, as being forbidden by statute or injurious to the public welfare"—there was no crime.

On the other hand, in what the dictionary calls a "more general" use of the term—"an evil or injurious act; an offence, a sin"†—the existence of a crime is a question of opinion. What is not open to question is that the omission of the standard silver dollar from the list of coins to be minted was intentional, in full knowledge of the likely consequences and in the belief that those consequences were desirable. That was made clear by H. R. Linderman, who was the director of the U.S. Mint at the time of the passage of the act, in a book published not long afterward (1877, chapter 9). In his Report to the Secretary of the Treasury in November 1872, when the coinage act was pending in Congress, he wrote: "The fluctuations in the relative value of gold and silver during the last hundred years have not been very great, but several causes are now at work, all tending to an excess of supply over demand for silver, and its consequent depreciation" (cited in 1877, p. 48).

On the consequences of the act, Linderman wrote: "The declaration in the Coinage Act of 1873, that the gold dollar was to be thereafter the unit of value, and the omission of the silver dollar from the coins to be struck under

*They even cited one of their opponents in support: "As Professor Laughlin states . . . : 'The Senate occupied its time chiefly on questions of seignorage and abrasion and the House on a question of the salaries of the officials' " (National Executive Silver Committee 1890, p. 22).

†Definitions from the Oxford English Dictionary.

the provisions of the Act, placed the United States upon the single gold standard. . . . [T]he weight of opinion in Europe and America was against the practicability of maintaining a double standard on any basis which might be selected, and in favor of a single gold standard" (p. 44).

In a later chapter, he said: "The advocates of the restoration of the old silver dollar . . . appear to think that an error, if not a wrong, was committed in discontinuing its coinage; and they desire to correct the same without reference to the question, whether it would be possible to maintain concurrent circulation of gold and silver coins after resumption in 1879" (pp. 100–101).

Further, as Walter Nugent documents in great detail, Senator John Sherman, the chairman of the Senate Finance Committee, had been determined to demonetize silver from at least 1867, and he had arranged to have a bill to that effect drafted at the end of 1869. From then on, Senator Sherman, Linderman, John Jay Knox (the deputy comptroller of the currency and then the comptroller), and Secretary of the Treasury George Boutwell cooperated in pushing a coinage bill that included the demonetization of silver (1968, pp. 80, 88, 99, 103, 105). "Were Knox, Linderman, Boutwell, Sherman, and others aware of what they were doing when they planned to drop the silver dollar?" Nugent asks. "It is inconceivable," he goes on, "that they were not. . . . But did they urge it because they feared a drop in silver prices? No one made an explicit statement to that effect, but it was undoubtedly the case" (p. 137).

In addition, as Francis Walker wrote two decades later: "So completely without observation was this measure passed, that it was not for a year or two that the fact of demonetization was popularly known." In an attached footnote, Walker added: "The writer was in 1873

Professor of Political Economy at Yale, and was actually engaged in lecturing upon the topic of money. He was, also, a pretty good newspaper reader, and by the accidents of position and personal acquaintance, was fairly well in touch with the men of commerce and banking in the neighboring city of New York. Yet it was long after the passage of the act of 1873 that he first learned of the demonetization of the silver dollar" (1893, pp. 170–71).

As Paul O'Leary summarized the evidence: "[I]t seems only reasonable to conclude that the failure to include provision for the standard silver dollar in the Coinage Act of 1873 was based not upon recognition of the existing economic facts but rather upon calculated hostility to silver as a part of the monetary standard. The Act anticipated the future. It was purposive and deliberate in the mind of the man [according to Nugent, "men"] who largely framed the legislation and saw it through the Congress. In this sense, the silver people are correct in holding that it was the result of 'malice aforethought.' It was expected to accomplish and did accomplish a result going far beyond a mere 'tidying up' of our coinage laws and procedures."

O'Leary went on to say: "For the next twenty-seven years the silver question bedeviled the politics and the finances of the United States. Silver never won back the place it would have enjoyed had the Act of 1873 not failed to include provision for the coinage of the standard silver dollar. The consequences of not striking down the free and unlimited coinage of the silver dollar could have been vast for subsequent American financial, economic, and political life. That is, however, another story" (1960, p. 392).*

A story to which we now turn.

*In a fascinating paper, Hugh Rockoff (1990) persuasively argues that Frank Baum's *The Wonderful Wizard of Oz* "is not only a child's tale but also a

The Consequences of the Coinage Act of 1873

Eliminating the free coinage of silver had major consequences because of one central fact cited by Linderman: the likely decline in the world price of silver relative to that of gold. Had there been no decline in the silver-gold price ratio—or, as it is more usually expressed, no rise in the gold-silver price ratio—it would have been irrelevant whether the fateful line was included or omitted in the act of 1873. In either event, the pre–Civil War situation of an effective gold standard would have continued when and if the United States resumed specie payments.

As it was, however, a rise in the gold-silver price ratio had started well before Congress passed the act of 1873 and was in full swing when the United States resumed specie payments in 1879. Resumption by the United States on the basis of gold was the final nail in the coffin of silver. The gold-silver price ratio, plotted in Figure 1, fluctuated around 15.5 (the mint ratio in France) for decades before the gold discoveries in California in 1848 and in Australia in 1851. It then fell to a low of nearly 15 by 1859, when it started an irregular but more or less steady rise.* The rise

---

sophisticated commentary on the political and economic debates of the Populist Era" (p. 739), that is, on the silver agitation generated by the so-called crime of 1873. "The land of Oz," according to Rockoff, "is the East [in which] the gold standard reigns supreme and where an ounce (Oz) of gold has almost mystical significance" (p. 745). Rockoff goes on to identify the Wicked Witch of the East with Grover Cleveland, the gold Democrat who, as president, "led the [successful] repeal of the Sherman Silver Purchase Act of 1893" (p. 746).

Similarly, Rockoff is able to identify many of the other places and characters, and much of the action, with places, people, and events that played a significant role in the final years of the free-silver movement.

*Though France certainly adopted the ratio of 15.5 to 1 because it was roughly the market ratio in 1803, France's successful maintenance of bimetallism undoubtedly helped to stabilize the ratio (see Walker 1896b, p. 87; Fisher 1911, p. 136).

Figure 1

Ratio of Price of Gold to Price of Silver, Annually, 1800–1914

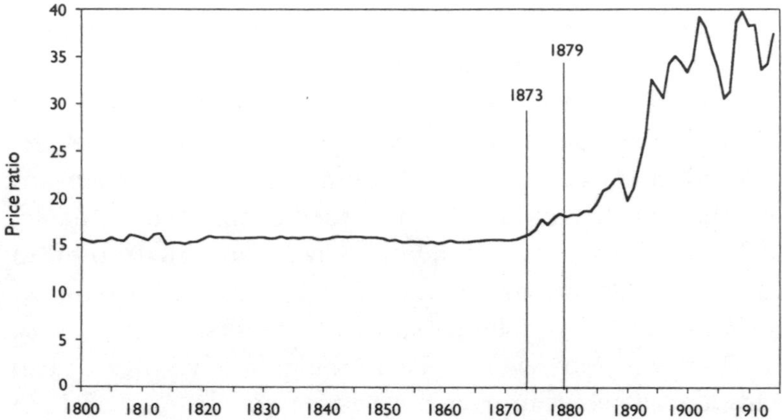

speeded up rapidly after 1870, as one European country after another shifted from a silver or bimetallic standard to a single gold standard—a tribute to the leadership of Britain, by then recognized as the dominant economic power. Germany shifted in 1871–73, after its defeat of France and imposition of a large war indemnity payable in funds convertible into gold. France, which had maintained a bimetallic standard since 1803, despite first major silver and then major gold discoveries, demonetized silver in 1873–74, along with the other members of the Latin Monetary Union (Italy, Belgium, and Switzerland). The Scandinavian Union (Denmark, Norway, and Sweden), the Netherlands, and Prussia followed suit in 1875–76, and Austria in 1879. By the late 1870s, India and China were the only major countries on an effective silver standard. The resulting increased demand for gold, along with the increased supply of silver for nonmonetary purposes, produced a dramatic rise in the gold-silver price ratio. From 15.4 in

1870, it jumped to 16.4 by 1873, 18.4 by 1879, and 30 by 1896, when "16 to 1" became the battle cry of the Bryan campaign.

By joining the movement to gold, the United States added to the upward pressure on the gold-silver price ratio, both by absorbing gold that would otherwise have been available for monetary use in the rest of the world and by failing to absorb silver. The effects were far from trivial. In preparation for resumption, the U.S. Treasury began accumulating gold; by 1879 the stock of monetary gold in the United States, both in the Treasury and in private hands, already amounted to nearly 7 percent of the world's stock. By 1889 the U.S. share had risen to nearly 20 percent. Even more dramatically, the increase from 1879 to 1889 in the U.S. stock of monetary gold *exceeded* the increase in the world's stock. The monetary gold holdings of the rest of the world declined from 1879 to 1883; then they rose, but did not surpass the earlier level until 1890.

For silver, the failure to absorb the metal via free coinage was offset to some extent by repeated special legislation for the benefit of silver interests. The legislation required the federal government to buy silver at market prices, and the first such measure, which preceded resumption, was the Bland-Allison Act of 1878. It authorized the Treasury to buy between $2 million and $4 million of silver each month at the market price and led to regular purchases from 1878 to 1890. Then the silver purchases were stepped up drastically, under the Sherman Silver Purchase Act, until the silver purchase clause was repealed in 1893.

Interestingly enough, the number of ounces of silver purchased under these acts was almost equal to 16 times the number of ounces of fine gold added to the country's monetary gold stock. On first blush, it looks as if political measures had absorbed as much silver as free coinage would have. However, that was not the case. As will become apparent in what follows, had the United States been on silver, the stock of money would have risen faster than it did, and hence the ounces of silver brought to the mint would have substantially exceeded 16 times the ounces of gold actually acquired.*

The most obvious, but by no means the most important, consequence of the U.S. return to gold rather than to a bimetallic standard was the sharp rise in the gold-silver price ratio. A far more important consequence was the effect on the nominal prices of goods and services in general. The increased world demand for gold for monetary purposes coincided with a slowing in the rate of increase of the world's stock of gold and a rising output of goods and services. These forces put downward pressure on the price level. Stated differently, with gold scarcer in relation to output in general, the price of gold in terms of goods went up and the nominal price level (under a gold standard, the price level in terms of gold) went down. The downward pressure was relieved somewhat by a rapid expansion of the banking system, which increased the amount of money that could be pyramided on each ounce of gold. On the other hand, rising real income, plus the spreading monetization of economic activities, plus the declining price level itself, increased the downward pressure on prices by leading the public to hold larger cash balances relative to their income (that is, velocity declined).

*According to the estimates discussed in the next section of this chapter, 26 times as many ounces of monetary silver would have been accumulated as the ounces of gold actually acquired.

The outcome was deflation from 1875 to 1896, at a rate of roughly 1.7 percent a year in the United States and 0.8 percent a year in the United Kingdom (which means in the gold-standard world). In the United States, the 1875–96 deflation followed the even sharper deflation after the Civil War. That sharper deflation was an essential requisite for successful resumption on gold at the prewar parity between the U.S. dollar and the British pound. It also produced wide unrest and dissatisfaction, particularly in rural areas. The unrest led to the formation in 1876 of the Greenback party, to continue the earlier agitation for the issuance of more greenbacks as a way to replace deflation with inflation. The political agitation ended the retirement of greenbacks, which had started after the Civil War, and led to the adoption in 1878 of the Bland-Allison bill, authorizing the Treasury to purchase a limited amount of silver at market prices.

Though this silver was purchased at market prices, it was valued for monetary purposes at the higher legal price, the difference being treated as seignorage. The silver was mostly coined into standard silver dollars. However, most of the coins were stockpiled in the Treasury as reserves for pieces of paper called silver certificates, or, after 1890, treasury notes of 1890. These were nominally convertible into silver, but they were also legal tender effectively convertible into gold. Hence, it was cheaper to get silver by using the paper money to buy it on the market, rather than convert the paper money into silver at the fictional legal price. In effect, the silver certificates were fiat money, differing from the greenbacks only because the historic role of silver as money made it more acceptable for the government to increase the money supply by buying silver rather than by openly issuing fiat money. Increasing the money supply in that way also had the political effect of harnessing the silver interests to the populist cause of inflation. The stock of silver in the Treasury was the counterpart to the stock of wheat the U.S. government currently holds as a result of its attempt to prop up the price of wheat.

A 1.7 percent per year decline in prices may seem too mild to generate the kind of agitation that bedeviled the country in the two decades from resumption to the end of the century. But several considerations argue otherwise. First, the 1.7 percent is for a price index that covers all goods and services (the implicit price deflator). The wholesale prices of agricultural and other basic commodities doubtless fell at a greater rate (3.0 percent a year by one index). At least as important is the fact that we all want the prices of the things we sell to go up, not down; sellers of goods and services are almost invariably inflationists. True, we want the prices of the things we buy to go down. But as consumers we buy many things, whose prices are moving in different directions, and this makes us far less acutely aware of what is happening to the overall price level than of what is happening to the specific prices of the things we sell. And that was much truer in the nineteenth century, when data on the economy as a whole were few and far between, than it is now. Moreover, at all times, sellers tend to be relatively few in numbers and to be organized, so that they have more political clout than the dispersed consumers who benefit from declining prices. That was particularly true of the producers of silver, who clearly had much to gain by the adoption of a silver standard. Though few in number, they were politically influential because the sparsely populated silver states had the same representation in the U.S. Senate as the densely populated urban states did. (For a much later manifestation of their political clout, see chapter 7.)

An additional factor was that farmers are generally net monetary debtors. As such, they are harmed by a fall in prices, which raises the real value of their debt, and are benefited by a rise in prices, which reduces the real value of their debt. As debtors, they were particularly susceptible to the propaganda representing "the crime of 1873" as the evil machinations of a cabal of eastern and foreign capitalists: Wall Street versus Main Street.*

One paradoxical result of the agitation for inflation via silver was that it explains why *deflation* was more severe in the United States than in the rest of the gold-standard world (1.7 percent versus 0.8 percent). As Anna Schwartz and I concluded (1963, pp. 133–34): "This entire silver episode is a fascinating example of how important what people think about money can sometimes be. The fear that silver would produce an inflation sufficient to force the United States off the gold standard made it necessary to have a severe deflation in order to stay on the gold standard. In retrospect, it seems clear that either acceptance of a silver standard at an early stage or an early commitment to gold would have been preferable to the uneasy compromise that was maintained, with the uncertainty about the ultimate outcome and the consequent wide fluctuations to which the currency was subjected."

Which Would Have Been Better: Silver or Gold?

Given that either extreme would have been preferable to the uneasy compromise, which extreme would have been better: the early adoption of silver as the single standard at the monetary value of $1.2929. . . an ounce, or the early commitment to gold as the single standard? Or, seemingly

*I owe this observation to Hugh Rockoff.

a third choice between the extremes, the continuation of nominal bimetallism? An answer requires a thorough examination of the quantitative consequences of the three choices.

As it happens, that examination, presented in chapter 4, makes it clear that resumption under a continuation of the bimetallic standard would have been to silver, not to gold, and would have occurred in 1876, a year after the passage of the Resumption Act. As a result, the gold-silver price ratio would have behaved very differently than it did.

Figure 2 plots the legal gold-silver price ratio (16 to 1), the actual market price ratio, and an estimate of the hypothetical price ratio that would have prevailed if legal bimetallism had continued. The actual ratio skyrocketed, especially after 1890, when it rose to more than 30 and stayed there. In sharp contrast, the estimated hypothetical

Figure 2

Gold-Silver Price Ratio: Legal, Actual, and Hypothetical, 1865–1914

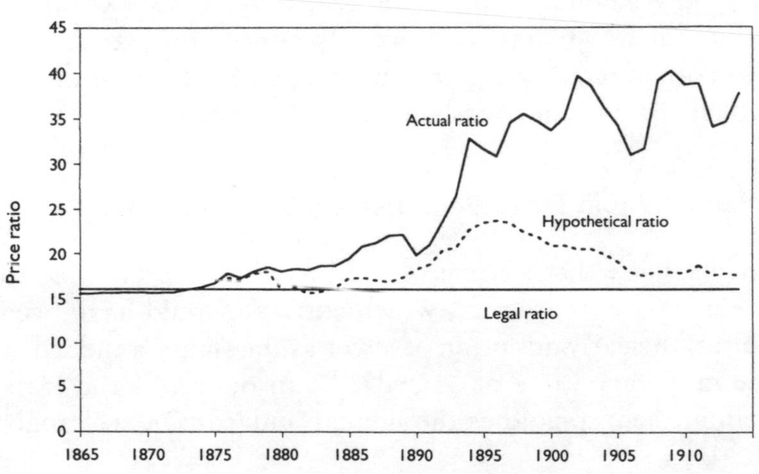

ratio departs widely from the legal ratio only between 1891 and 1904. Before 1891, it fluctuates narrowly around the 16 to 1 ratio. From 1906 to 1913, it remains between 17 and 18. The years during which the ratio departs widely from 16 to 1 are not the result of chance. The ratio's rise to well above 16 to 1 comes during the years of maximum political agitation about free silver surrounding the Bryan free-silver campaign of 1896 and the subsequent unwinding of the effects of that agitation. If the critical line about silver had been retained in the Coinage Act of 1873, that agitation would never have occurred, because the United States would have been on a silver standard. The hypothetical price ratio falls to a lower level during the period when world gold production, which started rising rapidly in 1897, reached peak levels, tending to depress the real price of gold.

These estimates allow (as fully as I could) for the changed economic circumstances that would have followed the continuation of legal bimetallism—the higher world price level and lower real price of gold, the reduction in the amount of silver available for nonmonetary use, and so on. But I have not been able to allow for some of the predictable effects, notably changes in real income and in the production of silver and gold, let alone for the change in the political climate. No doubt the political vacuum created by the disappearance of the free-silver issue would have been filled by other issues—very likely, pressure for the United States to convert to a gold standard—but there is no way of conjecturing what effect these issues would have had on the gold-silver ratio. Any attempt to do so would carry this exercise in history as it might have been into the realm of fantasy.

My conclusion is that the adoption of silver would in

practice have produced ratios throughout the period that would have fluctuated not far from 16 to 1 and that would have varied even less before 1891 and after 1904 than the hypothetical estimates plotted in Figure 2. In short, I believe that the United States could have played the same role after 1873 in stabilizing the gold-silver price ratio that France did before 1873.* If I am right, the fears of the opponents of bimetallism that a bimetallic standard would involve continual shifting between silver and gold would have proved false. With the United States effectively on silver and the United Kingdom and other major countries on gold, changes in the gold-silver ratio would have been directly reflected in the exchange rate between the dollar and other currencies. A rise in the ratio would have produced a dollar depreciation, a decline in the ratio a dollar appreciation. Here again, a relatively steady gold-silver ratio would have meant relatively steady exchange rates—varying for sterling not far from the level of $4.86 that actually prevailed. (These issues are considered in greater detail in chapter 6.)

The gold-silver price ratio is of no great importance in and of itself—except to gold and silver dealers—but it is vitally important for the price levels that would have prevailed in the silver-standard countries (by assumption, including the United States) and in the gold-standard countries. Figure 3 plots the actual U.S. price level and alternative hypothetical price levels corresponding to the gold-silver price ratios in Figure 2. The naive estimate simply assumes that the gold-silver price ratio and the real

*From 1803 to 1873, when France successfully maintained a bimetallic standard at a legal gold-silver ratio of 15.5 to 1, the lowest market ratio was 15.19 in 1859, the highest 16.25 in 1813. Most of the time the range was much narrower (Warren and Pearson 1933, table 25, p. 144).

Figure 3

U.S. Price Level: Actual and Alternatives under Silver Standard, 1865–1914

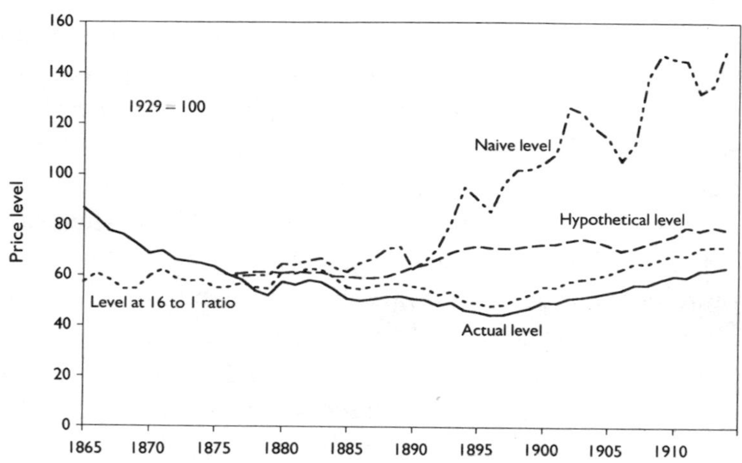

price of silver would have been what they actually were. On that assumption the price level is readily calculated. It is necessary only to multiply the price level that actually prevailed by the ratio of the legal price of silver ($1.2929) to the market price. However, this naive estimate clearly produces a great overestimate of the price rise that would have occurred. The 16 to 1 estimate goes to the other extreme; it underestimates the effect on the price level of the adoption of a silver standard by assuming that the actual ratio would have been precisely 16 to 1 throughout. The hypothetical estimate is in between these two, but for most of the period is considerably closer to the 16 to 1 estimate than to the naive estimate. However, the 16 to 1 estimate probably gives a more accurate picture of the likely year-to-year pattern than either of the other estimates do. Both the naive and the hypothetical estimates are bedeviled by purely statistical "noise." In addition, U.S. bimetallism would have provided an incentive for worldwide stabilizing speculation in silver that would have eliminated erratic movements.

The actual price level in the United States fell at a rate of 1.5 percent a year from 1876 to 1896 and then rose at a rate of 2.0 percent a year until 1914. The 16 to 1 price level first falls by 0.7 percent a year to 1896 and then rises by 2.3 percent a year to 1914. The hypothetical price level falls at a rate of 0.2 percent a year from 1876 to 1887 and then rises at the rate of 1.1 percent a year to 1914. Either alternative would have cut the initial rate of decline in half. The 16 to 1 alternative implies a slightly more rapid subsequent rise, the hypothetical alternative a much milder rise. If my estimates are anywhere near correct, a bimetallic standard—really a silver standard—would have produced a considerably steadier price level than did the gold standard that was adopted.

In addition, a silver standard almost surely would have avoided what Anna Schwartz and I, in our *Monetary History,* dubbed "the disturbed years from 1891 to 1897" (1963, p. 104)—years that encompassed the very sharp contraction of 1892 to 1894, a brief and mild recovery from 1894 to 1895, another contraction from 1895 to 1896,* widespread bank failures plus a banking panic in 1893, and a run on U.S. gold reserves by foreigners fearful that silver agitation would force the United States off the gold standard. Confidence was restored and a departure from gold prevented by a private syndicate headed by J. P. Morgan and August Belmont, under contract to the U.S. Treasury. "The allegedly onerous terms of the contract, arranged secretly through agents long identified in Populist litera-

*These are the annual reference dates used in Friedman and Schwartz (1982).

ture as 'the conspiracy of international bankers,' became an issue in the campaign of 1896" (Friedman and Schwartz 1963, p. 112n.).

The effects would not have been limited to the United States, of course. I have not been able to make anything like as thorough an empirical study for the rest of the world as for the United States. However, in the course of preparing the U.S. estimates, it was necessary to estimate the effect on the price level in the gold-standard world, for which I used Britain as a proxy. Figure 4 gives the actual and hypothetical level of prices in Britain. The estimated effect, though smaller than in the United States, is clearly substantial. The price level would have been consistently higher. The decline in the price level from 1875 to 1895 would have been cut from 0.8 percent a year to 0.5 percent; the subsequent rise would have been increased from 0.09 percent a year to 1.1 percent. Here too, however, effects

Figure 4

U.K. Price Level: Actual and Hypothetical, under U.S. Silver Standard, 1865–1914

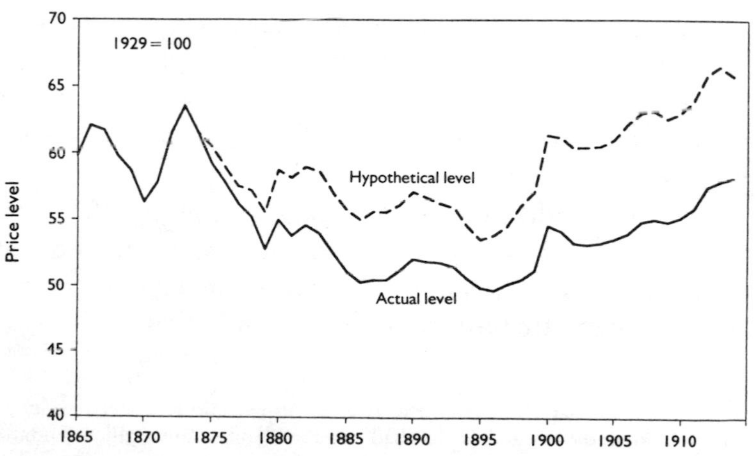

other than those encompassed in our simple calculation would clearly have been present. The changes in the United States would doubtless have produced echoes elsewhere. A healthier U.S. economy would have meant a healthier world economy. In addition, the consistently lower real price of gold would have reduced the incentive to produce gold. That might have delayed the introduction of the cyanide process for extracting low-grade ore, which was responsible for the flood of gold that produced worldwide inflation after 1896. I have not allowed for any such effects.

Whether or not a verdict of guilty would have been appropriate in a court of law for "the crime of 1873," that verdict is appropriate in the court of history. The omission of the fateful line had momentous consequences for the subsequent monetary history of the United States and, indeed, to some extent, of the world. The rhetoric was overheated, but the importance of the issue was not overstated. The real issue was the monetary standard: gold and silver bimetallism, which in practice in the United States had meant alternating silver and gold standards. The act of 1873 cast the die for a gold standard, which explains its significance. Moreover, while the conventional view is Laughlin's, that "the act of 1873 was a piece of good fortune" ([1886] 1895, p. 93), my own view is that it was the opposite—a mistake that had highly adverse consequences.

I hasten to add that this is a judgment about 1873, not 1896. By 1896 it was too late to undo the damage, for reasons discussed in chapter 5. Bryan was trying to close the barn door after the horse had been stolen.*

*The estimate in chapter 4 is that the market ratio would have been about 24 to 1 in 1896 if the United States had remained on a bimetallic standard.

I also hasten to add that this judgment is not intended either to denigrate or to praise the character or the intentions of the various parties in the long-running dispute. The pro-silver group contained silver producers seeking to promote their special interests, inflationists eager to seize any vehicle for that purpose, and sincere bimetallists who desired neither inflation nor deflation but were persuaded that bimetallism was more conducive to price stability than monometallism was. Similarly, the pro-gold group contained producers of gold, deflationists (pilloried by the free-silver forces as Wall Street bankers), and sincere believers that the gold standard was the only satisfactory pillar for a financially stable society. Motives and intentions matter far less than the outcome. And, in this as in so many other cases, the outcome was very different from that intended by the well-meaning advocates of the Coinage Act of 1873.

However, as indicated in the text, I suspect that that is a considerable overestimate.

CHAPTER 4

A Counterfactual Exercise: Estimating the Effect of Continuing Bimetallism after 1873*

This chapter provides the analysis that underlies the conclusions in the final section of the preceding chapter about the likely effects of continuing bimetallism after 1873. It is a what-if examination of a hypothetical development that, as I have argued in chapter 3, would have had major and far-reaching effects, not only in the United States but in the entire world. As such, my results are

*Many years ago, I suggested to Louis Drake, then professor of economics at the University of Southern Illinois, that he estimate the effect on U.S. and world prices of the United States' having remained on a bimetallic standard. He worked on the project for years and accumulated much data, but he was never sufficiently satisfied with his results to publish them. After his death in 1982, colleagues and friends edited a preliminary paper found in his files that retained in full his original calculations, and published the result in Drake (1985, pp. 194–219). When I began the paper which became chapter 3, I thought that I could simply use his results. However, when I read his paper in detail, I appreciated the reservations about his results that presumably had led him to refrain from publication. In consequence, I have produced an independent set of estimates, though benefiting from some of his data and analysis. Not surprisingly, my final results differ drastically from his.

inevitably subject to much uncertainty and wide margins of error, which I have tried to allow for in reaching the conclusions stated in chapter 3. This chapter is also highly technical and detailed. I suspect it will be of interest primarily to fellow practitioners of technical economics. Other readers may well prefer to proceed directly to later chapters.

1. **Objective.** To estimate the price level and gold-silver price ratio that would have prevailed if the Coinage Act of 1873 had contained provision for the free coinage of the standard silver dollar of 371.25 troy grains of pure silver, so that the legal and market price of silver had remained $1.2929. . . .

2. **Naive Estimate.** The real price of silver is simply the nominal price divided by the price level *(PS/P)*. On the naive assumption that this price remained unchanged, the real price of silver would have been 1.2929/*PHN*, where *PHN* is the naive estimate of the hypothetical price level under a silver standard. Equating the two and solving for the naive hypothetical price level gives

$$(1) \qquad PHN = 1.2929 \ldots \cdot \frac{P}{PS},$$

where *P* is the actual price level and *PS* is the actual nominal price of silver.* (For subsequent definitions of notation, see the Record of Notation at the end of the chapter.) The naive estimate is less than the actual price level from 1865 to 1876. In 1876 the two are equal; hence, if the fateful line had not been omitted from the Coinage Act of 1873, resumption on the basis of silver would have

*For sources of data for these and succeeding variables, see the Source Notes at the end of the chapter.

occurred in 1876, a year after the passage of the Resumption Act. Figure 3 of chapter 3 plots the subsequent naive estimate of the price level; Table 1 gives the numerical values.

Defects of the naive estimate: (1) The United States would probably have added to its silver stock under a silver standard even more than it did in response to the silver interests under a gold standard. That would have tended to raise the real price of silver. (2) The United States would also have exported gold rather than accumulating gold, which would have added to the rest of the world's monetary and nonmonetary stocks of gold and raised nominal prices in the gold-standard world. That would have lowered the real price of gold. (3) On both scores, the gold-silver price ratio would have been lower than it actually was.

3. **16 to 1 Estimate.** Assume that the adoption of a silver standard by the United States would have been effective in establishing 16 to 1 as the actual gold-silver price ratio and that the United States stayed on a strict silver standard (that is, the ratio was trivially above 16 to 1). As we shall see, this is not as farfetched as it seems.

To estimate the hypothetical U.S. price level under this assumption, we need an estimate of the hypothetical real price of gold. Assume that the United States disposed of the whole of its monetary gold stock when it adopted a silver standard and that the gold released was divided between nonmonetary use (by the United States and the rest of the world) and the monetary gold stock of the rest of the world in the proportion that actually prevailed between these two components of the total gold stock.*

*I owe this approach to Hugh Rockoff. It replaces a less attractive assumption I had made initially.

Table 1

Estimated Effect on U.S. and U.K. Prices of U.S. Being on Silver Standard, 1865–1914

Year	U.S. Price Level				UK Price Level		Gold-Silver	
	Actual	Hypothetical			1929 = 100		Price Ratio	
		Naive	16–1	Soph.	Actual	Hyp.	Actual	Hyp.
1865	86.5		57.3		59.8		15.4	
1866	82.6		60.8		62.0		15.5	
1867	77.6		58.2		61.6		15.6	
1868	76.2		54.6		59.8		15.6	
1869	72.7		54.7		58.7		15.6	
1870	68.7		59.8		56.3		15.6	
1871	69.8		62.5		57.8		15.6	
1872	66.3		59.0		61.4		15.6	
1873	65.5		57.6		63.5		15.9	
1874	64.8		58.3		61.5		16.2	
1875	63.3		55.1		59.2		16.6	
1876	60.4	60.2	55.4	60.4	57.8	59.0	17.8	17.2
1877	58.2	59.8	56.8	60.8	56.2	57.5	17.2	17.1
1878	53.9	60.1	55.4	61.4	55.2	57.2	17.9	17.7
1879	52.0	60.0	54.7	61.4	52.8	55.6	18.4	18.0
1880	57.4	64.5	61.3	61.0	55.0	58.7	18.0	15.9
1881	56.3	64.4	60.8	61.5	53.8	58.1	18.3	16.2
1882	58.1	66.0	62.8	61.1	54.6	59.0	18.2	15.5
1883	57.4	66.8	62.3	61.3	54.0	58.6	18.7	15.7
1884	54.4	63.2	59.1	59.7	52.5	57.0	18.7	16.2
1885	50.8	61.6	55.4	59.6	51.1	55.7	19.4	17.2
1886	50.1	65.1	54.8	59.2	50.3	55.0	20.9	17.3
1887	50.6	66.8	55.8	59.2	50.5	55.7	21.1	17.0
1888	51.5	70.9	56.7	59.7	50.5	55.6	22.0	16.8
1889	51.8	71.5	56.8	61.3	51.2	56.1	22.0	17.3
1890	50.8	62.8	55.8	63.4	52.1	57.1	19.7	18.2
1891	50.3	65.8	55.0	64.4	51.9	56.7	20.9	18.7
1892	48.3	71.3	52.5	66.7	51.8	56.2	23.8	20.3
1893	49.5	81.8	53.8	69.4	51.5	55.9	26.6	20.6
1894	46.4	95.2	50.0	70.9	50.6	54.6	32.9	22.7
1895	45.7	90.5	49.0	71.9	49.9	53.5	31.9	23.4
1896	44.4	85.5	48.1	71.3	49.7	53.9	30.5	23.7
1897	44.6	96.5	48.6	71.1	50.2	54.6	34.5	23.4
1898	45.9	101.8	51.0	71.3	50.5	56.1	35.5	22.4
1899	47.1	102.3	52.6	72.0	51.2	57.1	34.8	21.9

(continued on page 84)

Year	U.S. Price Level				UK Price Level		Gold-Silver	
	Actual	Hypothetical			1929 = 100		Price Ratio	
		Naive	16–1	Soph.	Actual	Hyp.	Actual	Hyp.
1900	49.6	104.5	55.8	72.6	54.6	61.4	33.8	20.8
1901	49.3	108.1	55.7	72.8	54.2	61.2	35.1	20.9
1902	51.0	126.5	57.9	74.0	53.3	60.4	39.7	20.5
1903	51.5	124.4	58.6	74.9	53.2	60.4	38.6	20.5
1904	52.3	118.2	59.4	73.8	53.3	60.5	36.2	19.9
1905	53.4	114.4	60.8	72.4	53.6	61.0	34.3	19.0
1906	54.5	105.4	62.7	70.1	54.0	62.2	31.0	17.9
1907	56.8	112.4	65.2	71.3	54.9	63.0	31.8	17.5
1908	56.7	138.6	65.0	73.1	55.1	63.2	39.1	18.0
1909	58.7	147.5	67.0	74.7	54.9	62.5	40.2	17.8
1910	60.2	145.6	68.7	76.4	55.2	63.0	38.7	17.8
1911	59.7	144.9	68.3	79.6	55.9	63.9	38.9	18.6
1912	62.3	132.4	71.4	78.2	57.5	65.9	34.1	17.5
1913	62.6	135.3	71.9	79.7	57.9	66.5	34.6	17.7
1914	63.5	149.7	71.8	78.6	58.2	65.8	37.8	17.5

Assume further that the world price level rose in proportion to the increased stock of gold. We then have

$$\text{(2)} \qquad RPGH = RPG \cdot \frac{EWMG + WNMG}{WMG + WNMG}.$$

Since the real price of silver is by assumption $\frac{1}{16}$ the real price of gold and by definition equal to the nominal price (= legal price) divided by the price level, we have

$$\text{(3)} \qquad PH16 = 1.2929\ldots \cdot \frac{16}{RPGH}.$$

The actual U.S. monetary gold stock became a steadily increasing fraction of the world's monetary gold from 1879 on, so that the 16 to 1 price roughly parallels the actual price, with the differential rising somewhat over the period (see Figure 3 of chapter 3). In 1876, when resumption on silver would have taken place, the price level as estimated from equation (3) was a trifle below the actual price level. By 1877, it was a trifle above.

The hypothetical real price of gold is also all that is needed to estimate the effect on the price level of the gold-standard world of the United States' being on a silver standard throughout the period. If we take the U.K. price level as representative of the price level of the gold-standard world, we have

$$UKPH = UKP \cdot \frac{WMG + WNMG}{EWMG + WNMG}. \quad (4)$$

(See Figure 4 of chapter 3.) The effect is clearly appreciable.*

4. A More Sophisticated Estimate. To go beyond these simple estimates requires finding a way to estimate the real price of silver, since we can use the counterpart of equation (3) to convert such an estimate into an estimate of the hypothetical price level.

*An interesting check on these estimates, discovered after they were completed, is provided by Irving Fisher, who in 1911 wrote: "If some way had been contrived by which gold and silver could have been kept together (say by world-wide bimetallism), prices would not have fallen so much [from the average of 1873–76] in gold countries, or risen so much (if at all) in silver countries, but would probably have fallen in gold countries slightly—probably about 10 per cent up to 1890–1893 and more up to 1896." He estimates that prices in fact fell 22 percent in gold countries between 1873–76 and 1890–93 and rose 17 percent in silver countries. According to Table 1, prices in the United States, a gold country, did fall 22 percent between the indicated dates, but in the United Kingdom, which I have taken as a representative gold country, they fell by 14 percent. The estimate of the hypothetical price index for the U.K. falls by half as much, or 7 percent, and then falls further to 1896, in both respects very close to Fisher's estimates, especially with respect to the fraction of the decline that would have been avoided.

As to silver countries, the estimate of the 16 to 1 U.S. price level in Table 1 falls 4 percent, of the hypothetical price level (discussed in point 4 of this chapter) rises 4 percent, consistent with Fisher's "if at all" (1911, pp. 244–45).

The real price of silver is determined by (a) the supply of and (b) the demand for silver for nonmonetary use in the world as a whole. The U.S. adoption of a bimetallic or silver standard would presumably not have significantly affected the world demand function for silver for nonmonetary use. To estimate that demand function (section b below) requires data on the actual nonmonetary use of silver (section a1). On the other hand, the U.S. adoption of a bimetallic or silver standard would clearly have altered significantly the supply of silver for nonmonetary use (section a2) because it would have increased the monetary demand for silver. Constructing acceptable estimates for the period in question (1875–1914) proved by far my most troublesome problem.

a1. *Actual Nonmonetary Use of Silver.* The supply of silver for nonmonetary use is equal to (1) the production of silver minus (2) the demand for silver for monetary use by the rest of the world minus (3) the demand for silver for U.S. monetary use. Or,

$$SNM = SPROD - EWMDS - UMDS \ . \tag{5}$$

Estimates for *SPROD,* the annual production of silver, and *EWMDS,* the increment in the monetary stock of silver by other countries, are readily available. I have constructed estimates for *UMDS,* the increment in the U.S. monetary stock of silver, for the fiscal years 1873 to 1894 from a report of the Treasury Department listing the U.S. purchases under the successive silver purchase acts and for later years from estimates of the total dollar value of the monetary stock of silver.

a2. *Hypothetical Supply of Silver for Nonmonetary Use.* Equation (5) gives actual nonmonetary use. Add an *H* to the relevant symbols and the equation gives hypothetical nonmonetary use under a silver standard. Item (1), silver production, depends in principle on the real price of silver. However, during the period in question the actual production of silver rose sharply, nearly tripling from 1880 to 1914, while at the same time the real price of silver fell to less than half its initial level. Supply was clearly being driven by exogenous discoveries and innovations. Moreover, much silver is a by-product of the mining of other metals and so is relatively inelastic in supply. Hence, I have assumed that silver production would have been what it actually was. This assumption introduces an error leading to an upward bias in the estimated real price of silver.

Regarding item (2), I have assumed that other countries would not have been affected by the U.S. adoption of a silver standard, either by themselves adopting silver rather than gold or by changing the amount of silver added to their monetary stocks. This assumption seems eminently justified. The major move from silver to gold by Germany, France, and others came before the United States would have moved to a silver standard and, indeed, was part of the reason why the United States itself moved to a gold standard. Hence, I have simply used the actual monetary demand by other countries as the hypothetical.

Item (3), the hypothetical increment in the U.S. monetary stock of silver, is the most difficult. We can tautologically express the hypothetical U.S. monetary silver stock (in ounces) as the product of the ratio maintained between specie and money *(SPR)* times the quantity of money divided by the legal price of silver, or, expressing the quantity of money by the ratio of nominal income to velocity and expressing nominal income as the product of real income and the price level, as follows:

$$(6)\quad UMSH = \frac{UMG\$}{UM} \cdot \frac{y}{V} \cdot \frac{P}{LP} = SPR \cdot \frac{y}{V} \cdot \frac{1}{RPSH} = k_1 \cdot \frac{1}{RPSH}.$$

y/V is the real money stock; multiplication by P converts it into nominal dollars. Only the product of SPR and y/V, which I have designated by k_1 and which equals the real value of the specie reserve, enters into the subsequent analysis. (In principle, all the symbols should be followed by an H, but since no confusion arises except for the real price of silver, I have omitted the H.)

The reason for expressing the money stock as the product of the real stock and the price level is because the price level is what we are seeking to estimate. The second form of stating the right-hand side of equation (6) introduces the hypothetical real price of silver in place of the nominal price level. From that, we can readily estimate the hypothetical nominal price level by using the counterpart of equation (1).

In computing the actual values in equation (5), we regarded silver in circulation or held by the Treasury as monetary silver. However, in estimating hypothetical values of the specie reserve ratio and of specie reserves for the gold-standard period, we cannot treat monetary silver as part of specie reserves, though it would have had that status under a bimetallic or silver standard. It was simply a governmental asset accumulated as part of an attempt to prop up the price of silver (like government stocks of wheat at present).

Accordingly, we have used only monetary gold stocks for the present purpose. Figure 1 plots the gold reserve ratio (the ratio of the dollar value of monetary gold to the quantity of money), the real value of the stock of money, and the real value of gold reserves (actual gold k_1). The

Figure 1

Gold Reserve Ratio, Real M2, and Gold Reserves, 1875–1914 (Money amounts in billions of 1929 dollars)

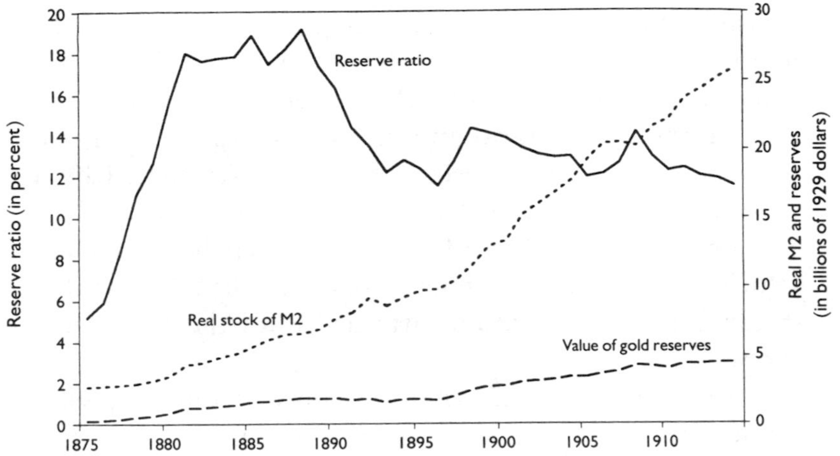

rapid rise in the reserve ratio during the first five years after the passage of the Resumption Act (1875 through 1879) was to be expected in preparation for resumption. Presumably, a similar rise would have occurred if resumption had been on silver instead of gold, with the sole difference that silver would have been accumulated rather than gold. In either case, the accumulation of reserves required a surplus on the current account of the balance of payment or capital inflows. And a sizable surplus was generated from 1876 to 1881, followed by sizable capital inflows. I see no reason to suppose that the initial buildup of reserves would have been different under silver than it was under gold.

By 1879, the specie reserve ratio reached roughly the same level as in the early 1900s, after the end of the period of uncertainty generated by the monetary disturbances of the 1880s and 1890s. The further rise after 1879 was prompted by an effort to persuade the public, not only at home but equally abroad, that the gold standard was here to stay. As agitation for a more expansive monetary policy mounted, however, that effort failed and, especially after the pro-silver movement gained steam, led to continuous pressures on gold reserves, producing a sharp decline in the reserve ratio and a slightly declining level of real reserves. After the defeat of Bryan in 1896, there was a temporary spurt in the reserve ratio and an even sharper rise in real reserves, as the higher reserve ratio was reinforced by a rapid increase in the real money supply—itself partly a consequence of a return of confidence that both lowered velocity and fostered a higher real income. Reasonably steady conditions were not attained until the end of the period.

After trying many alternative ways of estimating what specie reserves would have been under an unchallenged and fully accepted silver standard, I finally settled on a purely empirical expedient: a straight-line trend between the average values of gold reserves during the first five and the last five years of the period from 1875 to 1914. As Figure 2 shows, such a trend eliminates both the initial bulge and the later decline that, in the previous paragraph, I attributed to the monetary disturbances and their aftermath. For 1875–79 and 1901–14, it approximates the actual pattern.

The U.S. hypothetical annual monetary demand for silver is simply the increment in the U.S. hypothetical silver stock:

$$(7) \quad UMDSH(t) = \Delta UMSH = UMSH(t) - UMSH\,(t - 1)\,.$$

The possible errors in this approach are numerous. Some simply affect the year-to-year movements as a result of the use of a trend for k_1. Any systematic bias arises primarily from the assumption that the same specie re-

Figure 2

Actual and Hypothetical Gold Reserves (k_1), 1875–1914 (in billions of 1929 dollars)

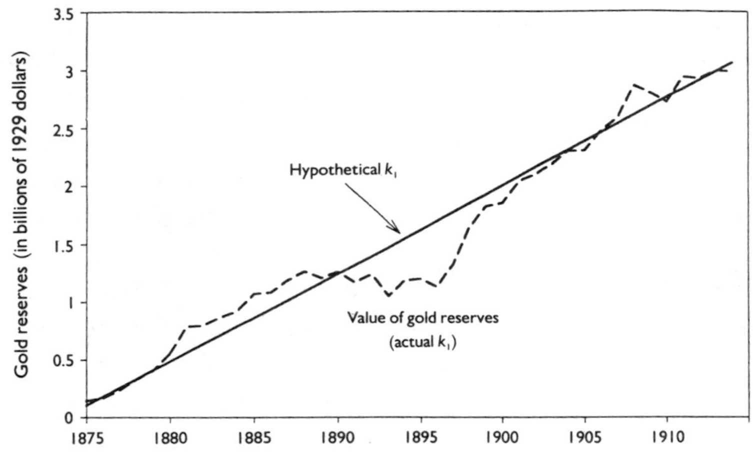

serves would have been maintained under a silver standard in the early and late years of the period as those maintained under a gold standard. The possible sources of error are different for the specie reserve ratio and the real stock of money. The desired specie reserve ratio might have been affected by a different pattern of prices. A rise in prices under a gold (silver) standard means that the real value of gold (silver) is falling, and conversely. A falling real value makes it less expensive to hold the specie reserves, and conversely. It is doubtful, however, that any such price effect has a significant influence on the decision by the monetary authority on how large a specie reserve is desirable—any financial benefit or loss is subtle and accrues to the government at large and not specifically to the monetary authority. A more important factor is surely the threat of a specie drain, which would have been largely absent under a secure silver standard.

The real stock of money would have been affected by the reduction in uncertainty as a result of settling on a definitive silver standard. The reduced uncertainty would have tended to lower velocity and raise real income, both of which would have raised the real money stock—as appears to have happened after 1896. Neglect of these effects produces an underestimate of the hypothetical silver stock. Such an underestimate introduces a downward bias in estimating the real price of silver, or a bias in the opposite direction from the possible bias introduced in estimating item (1), the production of silver.

b. *Demand for Silver.* The quantity of silver demanded for nonmonetary use depends primarily on world real income, the real price of silver, and the real price of gold. I have estimated a demand curve with these variables in two variants: linear and logarithmic. As a general rule, the logarithmic form is preferable. However, in this particular case I do not believe it is. The logarithmic form forces the nonmonetary demand for silver to be positive, yet it is easily possible for additions to monetary stocks of silver to exceed the world production of silver (as happened most recently under the silver purchase program of Franklin Delano Roosevelt in the 1930s). In that case, the quantity of silver available for nonmonetary purposes is negative if it is estimated in accordance with equation (5), which gives the nonmonetary supply of silver out of current production, not the nonmonetary use of silver.

As an estimate of world real income, I have used an index number of the physical volume of world production given by Warren and Pearson (1933).* For the real price of

*A footnote to the Warren and Pearson tables says that for 1865 to 1932 the index was prepared by Carl Snyder of the Federal Reserve Bank of New York.

silver and the real price of gold, I simply used the actual prices divided by the U.S. deflator. This procedure assumes that the real price of silver and the real price of gold were the same throughout the world, surely not an unreasonable assumption for those two monetary metals.*

The two equations are as follows for 1880–1914:

$$(8) \qquad \log SNM = \underset{(3.7)}{-6.96} + \underset{(4.0)}{1.27} \log WI - \underset{(4.0)}{1.28} \log RPS + \underset{(5.6)}{1.87} \log RPG\,,$$

$$(9) \qquad SNM = \underset{(0.8)}{58.28} + \underset{(4.0)}{2.13}WI - \underset{(4.0)}{66.21}RPA + \underset{(1.1)}{0.88}RPG,$$

where *WI* stands for world income. As usual, the values in parentheses are the absolute *t*-values. In the log equation, the coefficients are all highly significant; in the linear equation, only the coefficients of world income and the real price of silver are. However, there is little to choose between the equations in terms of the goodness of fit, as can be seen graphically in Figure 3 as well as from the adjusted

Warren and Pearson report similar index numbers of U.S. physical volume of production. The trend of the index of U.S. production is steeper than the trend of U.S. real income (estimates from Friedman and Schwartz 1982). On the other hand, the general ups and downs are very similar. Accordingly, I experimented with adjusting the Warren and Pearson index by subtracting out a trend at a rate equal to the difference between the logarithmic trends of U.S. production and U.S. real income, which was four-tenths of 1 percent per year. However, the effect on the final results was trivial and, if anything, rendered them slightly less significant statistically, so I have simply used the original index.

*However, it is not clear that it is preferable to use the U.S. rather than the U.K. deflator. I experimented with both. The difference in results was small, trivially in favor of the U.S. deflator. Still, a more decisive consideration was that I wanted to use the equation to estimate the hypothetical U.S. price level, so it was encouraging that substituting the U.K. deflator did not produce a statistical improvement.

Figure 3

Nonmonetary Demand for Silver, Actual and Predicted, Linear and Log Regression, 1880:1914

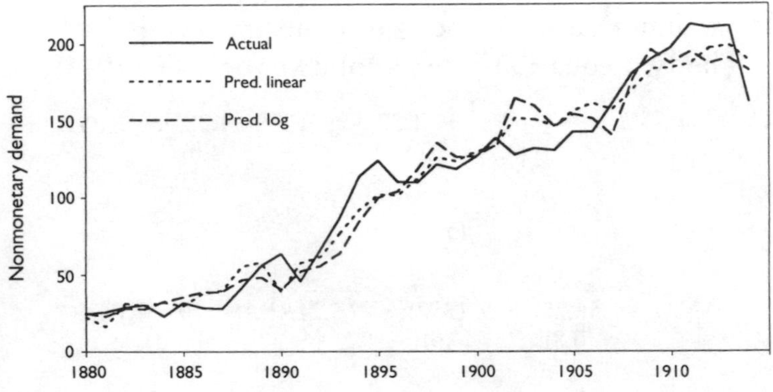

Note: Dependent variable: nonmonetary demand for silver (in millions of ounces); independent variables: world income, real prices of silver and gold.

R^2*s*, which are .949 for the log equation and .950 for the linear equation. The standard error of estimate for the log equation is .180, which is comparable to an estimate of the coefficient of variation for the linear equation. That is .138 if the denominator of the coefficient of variation is the arithmetic mean of the dependent variables and .177 if it is the geometric mean. Both estimates for the linear equation are lower than that for the log equation.

Estimating a hypothetical price level using the linear equation is mathematically far more tractable than using the log equation, and that reinforces the theoretical consideration in favor of the linear equation (that the silver available for nonmonetary use out of current production can be negative). Hence, from here on I use only the linear equation.

c. *Equating Supply and Demand.* Equating equations (5) and (9), and rearranging the terms:

$$UMDSH = SPROD - EWMDS - 58.28 - 2.13WI - 0.88RPGH + 66.21RPSH . \tag{10}$$

To simplify, let k_2 equal all the terms on the right-hand side of equation (10) except the last, and let x equal the hypothetical real price of silver that is our objective. All of these are also functions of time. However, given our assumptions up to this point, we have estimates of the values of k_1 and k_2 for all the years from 1874 to 1914.

In terms of these symbols, we can rewrite equation (7), using equation (6), as

$$UMDSH(t) = \frac{k_1(t)}{x(t)} - \frac{k_1(t-1)}{x(t-1)} . \tag{11}$$

Equating equations (10) and (11) and simplifying:

$$66.21x^2(t) + \left[k_2(t) + \frac{k_1(t-1)}{x(t-1)}\right] x(t) - k_1(t) = 0 . \tag{12}$$

Equation (12) is now in the form of a straightforward quadratic equation except for the troublesome presence of the term including $x(t - 1)$ in the denominator. This $x(t - 1)$ is one of the unknowns that we are trying to determine. As a first approximation, assume that the real price of silver does not change from year to year, in other words, that $x(t)$ equals $x(t - 1)$. That assumption converts equation (12) into the simplified equation (13), which involves only the current year's value of the unknown x, although it does involve the prior year's value of k_1, via substituting Δk_1 for $k_1(t) - k_1(t - 1)$.

$$66.21x^2 + k_2x - \Delta k_1 = 0 . \tag{13}$$

The solution to this equation is a first approximation to x.

For a second, third, and succeeding approximations, we can return to equation (12) and replace $x(t - 1)$ by the prior approximation estimate. The successive approximations do converge, though rather slowly. The main changes are not in the level or general pattern but, rather, in the year-to-year movements. However, each approximation involves losing one value at the beginning of the series. I stopped with the eleventh approximation, at which point 1884 is the first year for which there is an estimate. For earlier years, I used the earlier approximations, beginning with the third for 1876, the year in which the silver standard would have been adopted.* Given this estimate of the real price of silver, it is necessary only to divide the legal price by the real price to estimate the hypothetical price level under a silver standard. The resulting estimate of the hypothetical price level for the United States is plotted in Figure 3 of chapter 3.

d. *Gold-Silver Price Ratio.* Since we have already estimated the hypothetical price of gold, it is trivial to get the hypothetical price ratio of gold to silver. The result is plotted in Figure 2 of chapter 3, along with the actual and legal gold-silver price ratio. The actual gold-silver price ratio under a U.S. silver standard would almost surely have fluctuated much less than our estimates of the hypothetical gold-silver price ratio, given the arbitrary assumptions and inevitable measurement errors that affect our estimates and the extent to which they have been affected by the monetary uncertainty of the period.

These estimates suggest that, if the United States had returned to a bimetallic standard in 1879 and had stayed

*The year 1874 is the first for which I have an estimate for *EWMDS*, which explains why the first year for which I can estimate the first approximation is 1874.

on it consistently, the market gold-silver price ratio would have remained roughly equal to or only slightly above the U.S. legal price ratio—just as for close to a century the market ratio remained roughly equal to the legal price ratio in France. (Table 1 gives the numerical values for the curves plotted in Figures 2, 3, and 4 of chapter 3.)

5. **An Even More Sophisticated Estimate.** In principle, it would be possible to get a fully simultaneous solution for both the real price of silver and the real price of gold by following the same procedure for gold as for silver, namely, estimating (a) a demand equation for the nonmonetary use of gold and (b) the hypothetical quantity of gold that would have been demanded if the United States had gone on a silver standard. However, explorations along this line have proved disappointing. First, estimating the hypothetical nonmonetary demand is even more difficult for gold than for silver.* Second, estimated demand equations for gold yielded negative, though statistically not significant, coefficients for the real price of silver instead of the positive coefficient that would be expected for a substitute for gold.† That result is inconsistent with the

*A major sticking point is to specify precisely how the U.S. gold stock would have been disposed of. My earlier rough approximation evades this question. For a full solution, however, we cannot evade it. Demand functions for gold and silver refer to annual quantity demanded, and we need to equate that demand function with annual supply; this means that we would need to add to total gold production the amount of gold that the United States would have released to the rest of the world from its stock on a year-by-year basis. I see no way to estimate the annual release except by purely arbitrary assumptions.

†The calculated demand functions for nonmonetary use of gold are as satisfactory as those for silver in terms of goodness of fit, but not in terms of economic logic. The logarithmic and linear demand functions are as follows:

$$\text{(14)} \quad \log WNMG = \underset{(13.2)}{4.34} + \underset{(10.0)}{0.555} \log WI - \underset{(1.4)}{0.077} \log RPS - \underset{(4.5)}{0.259} \log RPG\ ,$$

positive coefficient for the real price of gold in demand equations for silver, a violation of the Slutsky cross-equation condition. Eliminating that contradiction requires estimating the silver and gold demand equations simultaneously, imposing the appropriate cross-equation restriction. Given the drastic difference between the two separate equations, I doubt that the result would deserve much confidence. Finally, these problems resolved, the simultaneous solution requires solving a fourth-degree equation in the U.S. price level.

I am thus left in a quandary. I am unhappy with what I have done but even more unhappy with the most obvious alternative, a simplified general equilibrium analysis. A comprehensive general equilibrium analysis would have to

---

$$(15)\quad \underset{}{WNMG} = \underset{(4.2)}{169.862} + \underset{(9.0)}{3.08} \log WI - \underset{(0.8)}{8.721RPS} - \underset{(2.8)}{1.482RPG},$$

where *WNMG* is the world nonmonetary demand for gold. As with silver, both equations give high multiple correlations (adjusted R^2s of .98 for the log equation and of .97 for the linear equation) and relatively small standard errors. The standard error of the log correlation is .031. The corresponding estimate for the linear equation of the coefficient of variation is .037, whether the denominator is an arithmetic mean or a geometric mean.

An appendix to chapter 4 of the Report of the U.S. Commission on the Role of Gold reports estimates of demand equations that are linear in the logarithms of the variables for the industrial demand for gold for 1950–80 and 1969–80 (1982, pp. 176–77). The independent variables are conceptually the same as those that I used: the real price of gold, the real price of silver, and real income. Both sets use two alternative deflators to estimate the real prices, the U.S. wholesale price index and the world consumer price index. The difference between the two sets of equations is that the one for the longer period uses U.S. income only, whereas that for the shorter period uses three alternative real income variables: for seven major industrial countries, for the United States, and for the world.

The four equations that use U.S. income give a negative coefficient for the real price of silver, though only one out of four comes close to statistical significance. On the other hand, the four others (all for the shorter period) are all positive, in line with theoretical expectations, though none comes close to statistical significance.

This evidence clearly does not contribute to resolving the puzzle.

include not only the determinants of gold production and silver production, which I have completely neglected, but also the determinants of the fraction of gold production and silver production that go into monetary and nonmonetary use. Construction of such an expanded general equilibrium model would be extremely laborious and would deserve little confidence. Under the circumstances, I am inclined to leave well enough alone, while at the same time acknowledging that the estimates are subject to a wide margin of error—particularly with respect to year-to-year movements.

Source Notes

(in the order in which the variables are introduced)

P 1869–1914: Friedman and Schwartz (1982, table 4.8); 1865–68: extrapolated backward from Hoover (1960, p. 142).

PS U.S. Bureau of the Census (1975, p. 606, series 270). For 1865 to 1878, original source gives price in gold dollars; adjusted to greenback price by multiplying by reciprocal of gold value of currency, from Warren and Pearson (1933, table 69, p. 351).

WMG, *WNMG* U.S. Commission on the Role of Gold (1982, table SC 7, p. 198).

UMG U.S. Commission on the Role of Gold (1982, table SC 9, p. 203); 1865–77 shifted from June 30 to December 31 date by two-year moving average of June 30 data for 1865–78.

EWMG = *WMG* − *UMG*.

RPG 1865–78: reciprocal of gold value of currency

(from Warren and Pearson 1933, table 69, p. 351) times legal price of gold ($20.67183) divided by *P;* 1879–1914: legal price divided by *P*.

UKP 1868–1914: Friedman and Schwartz (1982, table 4.9); 1865–67: extrapolated back from 1868 by price index implicit in Deane (1968).

SPROD Warren and Pearson (1933, table 24, p. 139). 1865–75: linear interpolation between centered five-year averages in table; thereafter, annual figures in table.

EWMDS Drake (1985, table A, pp. 208–209) gives estimates for successive five-year periods based on annual reports of the director of the U.S. Mint. I simply assumed that the same amount was accumulated each year during the successive five-year periods. The numbers are small and do not vary drastically from one period to the next, so not much error is introduced by this assumption. However, I suspect that the initial estimates are subject to a large margin of error.

UMDS Purchases under the silver purchase laws of February 12, 1873, January 14, 1875, February 28, 1878, and July 14, 1890, are given in U.S. Secretary of the Treasury (1899, p. 207). For the first two purchase laws, only the total is given; I have assumed the amount purchased was the same in each month of the period for which each law was in effect. For the final two laws, figures are given for fiscal years from 1878 to 1894. For later years, I have estimated the physical stock of silver from the dollar stock of silver dollars and subsidiary silver as reported in U.S. Secretary of the Treasury (1928, pp. 552–53) by dividing by the legal price, allowing roughly for the lesser amount of silver in subsidiary silver, and have differenced the series to get annual purchases. When the Treasury bought silver it paid the market price, but it valued the silver for monetary purposes at the legal price, which is why the physical stock can be estimated from the monetary stock by dividing by the legal price of silver. The allowance for the different treatment of subsidiary silver is rough, but the amounts involved are small, so no great error is introduced. The final estimates are for fiscal years ending June 30, whereas *SPROD* and *EWMDS* are for calendar years, so I have converted the fiscal-year data to calendar-year data by a two-year moving average.

UMG$ 1879–1914: Friedman and Schwartz (1963, table 5, pp. 130–31); 1866–78: estimates by Anna J. Schwartz based on same sources.

UM Friedman and Schwartz (1982, table 4.8).

y Friedman and Schwartz (1982, table 4.8).

V = Nominal income from Friedman and Schwartz (1982, table 4.8) divided by *UM*.

WI = Warren and Pearson (1933, table 12, pp. 85–86) index number of world's physical volume of production, 1880–1914 = 100, divided by 2.

Record of Notation

EWMDS	actual monetary demand for silver in rest of world (external)
EWMG	rest of world actual monetary gold stock
k_1 =	$SPR \cdot y/V$
k_2 =	$SPROD - EWMDS - 58.28 - 2.13WI - 0.88RPGH$
LP	legal price of silver
P	U.S. price level
PHN	naive estimate of price level
*PH*16	estimate of price level on assumption that gold-silver price ratio is 16 to 1
PS	nominal price of silver
RPG	real price of gold in 1929 dollars
RPGH	hypothetical real price of gold in 1929 dollars
RPS	real price of silver in 1929 dollars
RPSH	hypothetical real price of silver in 1929 dollars
*RPSH*16	hypothetical real price of silver on assumption of 16 to 1 ratio
SNM	silver available for nonmonetary use
SPR	specie reserve ratio
SPROD	total silver production
UKP	British price level
UKPH	hypothetical British price level
UM	U.S. actual stock of money
UMDS	actual annual monetary demand for silver in U.S.
UMDSH	hypothetical U.S. annual monetary demand for silver
UMG	U.S. monetary gold stock in ounces
UMG$	U.S. monetary gold stock in dollars

UMGR$	U.S. monetary gold stock in 1929 dollars
UMS	actual U.S. monetary stock of silver
UMSH	hypothetical U.S. monetary stock of silver
V	U.S. velocity
WI	real world income (including U.S.)
WMG	world monetary gold
WNMG	world nonmonetary demand for gold (including U.S.)
x	*RPSH*
y	U.S. real income

CHAPTER 5

William Jennings Bryan and the Cyanide Process

In 1896, William Jennings Bryan was nominated for president by the Democratic, the Populist, and the National Silver parties. He ran on a platform committed to "free silver" at "16 to 1"—that is, the adoption of a bimetallic monetary standard at mint prices for gold and silver whereby 16 ounces of silver would have the same value as 1 ounce of gold. His Republican opponent, William McKinley, ran on a platform committed to the retention of a monometallic gold standard. McKinley beat Bryan by a popular vote margin of less than 10 percent. That was the high point of the free-silver movement. Although Bryan was twice again the Democratic nominee, he lost by increasingly wide margins.

In 1887, three Scottish chemists—John S. MacArthur and Robert W. and William Forrest—had invented a commercially viable cyanide process for extracting gold from low-grade ore. The process turned out to be particularly applicable to the vast goldfields discovered at about that time in South Africa. The output of gold in Africa went from zero in 1886 to 23 percent of total world output by 1896, and to more than 40 percent of total world output during the first quarter of the twentieth century.*

Strange as it may seem, these two sets of events in nearly opposite parts of the globe were intimately related. Not long after the outbreak of the Civil War, the United States had replaced its bimetallic standard, under which gold and silver, or notes convertible into gold and silver, served as money, with a greenback standard, under which paper money not convertible into anything else was designated legal tender. The resulting wartime inflation produced a price level more than twice what it had been. When the war ended, there was a widespread desire to return to a commodity standard. But to do so at the prewar legal price of the precious metals, which meant at the prewar exchange rate between the dollar and the British pound, required the cutting of the price level by more than half. That took fourteen years. As chapter 3 explains, the Coinage Act of 1873 was passed to prepare for resumption, though its real function was to replace the pre–Civil War bimetallic standard with a monometallic gold standard. The Resumption Act of 1875 was the next major step. It specified that resumption of specie payments—that is, the full convertibility of paper money into gold, and conversely—should take place on January 1, 1879.

Resumption on the basis of gold did occur on schedule in 1879. Together with the roughly concurrent adoption of a gold standard by most European nations, the result produced worldwide deflation in the 1880s and 1890s. That deflation, particularly serious in the United States, was

*Data for 1896 from *Encyclopaedia Britannica,* 11th ed. (1910), s.v. "Gold"; first-quarter-century figure from Warren and Pearson (1935, p. 122).

what energized the free-silver movement, which had arisen after the demonetization of silver, and ultimately led to Bryan's nomination in 1896 on a free-silver platform.

By making gold more valuable in terms of other goods, the price deflation also encouraged the invention of the cyanide process. And the successful application of the cyanide process in South Africa, in turn, doomed Bryan and the cause of free silver to defeat and political decline by producing a flood of gold that achieved the free-silver movement's primary objective—inflation—by other means.

Bryan's Nomination and Subsequent Political Career

The Democratic national convention of 1896 was held in Chicago, in tents erected in open fields at Sixty-third Street and Cottage Grove. The site was near the terminus of the recently constructed elevated railway, enabling delegates to reach the tent city rapidly from their Loop hotels. (The area later became highly developed and acquired an unsavory reputation. In the 1930s, when I was a student at the nearby University of Chicago, Sixty-third Street and Cottage Grove was known as "Sin Corner.")

This was the convention at which William Jennings Bryan, a delegate and a masterful orator, electrified the audience with his famous speech containing the passage "You shall not press down upon the brow of labor this crown of thorns, you shall not crucify mankind upon a cross of gold."

Bryan's previous activities on behalf of the free coinage of silver at a ratio of 16 ounces of silver to 1 ounce of gold had made him a leading contender for the presidential nomination on the Democratic ticket. Prior to the convention, the western and southern Silver Democrats had wrested control of the party machinery from the eastern Gold Democrats, with whom it had long resided. However, Bryan was only one of a number of Silver Democrats considered as possible candidates. His stirring speech—characterized by historian Richard Hofstadter (1966, 2:573) as "probably the most effective speech in the history of American party politics"—settled the matter and led to his nomination at age thirty-six as the presidential candidate of the Democratic party. He later was nominated also by the Populist and the National Silver parties.

After a bitter and hard-fought campaign, Bryan was defeated by his Republican opponent, William McKinley, who received 271 electoral votes to Bryan's 176. Though the electoral vote exaggerates the margin of victory, McKinley's victory was decisive. His popular vote majority was nearly 10 percent, a remarkable accomplishment under the circumstances. Eighteen ninety-six was itself a year of deep depression, following a number of years of hard times. Unemployment was high and rising; industrial output was low and falling; agricultural prices were low and falling. While somewhat less extreme, the economic situation resembled that of 1932.

The political situation was, however, very different. The incumbent president was a Democrat, Grover Cleveland, a Gold Democrat who had engineered the repeal of the Sherman Silver Purchase Act (Timberlake 1978). The party was split on the silver issue. The Gold Democrats organized a National Democratic party, which ran its own candidate, but this splinter party did not poll many votes. Rather, as James Barnes writes in an authoritative discussion of the Bryan campaign, "Bryan was defeated by that fear of something we know not of, for the bare bodkin of free silver on the tongues of the gold advocates conjured up evils more formidable even than those that existed. . . . Bryan . . . in part defeated himself by permitting the gold men to draw him on to their own battlefield and slay him with a single sword. A brilliant offensive that had begun on a wide field in July with the cry 'We defy them' had by November turned into a defense on a narrow money front. There was sense in Mark Hanna's comment [Mark Hanna was McKinley's campaign manager], 'He's talking Silver all the time, and that's where we've got him,' for the army that girded itself in midsummer could not be held together on the single question of the standard of value" (1947, pp. 399, 402). In an attached footnote, Barnes adds: "In the beginning they were attacking with confidence privilege, monopoly, high prices, exactions by the money lenders, corruption in government, and a social and economic order that had neglected the mass of the people. By November they were fighting on the single question of a silver dollar versus a gold dollar, and many were both scared and bewildered" (pp. 399–400).*

Bryan was nominated for president again in 1900 and in 1908. On both occasions, he was defeated by a wider popular and electoral vote majority than in 1896. He remained influential in the Democratic party, serving as Woodrow Wilson's secretary of state from 1913 to 1915, when he resigned. As an avowed pacifist, he objected to what he took to be Wilson's departure from absolute neutrality—one of the all too rare instances when a cabinet

*As noted in the footnote on pages 64–65, chapter 3, Hugh Rockoff (1990) argues that *The Wonderful Wizard of Oz* is a fictional retelling of the silver agitation and this campaign.

member has resigned on grounds of principle. Nonetheless, 1896 had clearly been the peak of his political career. It was all downhill after that.

He died in 1925, a few days after his last great battle—the famous Scopes trial, which pitted Bryan, as a fundamentalist defending a Tennessee statute outlawing the teaching of evolution, against Clarence Darrow, as a modernist opposing the statute as a violation of free speech. Bryan won the battle (the defendant, John Scopes, was found guilty of violating the law and was fined) but lost the war (the decision was later overruled). And, the legal verdict aside, it was Darrow, not Bryan, who was undoubtedly the hero in the court of public opinion.

While conventional wisdom identifies both Bryan and the 1896 campaign almost exclusively with silver, free silver was not the only plank in the Democratic platform, as Barnes (1947) suggests, and many of the other planks ultimately fared much better. As Henry Commager wrote in 1942: "Few statesmen have ever been more fully vindicated by history. Item by item the program which Bryan had consistently espoused, from the early nineties on into the new century, was written onto the statute books—written into law by those who had denounced and ridiculed it. Call the list of reforms: government control of currency and banking, government regulation of railroads, telegraph and telephone, trust regulation, the eight-hour day, labor reforms, the prohibition of injunctions in labor disputes, the income tax, tariff reform, anti-imperialism, the initiative, the referendum, woman suffrage, temperance, international arbitration" (p. 99). Personally, I have considerably more sympathy for Bryan's support of bimetallism than conventional wisdom does and considerably less for many of the other reforms he sponsored.

McKinley's career was quite different: politically successful, personally tragic. He was assassinated by an anarchist in 1901, but he also presided over the Spanish-American War, was reelected in 1900 by a substantially wider margin than he had achieved in 1896, and witnessed a rapid economic revival—indeed, something close to a boom—in the United States.

The Triumph of the Gold Standard

Both the free-silver movement and the incentives that spurred the development and application of the cyanide process for mining gold have their roots in monetary developments of the 1870s and even further back, after the Napoleonic wars, in Britain's adoption of a gold standard in 1816 and resumption of specie payments on the basis of gold in 1821. Britain's subsequent rise to world economic dominance doubtless played a major role in endowing the gold standard with an aura of superiority and in inducing other countries to follow Britain's example.

France successfully maintained a bimetallic standard at a ratio of 15.5 to 1 from 1803 on. However, it was forced off that standard in 1873 by its defeat in the Franco-Prussian War. Germany exacted a huge indemnity, which it used to finance the adoption of a gold standard. In the process, Germany disposed of large amounts of silver, simultaneously putting upward pressure on the price of gold and downward pressure on the price of silver. The combination made it impossible for France to continue maintaining the price ratio of 15.5 to 1. France and most other European countries subsequently replaced bimetallic or silver standards with gold standards.

At the time, the United States was still on the paper

standard—the greenback standard—that it had adopted not long after the outbreak of the Civil War. Chapter 3 tells the detailed story of the developments that led the United States to resume specie payments in 1879 on the basis of gold. The U.S. action was the final step, and a major one, in the transition of the Western world to a gold standard.

The resulting sharp increase in the demand for gold for monetary purposes was superimposed on a slowing supply, as the flood of gold from the California and Australia discoveries of the 1840s and 1850s started to ebb. The inevitable result was worldwide deflation. (Figure 1 plots

Figure 1

U.S. and U.K. Price Level, Annually, 1865–1914

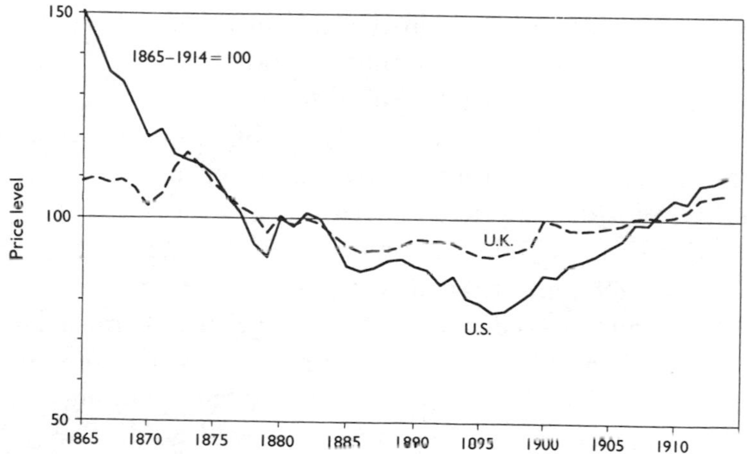

SOURCES: Data from 1869 on for the U.S. and 1868 on for the U.K. from Friedman and Schwartz (1982, tables 4.8 and 4.9). Earlier data extrapolated from later data by the use of a number of available indexes.

the price level in the United States and the United Kingdom from 1865 to 1914.)

The price decline was particularly severe in the United States because of the aftermath of the Civil War greenback inflation. By 1879, when the United States resumed specie payments, prices were already less than half their level at the end of the Civil War. That sharp price decline was what made resumption possible at the pre–Civil War parity between the dollar and the British pound sterling. In its turn, resumption brought temporary relief from the falling prices. However, within a few years deflation began again, accelerating after 1889 as the growing political agitation for free silver spread doubts that the United States would stay on the gold standard.

Deflation and the Cyanide Process

Deflation meant a decline in prices expressed in gold. It was equivalent to a rise in the real price of gold, that is, in the quantity of goods that an ounce of gold would purchase on the market. Put differently, the prices that were declining included those entering into the cost of producing gold, so that gold mining became more profitable. Worldwide prices in terms of gold, as measured by the British price index, fell by more than 20 percent from 1873 to 1896, and that meant a similar reduction in the cost of mining gold. Such a reduction in cost must have multiplied the profit margin at prior levels of production severalfold. In other words, it justified the spending of up to 20 percent more to extract additional gold. The gold discoveries in South Africa, the development of the cyanide process, and its commercial application would very likely have occurred in any case. But they were speeded up, perhaps significantly, by the additional incentive arising from the price deflation.

Deflation and the Silver Movement

Deflation did not prevent rapid economic growth in the United States. On the contrary, rapid growth was the active force that produced the deflation after the Civil War. The desire to return to a specie standard encouraged restraint in monetary growth, but the restraint was not potent enough to prevent the quantity of money from being higher in 1879 than it was in 1867 (the first year for which we have satisfactory data). Prices came down as rapidly as they did only because output was rising so much faster than the quantity of money was. Similarly, the evidence "suggests little significant change in the rate of growth over the period [from 1879 to 1914] as a whole, but rather a sharp retardation from something like 1892 to 1896, and then a sharp acceleration from 1896 to 1901, which just about made up for lost time. If this be right, generally declining or generally rising prices had little impact on the rate of growth, but the period of great monetary uncertainty in the early nineties produced sharp deviations from the longer term trend" (Friedman and Schwartz 1963, p. 93).

Nonetheless, the price decline produced great dissatisfaction both in the United States (as discussed in some detail in chapter 3) and in the rest of the gold-standard world. The reason is partly what economists call "money illusion," the tendency of individuals to pay primary attention to nominal prices rather than to real prices or to the ratio of prices to their incomes. Most people receive their incomes from the sale of a relatively few goods or services.

They are especially well informed about those prices, and they regard any rise in them as a just reward for their enterprise and any fall as a misfortune arising from forces beyond their control. They are much less well informed about the prices of the numerous goods and services they buy as consumers and are much less sensitive to the behavior of those prices. Hence, there is the widespread tendency for inflation, provided it is fairly mild, to give rise to a general feeling of good times; of deflation, even if it is mild, to give rise to a general feeling of bad times.

An equally important reason for dissatisfaction is that deflation, like inflation, affects different people differently. Of particular relevance to the greenback, populist, and free-silver agitation in the United States is the fact that deflation affects debtors and creditors in very different ways. Most farmers at the time were debtors, and so were most small businessmen, and most of their debts were in fixed dollar terms at specified nominal interest rates. Falling prices make the same number of dollars correspond to a larger volume of goods. Hence, debtors tend to lose from deflation, creditors to gain.*

"The silver movement that came to a climax in the Bryan campaign of 1896," writes Barnes (1947, p. 371), "was founded primarily . . . upon the resumption law of 1875. The basic want of the people was for more money; the legislation that stripped them of paper turned them to silver." In the early years of falling prices after the Civil War, the pressure was for creating more greenbacks

*Strictly speaking, this statement is correct only for unanticipated deflation. If deflation is anticipated, the interest rate can be adjusted to allow for the expected deflation. However, there is ample evidence that, certainly during the nineteenth century, deflation and inflation were only imperfectly anticipated and then only after a considerable time lag (see chapter 2 and Fisher 1896).

instead of retiring them—from which came the name of the Greenback party (born in 1875, died in 1885). But once the passage of the Resumption Act documented the widespread opposition to paper money and the equally widespread belief in a specie standard as the natural order, the populists, as Barnes said, turned to silver as the vehicle for achieving inflation. In doing so, they acquired both a powerful ally—the silver miners in a number of sparsely settled western states, who wielded political power out of all proportion to their numbers—and a convenient devil—Wall Street and the eastern bankers, whom they accused of "the crime of 1873." They demanded a return to what they described as the "legal tender of the Constitution," gold *and* silver at the pre–Civil War ratio of 16 to 1.

The price decline of the 1870s that is recorded in Figure 1 affected silver as well as other commodities. By 1876, the dollar price of silver was lower than the official legal price. As explained in chapter 3, if provision for the free coinage of silver had not been omitted from the Coinage Act of 1873, the United States would have resumed specie payments in 1876 on the basis of silver, not gold. Dollar prices would have ceased to decline or would have declined at a lower rate, and most of the monetary agitation of the following decades would not have occurred.* As it was, the price level continued to fall and the agitation to increase. The result was a number of bills in the late 1870s, culminating in the Bland-Allison Act of 1878, which provided for the government's purchase of a limited amount of silver each month as a sop to the silver interests. A brief price rise after the enactment of resumption quieted the agitation for a

*Chapter 4 presents estimates of the hypothetical price level under these assumptions.

time, but when prices again started to fall, the agitation again mounted. It produced the Sherman Silver Purchase Act, passed in July 1890 "by a Republican Congress as a purported concession to the West for the support of the protectionist McKinley Tariff Act of 1890, sought by the industrial East" (Friedman and Schwartz 1963, p. 106). By comparison with the Bland-Allison Act, the Sherman Act roughly doubled the amount of silver the government was required to purchase. "The year 1890 [also] produced a great number of free-coinage planks in state political platforms. . . . After 1890 the silver movement began to sweep into flood tide" (Barnes 1947, p. 372). The rising tide of agitation explains why prices in the United States fell so much more sharply after 1888 than they did in Britain. "The disastrous panic year of 1893 . . . was fruitful in stirring the demand for free silver over the stricken nation" (Barnes 1947, p. 372). By 1896, it was a foregone conclusion that the Democrats would embrace free silver—and would split in two, with the eastern Gold Democrats in revolt.

Was 16 to 1 a Crackpot Idea?

The price of silver fell throughout the 1870s, '80s, and '90s. The price of gold was fixed under the gold standard at $20.67. Accordingly, the gold-silver price ratio rose from about 16 to 1 in 1873, when the fateful line was omitted from the Coinage Act, to 30 to 1 at the time of Bryan's nomination. However plausible 16 to 1 might have seemed as a legal ratio in 1873, by 1896 it seemed to the financial community a recipe for disaster. Its adoption would, they believed, produce an outrageous inflation. Bryan and his followers were proposing to nearly double the nominal price of silver, from the then prevailing market price of 68 cents an ounce to the legal price still on the books of $1.29. It seemed plain to the financial community that other prices would have to rise in proportion, in particular the price of gold. But that would break the monetary link between the U.S. dollar and gold-standard currencies, would produce a major depreciation in the exchange rate between the U.S. dollar and the gold-standard currencies, and, in the financial community's view, would devastate the channels of international trade. What a crackpot idea!

This conclusion, though not necessarily the precise reasoning, has become the conventional wisdom among both economic and other historians, as has the related view that the termination of the free coinage of silver by the Coinage Act of 1873 was, as James Lawrence Laughlin put it in 1886, "a piece of good fortune, which saved our financial credit and protected the honor of the State. It is a work of legislation for which we can not now be too thankful" (1895, p. 93).

In chapter 3, I concluded that Laughlin was wrong, that the act, far from being "a piece of good fortune," "was the opposite—a mistake that had highly adverse consequences" for both the United States and the world. I concluded that the retention of bimetallism at 16 to 1 as the legal monetary standard would have greatly reduced the subsequent deflation in the United States and would have avoided the monetary and political agitation and uncertainty that the deflation produced. To a lesser extent, it would also have reduced the deflation in the rest of the world. Under those circumstances, Bryan's genius as an orator and a politician would almost surely have still brought him fame, though fame under a very different banner.

But this is a judgment about 1873, when the Coinage

Act was passed, or about 1879, when resumption on the basis of gold occurred. By 1896, was it not too late to undo the damage? Wasn't Bryan trying to close the barn door after the horse had been stolen? Although the reasoning I have attributed to the financial community is naive, I believe that the fundamental conclusion was correct. A measure that would have been of great benefit to both the United States and the rest of the world in 1873 would have done great harm to both after 1896, in part precisely because it was not adopted in 1873. For reasons developed at some length in chapter 6, I believe that a bimetallic standard is a better monetary standard than a monometallic gold standard. That was true in 1896 as in 1879. However, circumstances do alter cases. Under the changed circumstances of 1896, the gold-silver price ratio at which bimetallism would have been a boon rather than a disaster was a ratio equal to or higher than the then current market ratio, not lower.

Bimetallism at 16 to 1 would have been a boon in 1879 because it would have prevented or eased the deflation threat posed by the widespread shift to gold. Moreover, it would have done this without a discontinuous transition. The market gold-silver price ratio was only a trifle below 16 to 1 in 1873, reached that level by 1875 or 1876, and exceeded it only slightly by 1879, so the transition would have been smooth and prompt.

In 1896 the threat was inflation, not deflation. The flood of gold from South Africa was raising the stock of money in the gold-standard countries, and the only countervailing force this time was the continued increase in output. By 1914, the price level was 17 percent higher in Britain and 44 percent higher in the United States than in 1896. The greater rise in the United States than in Britain reflected the reaction to the greater decline in the early 1890s.

The United States' adoption of bimetallism at a 16 to 1 ratio in 1896 would have sharply increased the demand for silver relative to the demand for goods in general and would have produced an outflow of gold from the United States. The market gold-silver price ratio could not have remained at 30 to 1. It might not have come all the way down to 16 to 1, but even that cannot be entirely ruled out. The calculations in chapter 4 of the hypothetical gold-silver price ratio that would have prevailed if the United States had remained on a legal bimetallic standard suggest that the ratio would have tended to fluctuate around 16 to 1 throughout the period from 1873 to 1914. According to those estimates, the highest ratio would have occurred in 1896, at about 24 to 1. However, I believe that that is very likely an overestimate both of what the ratio would have been under the hypothetical circumstances and of what it would have fallen to if Bryan's monetary program had been enacted.*

Whatever happened to the ratio, the effect would have been to raise the rate of growth of the quantity of money in both the United States, which would have accumulated silver, and in the rest of the world, which would have

*The reasons for the overestimate are different for the two cases. My estimates for the continuation throughout of the free coinage of silver necessarily use data affected by monetary disturbances that would not have occurred if free coinage had been continued. However, that does not make those estimates valid for the actual circumstances. The reason is that in making my estimates I have assumed a very different prior pattern of accumulation of both gold and silver than actually occurred. Had free coinage at 16 to 1 been enacted in, say, 1897, there would have been an immediate change in the conditions of demand and supply of silver and gold much larger than the gradual change I have postulated. I conjecture that that would have produced a market ratio lower than my estimate of 24 to 1.

received the outflow of gold from the United States. Inflation would have been even higher than it actually was. And the transition would have been anything but gradual for the United States. The financial community was right that the immediate result would have been a sharp depreciation in the exchange rate between the dollar and the currencies of the gold-standard countries, a depreciation that would indeed have created great transitional difficulties for the international trade and financial activities of the United States.

On the other hand, suppose bimetallism had been adopted in 1896 at a ratio of, say, 35 to 1. The immediate effect would have been negligible. The United States would have remained on an effective gold standard. There would have been no immediate additional demand for silver or additional supply of gold. The only effect on the price of either silver or gold would have been on expectations about possible future developments. The reaction to the depressed 1890s in the United States, and to the inflation in the rest of the world, would have proceeded for the time being as it actually did. The hypothetical adoption of bimetallism at 35 to 1 would not have made any real difference until about 1901 or 1902, when the market gold-silver price ratio began to rise above 35 to 1 by more than trivial amounts and for more than brief periods. The ratio remained above 35 to 1 until 1905 and then fell below 35 to 1 for a few years, before rising above it again for most of the period until 1914.

From 1902 on, bimetallism in the United States would doubtless have kept the ratio at 35 to 1. However, in view of the actual course of the price ratio, that would not have required large silver purchases by the United States or resulted in large gold outflows, would have involved no change in the exchange rate of the dollar in terms of the currencies of gold-standard countries, and would have produced greater stability of the exchange rate in terms of the currency of the few silver-standard countries, of which the principal one was China. In retrospect, the minor increase in inflation in both the United States and the gold-standard world that might have occurred would have been a low price to pay for a superior monetary system.

Unfortunately, the heated political atmosphere surrounding the silver issue prevented serious consideration of any alternative to a 16 to 1 ratio. As Simon Newcomb, an internationally famous mathematician and astronomer as well as one of the ablest economists and monetary theorists of the period, wrote in an 1893 article: "The writer has no objections to the principles of bimetallism, if properly and correctly applied. One of the misfortunes of the monetary situation is that the logical and consistent bimetallist seems to have disappeared from the field of battle, leaving only silver monometallists and gold monometallists. Every one ought to know that the free coinage of silver on the present basis means silver monometallism. . . . Free coinage on the present ratio of 16 to 1 would at the present moment be a simple cataclysm, and it is not likely that a ratio of 20 to 1 would work much better" (p. 511).

One "logical and consistent bimetallist" was General Francis A. Walker, described in the *New Palgrave* dictionary as "internationally the most widely known and esteemed American economist of his generation" and successively a professor of political economy and history at Yale University and the president of the Massachusetts Institute of Technology. He supported international bimetallism—that is, an agreement by a number of countries to adopt a bimetallic standard at the same gold-silver price ratio—but he opposed the adoption of bimetallism in a single country and hence did not favor Bryan's free-silver plank. I do not know whether he was active in the 1896 campaign in opposition to Bryan. However, in the "Address on International Bimetallism" that he delivered a few days after the 1896 election, he referred to the defeat of Bryan as "the passing of a great storm" ([1896a] 1899, 1:251). So far as I know, he never suggested the unilateral adoption of bimetallism at a ratio other than 16 to 1, and, indeed, he continued to favor the adoption of international bimetallism, even at a ratio of 15.5 to 1, the ratio that France had maintained (1896b, pp. 212–13).

Had the United States adopted bimetallism in 1896, whether at the ratio of 16 to 1 or 35 to 1, it is not impossible that other countries would have joined and adopted the same ratio. By 1896, the United States was probably a greater power in relation to the rest of the world than France had been in the early decades of the century. Yet France was able to hold the ratio at 15.5 to 1 from 1803 to 1873, despite first the major silver discoveries and then the major gold discoveries. There was substantial sentiment in favor of bimetallism in many European countries. India had only recently terminated the free coinage of silver, and China would remain on a silver standard until Franklin D. Roosevelt drove it off silver with his silver purchase program in the 1930s (interestingly enough, a politial sop to some of the same forces that had been behind the U.S. silver movement in the nineteenth century, as detailed in chapter 7). We have become so accustomed to regarding gold as the natural monetary metal that we have forgotten that silver was a far more important monetary metal than gold for centuries, losing first place only after the 1870s.

Had other countries joined the United States at 16 to 1, the damage done would have been even greater. On the other hand, had they joined at 35 to 1, the long-term results might well have been favorable. The outbreak of World War I in 1914, only a short time after the market ratio and the legal ratio would have come together, means that the effects, if any, would have been minor until after the war. After 1915 the market ratio fell sharply, to below 16 to 1 by 1920, and then rose sharply to a level over 35 by 1927. The postwar pattern doubtless would have been different had bimetallism become the legal standard for a number of countries, including the United States. The gold-exchange standard was adopted after World War I because of a concern that there would be a shortage of gold, and bimetallism would have relieved that concern. However, we are getting too far from our historical base for such speculation to be productive.

The Cyanide Process and Bryan's Political Decline

The final chapter in our story concerns the effect on Bryan's political career of the application of the cyanide process. That chapter is soon told. As we have seen, the flood of gold from South Africa produced the inflation that Bryan and his followers had sought to achieve with silver, "but when followers like the sociologist E. A. Ross pointed out to Bryan that the new gold supplies had relieved the money shortage and undermined the cause of silver, the Commoner was unimpressed" (Hofstadter 1948, p. 194). The result was inevitable. Bryan's political career had passed its peak.

Conclusion

Bryan labeled his account of the 1896 campaign *The First Battle*. From the outset, he clearly had viewed himself as a general at the head of an army engaged in a war—or a crusade—for a holy cause. He started his great speech at the 1896 Democratic convention by remarking, "This is not a contest between persons. The humblest citizen in all the land, when clad in the armor of a righteous cause, is stronger than all the hosts of error. I come to speak to you in defense of a cause as holy as the cause of liberty—the cause of humanity." The rhetoric rolls on: the "zeal which inspired the crusaders who followed Peter the Hermit," "our war is not a war of conquest," "crown of thorns," "crucify," "cross of gold."

The crusaders who followed Bryan were a mixed lot, as they are in every broad-based political movement. The silver miners had narrow sectional interests. The agrarian reformers were motivated by the age-old conflict between country and city, the populists by the equally ancient conflict between the masses and the classes—Main Street versus Wall Street. No doubt Bryan's followers included many who were disturbed by the evident economic difficulties that the country had experienced in the prior decade and who thought monetary expansion a possible, or the only, cure. Unfortunately, they included few if any "logical and consistent bimetallists."

His opponents were an equally mixed lot: persons with interests in gold mining; deflationists castigated by the free-silver forces, with some justice, as "Wall Street"; convinced monometallists who interpreted the economic preeminence of Britain as testimony to the virtues of a gold standard and the move by many European countries in the

1870s from bimetallism to gold as testimony to the fragility of bimetallism; persons for whom silver was not the major issue but who objected to other planks in the populist platform. No doubt his opponents also included many who were as disturbed as his followers were by the economic difficulties that the country had experienced in the prior decade but who—correctly, I believe—regarded the proposed cure of 16 to 1 as likely to make the disease even worse.

In the event, the ultimate result was decided by none of the issues raised or arguments offered by either side in the heated political contest. It was decided by faraway events in Scotland and South Africa that never entered into the domestic debate. A fascinating example of the far-reaching and mostly unanticipated effects of a seemingly minor monetary development.

CHAPTER 6

*Bimetallism Revisited**

Throughout recorded history, monetary systems have generally been based on a physical commodity. Metals have been the most widely used, the precious metals of silver and gold above all. As between them, "silver composed nearly the entire circulating metallic currency of Europe" until at least the late nineteenth century (Martin 1977, p. 642), and also of India and other parts of Asia. Gold was used much less, primarily for high-valued transactions.

The rate of exchange between silver and gold was sometimes specified by the authorities, sometimes left to the market. If a legal rate was specified, the result was a bimetallic system (as described in chapter 3) under which an authorized mint stood ready, for anyone who requested it to do so, to turn either silver or gold into coins of designated face value and specified weight and fineness on demand (free coinage). Typically there was a small seignorage charge to cover the cost of minting, though

*I am indebted for helpful comments on earlier drafts to Angela Redish, Hugh Rockoff, and Anna J. Schwartz. In addition, I have benefited greatly from detailed comments by the editors of the *Journal of Economic Perspectives*.

sometimes, as in Great Britain and the United States, there was none. The legal price ratio was determined by the weights assigned to the silver and gold coins. For example, from 1837 to the Civil War, the U.S. gold dollar was defined as equal to 23.22 grains of pure gold, the silver dollar as equal to 371.25 grains of pure silver—or 15.988 times as many grains of silver as of gold, rounded in common parlance to a ratio of 16 to 1.

A strictly equivalent way to define a bimetallic standard is in terms of a government commitment to buy either gold or silver at a fixed price in money designated as legal tender. For the U.S. example, the corresponding fixed prices were $20.67 per fine ounce of gold and $1.29 per fine ounce of silver.* That remained the legal price of gold until 1933, when President Franklin D. Roosevelt raised it by stages and then fixed it at $35 an ounce in early 1934. There it remained until it was raised to $42.22 in early 1973, the price at which the gold holdings of the U.S. government are still valued on the books, though the market price is currently (1991) about nine times the official price.

While either silver or gold could legally be used as money, in practice (as was explained in chapter 3) only one of the metals might be so used. In addition to their use as money, both silver and gold have important nonmonetary, or market, uses, for jewelry and for industrial purposes. When the market price ratio differed substantially from the legal ratio, only the metal that was cheaper at the market price than at the legal ratio would be brought to the mint

*These are the rounded prices. There are 480 grains in a fine ounce of gold, so the exact legal price of gold was 480/23.22, or $20.6711835 . . . , and of silver, 480/371.25, or $1.2929 . . . .

for coinage. For example, if 1 ounce of gold sold on the market for the same number of dollars as 15.5 ounces of silver when the legal ratio was 16 to 1, a holder of silver, rather than taking the silver directly to the mint, would do better to exchange his silver for gold at the market ratio and then take the gold to the mint.

The situation in the United States from 1837 to the Civil War was roughly as just described: the legal ratio was 16 to 1, the market ratio 15.5 to 1. The result was that the United States was effectively on a gold standard. Silver might still be used for less than full-bodied minor coins (coins containing less silver than the amount that, at the legal price, would equal the face value of the coin) and for international monetary transactions, but at a premium, not at its par value.

Beginning in the early 1870s, most advanced countries, including the United States in 1879, shifted to a monometallic gold standard, that is, a standard under which only the price of gold was legally fixed. This left India and China as the only two populous countries relying primarily on silver. Silver was still used elsewhere, but just for minor coinage. After World War I the link between money and gold was progressively loosened, with a gold-exchange standard—a commitment by governments to redeem their money either in gold or in a foreign currency that was redeemable in gold—replacing a strict gold standard as the norm. After World War II, the Bretton Woods agreement setting up the International Monetary Fund gave gold an even smaller role, requiring convertibility into gold only for the United States and only for external purposes. This final link was ended by President Richard Nixon on August 15, 1971, when, in monetary jargon, he "closed the gold window" by refusing to honor the U.S. commitment under the International Monetary Fund agreement to sell gold to foreign central banks at $35 an ounce. Since then, every major country has adopted an inconvertible paper or fiat standard, not as a temporary emergency measure but as a system intended to be permanent. Such a worldwide fiat monetary system has no historical precedent.

Up to the present, the fiat monetary system has been characterized by wide fluctuations in price levels, interest rates, and exchange rates, as the major nations have tried to learn how to navigate in these uncharted waters, have tried to find some anchor for the price level other than conversion into a commodity. Whether the fiat system will lead to acceptable results—and, if so, when—remains an open question, which is examined in chapter 10. Hence, a discussion of perhaps the most common earlier world system, bimetallism, may be of more than historical interest.

In a 1936 article entitled "Bimetallism Reconsidered," Lewis Froman wrote: "Economists in general are almost unanimously in agreement that bimetallism does not provide a satisfactory monetary system" (p. 55). Until recently I shared that view, which I believe remains the conventional view of monetary economists: namely, that bimetallism is an unstable and unsatisfactory monetary system involving frequent shifts between alternative monometallic systems; that monometallism is preferable, with gold monometallism preferable to silver monometallism.*

*It is not easy to document that this remains the conventional view, since few contemporary textbooks on money or macroeconomics even mention bimetallism. They almost all have some reference to the gold standard, but typically take it for granted that a gold standard is the only kind of commodity standard that needs to be mentioned. I have examined seven popular monetary and macroeconomics texts, dated from 1968 to 1986. Only two mention a bimetallic standard; only the earliest has any reasoned discussion of its advantages and disadvantages, and that in a footnote, which notes that "criticism of the

In the course of doing research on the U.S. monetary history of the nineteenth century for chapters 3, 4, and 5, I discovered, much to my surprise, that the conventional view is dubious, if not outright wrong, with respect to both the superiority of monometallism over bimetallism and the superiority of gold monometallism over silver monometallism.

Historical Experience

In his 1791 Treasury Report on the Establishment of the Mint, in which he recommended the adoption of a bimetallic standard, Alexander Hamilton ([1791] 1969, pp. 167–68) wrote: "Gold may, perhaps, in certain senses, be said to have greater stability than silver: as, being of superior value, less liberties have been taken with it, in the regulation of different countries. Its standard has remained more uniform, and it has, in other respects, undergone fewer changes; as being not so much an article of merchandise, . . . it is less liable to be influenced by circumstances of commercial demand."

Hamilton nonetheless chose bimetallism, on the purely pragmatic grounds that silver was the metal in more

system [bimetallism] has doubtless been overdone" (Culbertson 1968, p. 133n.). I have also examined seven texts on American economic history, dated from 1964 to 1987. All discuss the use of different commodities as monetary standards, bimetallism, and the shift to a gold standard. However, the general approach is strictly factual and, with one exception, conventional. For example, the most recent (and, I understand, the most widely used) text states flatly: "Bimetallism is a poor metallic system to use because the two metals fluctuate constantly *against each other* in price with strange results" and "Silver had been driven from circulation by the rise in gold supplies in the 1840s and 1850s. . . . Therefore, in 1873 the Coinage Act omitted any provision for the resumption of the minting of silver dollars" (Hughes 1987, pp. 175–76, 360).

common use, that most specie in the original thirteen states was silver, in the form of foreign coins, and that gold was rare. He chose a ratio of 15 to 1 because that was the market ratio at the time, while also recognizing that the ratio was subject to variation and urging that "care be taken to regulate the proportion between [the metals], with an eye to their average commercial value" ([1791] 1969, p. 168). Very shortly, however, the market ratio rose, conforming with the legal ratio in France of 15.5 to 1. Congress did not heed Hamilton's counsel, but left the legal ratio at 15 to 1 until 1834. As a result, silver became the de facto standard until 1834, when Congress altered the legal ratio to 16 to 1, and gold became the de facto standard from then to the Civil War. In 1862, redemption of currency in specie was suspended, and a pure fiat currency, popularly known as greenbacks, was issued to help finance the war. The 1873 coinage act ended the free coinage of silver and limited its legal-tender status, so that when resumption (the convertibility of legal tender into specie) was achieved in 1879, it was on the basis of gold. That in turn unleashed the free-silver movement of the 1880s and 1890s, which culminated in William Jennings Bryan's 1896 presidential campaign under the flag of 16 to 1.

The U.S. experience doubtless helped form the conventional view, as stated for example by Ludwig von Mises (1953, p. 75), that the bimetallic "standard was . . . turned, not into a double standard, as the legislators had intended, but into an alternative standard."

While such an alternative standard is possible and has often been the case, as it was in the United States before the Civil War and in Britain for several centuries before the Napoleonic wars, it is not at all inevitable. As Irving Fisher

(1911, p. 132) points out: "The history of France and the Latin Union during the period from 1785, and especially from 1803, to 1873 is instructive. It affords a practical illustration of the theory that when conditions are favorable, gold and silver can be kept tied together for a considerable period by means of bimetallism. During this period the public was ordinarily unconscious of any disparity of value, and only observed the changes from the relative predominance of gold to the relative predominance of silver in the currency and *vice versa.*"

France's success in maintaining full-bodied gold and silver coins in circulation simultaneously over such a long period reflected several factors. The first was France's economic importance in the world, which was far greater than it is now. A second was the exceptionally high propensity of the French people to use specie as money, both directly as coins and indirectly as reserves for paper currency and deposits.* These two factors made France a major participant in the market for silver and gold, an important enough participant to be able to peg the price ratio despite major changes in the relative production of silver and gold.† In Fisher's words (1911, pp. 133–34):

*In 1880, gold and silver coins accounted for more than 70 percent of all transactions balances (coins plus paper money plus bank deposits); the corresponding fraction for the United States was about 15 percent. Source for France, Saint Marc (1983, pp. 23–33); for the United States, Friedman and Schwartz (1963, pp. 131, 174).

†To illustrate France's importance, in both 1850 and 1870 monetary silver in France amounted to more than 10 percent of all the silver produced in the world from 1493 on; in 1850 monetary gold in France was about one-third of the world's monetary gold stock; in 1870 more than one-half. (I have been unable to find estimates of the world's monetary silver stock, which is why I have compared the French monetary silver with total production.) Source for France, Saint Marc (1983, pp. 23–33); for the world gold stock, Warren and Pearson (1933, pp. 78–79).

> From 1803 until about 1850 the tendency was for silver to displace gold. . . . By 1850, . . . [b]imetallism would have broken down and resulted in silver monometallism . . . , except for the fact that, as though to save the day, gold had just been discovered in California. The consequence of the new and increased gold production was a reverse movement, an inflow of gold into the French currency and an outflow of silver. . . . It seemed probable that France would be entirely drained of her silver currency and come to a gold basis. . . . But the new gold mines were gradually exhausted, while silver production increased, with the consequence that there was again a reversal of the movement.

France absorbed into its money stock more than half of the world's total output of gold from 1850 to 1870, while holding the amount of silver almost constant.* As a result, the market price ratio, which was 15.7 in 1850, never fell below 15.2 (in 1859) and was back up to 15.6 by 1870 (Warren and Pearson 1933, p. 144).

The conventional view implicitly assumes that the legal gold-silver price ratio is a knife-edge, so that the least departure of the market ratio from the legal ratio would rapidly send all the coins minted from the now more valuable metal to the melting pot for sale on the market. That turned out not to be the case in France. The situation is comparable to that of the exchange rates between currencies under a strict gold standard. The legally specified specie contents of the national currencies define a par exchange rate (for example, from 1879 to 1914, $4.86649 . . . for one British pound).† If the market

*The ratio of ounces of silver to ounces of gold in its monetary stock fell from 41 to 8, entirely via an increase in gold.

†The pound sterling was defined as 113 grains of pure gold, the U.S. dollar as 23.22 grains; the ratio of these two numbers gives the par exchange rate.

As an aside, a classic story illustrating British provincialism in the exchange rate deviates from par, there is opportunity for arbitrage by exchanging the cheaper currency for gold, shipping the gold to the other country, converting the gold into the other currency, and converting the proceeds into the cheaper currency on the market. For the arbitrage to be profitable, the difference between the market exchange rate and par must be large enough to cover the costs of insurance, shipping the gold, and any other expenses. The par exchange rate plus or minus these costs defines the so-called gold points between which the market exchange rate can fluctuate without shipment of gold in either direction.

In precisely parallel fashion, under a bimetallic standard costs are incurred in converting the undervalued coins into specie and selling the specie on the market. These costs define the upper and lower gold-silver price ratio points between which the market ratio can vary without producing the complete replacement of one metal by the other. The width of the range depends on the seignorage charge, the cost of melting coins, insurance fees, delays and the associated loss of interest, and so on.*

France's bimetallic standard ended when it did because of the Franco-Prussian War of 1870–71. France suffered a devastating defeat and was forced to pay Germany a huge war indemnity in funds convertible to gold.

Victorian era has an American taking an English gentleman to task for the complexity of the British currency: "12 pence to the shilling, 20 shillings to the pound, 21 shillings to the guinea." Responds the English gentleman: "What are you Americans complaining about? Look at your awful dollar—4.8665 to the pound."

*In a private communication dated April 24, 1989, Angela Redish suggests that the widest plausible limits, allowing for mint costs and 1 percent transactions costs, were 15.3 and 15.89. The limits of the market ratio cited are imperfect estimates, and so are not seriously in conflict with her estimated range.

Germany used the money to finance its own shift from a silver standard to a gold standard—a tribute to the example of Britain, which German leaders desperately wanted to surpass in economic power and which had been on gold since 1821. In the process, Germany also dumped on the market large quantities of silver that was withdrawn from circulation. France was not willing to accept the major inflation (in terms of silver) that would have been produced by the combined effect of the drain of gold and the flood of silver. Accordingly, France closed its mints to the free coinage of silver and subsequently adopted a gold standard.*

A remarkable feature of the French experience under bimetallism is that "through twenty years of war, at times against half Europe, [Napoleon] never once allowed a resort to the delusive expedient of inconvertible paper money" (Walker 1896b, p. 87). That was almost certainly a tribute to the cautionary example of the *assignat* hyperinflation (White 1896) that had helped bring Napoleon to power, rather than to any peculiar virtue of bimetallism over monometallism. After the *assignat* experience, any attempt by Napoleon to issue inconvertible paper money on the promise of returning to specie payments would have had no credibility, and there would have been a large-scale flight from the currency. To the best of my knowledge, no other major war has ever been conducted without resort to depreciation of the currency (in earlier times, by adulterating the currency, changing the nominal value of the coinage, and similar expedients; in recent centuries, by suspending specie payments and resorting to inconvertible

*Walker (1896b, chapters 4, 5, and 6) has an excellent discussion of this episode, as well as of prior French experience.

paper money). France's behavior contrasts sharply with that of Britain. Britain, which had been on a legal bimetallic but a de facto gold standard, ended specie payments in 1797 and did not resume them until 1821. Its promise to return to specie payments had credibility, however, because of the long earlier period during which a specie standard had prevailed.

During the 1870s, not only Germany and France but many other countries shifted from bimetallism to gold, culminating in the U.S. resumption in 1879. The effect was a rapid fall and wide fluctuations in the market price of silver relative to gold, so that the market gold-silver price ratio had nearly doubled by 1896, when Bryan gave his famous "Cross of Gold" speech and made 16 to 1 his battle cry.

In chapter 4, I have estimated the hypothetical U.S. price level and, as a by-product, the hypothetical gold-silver price ratio that would have prevailed if the United States had returned to the prewar bimetallic standard after the Civil War. These estimates indicate that the market gold-silver price ratio would have remained fairly close to 16 to 1 until at least 1914, when World War I started. The ability of France to maintain an effective bimetallic standard for seventy years, despite wide swings in the relative supplies of silver and gold, strengthens my confidence in these estimates. If I am anywhere close to right, as I wrote in chapter 3, "the United States could have played the same role after 1873 in stabilizing the gold-silver price ratio that France did before 1873" (see p. 74). The result would have been a more stable price level in both the United States and the gold-standard countries.

The Scholarly Literature on Bimetallism

Like the historical evidence, the scholarly literature of the time does not support the conventional view. On the contrary, as Schumpeter put it in his *History of Economic Analysis* (1954, p. 1076): "[B]imetallism was the chief hunting ground of monetary monomaniacs. Nevertheless, it is the fact—a fact that these semi-pathological products and also the victory of the gold party tend to obliterate—that, on its highest level, the bimetallist argument really had the better of the controversy, even apart from the support that a number of men of scientific standing extended to the cause of bimetallism." Schumpeter adds in a footnote that the "outstanding purely analytic performance on bimetallism is that of Walras (*Éléments, leçons* 31 and 32)" (1954, p. 1076).* As Walras (1954, lesson 32, p. 359) put it, in a carefully qualified statement: "In short, bimetallism is as much at the mercy of chance as monometallism so far as the stability of value of the monetary standard is concerned; only bimetallism has a few more chances in its favour."

Schumpeter may be right in his judgment of the quality of Walras's analysis. However, Irving Fisher's analysis is equally rigorous and far more accessible. His succinct conclusion (1911, chap. 7, pp. 123–24) is that "bimetallism, impossible at one [legal] ratio [between the prices of the two monetary metals], is always possible at another. There will always be two limiting ratios between which

*Schumpeter makes it clear that the "monetary monomaniacs" he refers to are among "the silver men," not the "sponsors of gold." In that respect, he shared the conventional view. My own opinion, like that of Francis A. Walker—to whose work Schumpeter refers as "of undoubted scientific standing"—is that the pro-gold cause had its share of monetary monomaniacs.

bimetallism is possible." Note that Fisher's limiting ratios are not the gold-silver price ratio points referred to earlier: those define the range of *market* price ratios consistent with a fixed legal price ratio. Fisher's limiting ratios define the range of *legal* price ratios at which it would be feasible to keep both gold and silver in circulation under given conditions of demand and supply of gold and silver. A different division of new production of gold and silver would correspond to each such legal ratio. At the lower limiting gold-silver price ratio, the bulk of new gold production would go to nonmonetary uses, and the bimetallic standard would be on the verge of becoming a monometallic silver standard; at the upper limiting ratio, the bulk of new silver production would go to nonmonetary uses, and the bimetallic standard would be on the verge of becoming a monometallic gold standard.

No great importance attaches to the maintenance of one or another market ratio for its own sake (except perhaps to persons involved in the mining of silver or gold). The important general question is the behavior of the price level. Which monetary system, bimetallism, silver monometallism, or gold monometallism, will lead to the most stable price level over time, that is, to the most stable real value of the monetary unit? Fisher's answer (1911, chap. 7, pp. 126–27) is that, when the legal bimetallic ratio is effective, then "in a series of years, the bimetallic level [of the real value of the monetary unit] remains intermediate between the changing levels which the two metals would separately follow. Bimetallism spreads the effect of any single fluctuation over the combined gold and silver markets. . . . It should be pointed out that the equalizing effect maintained is relative only. It is conceivable that one metal would be steadier alone than when joined to the other."* In other words, a bimetallic standard always yields a steadier price level than at least one of the two alternative monometallic standards and may yield a steadier price level than either. This is what Walras meant by "more chances."

Proponents and Opponents of Bimetallism

Writing in 1896, at the height of the agitation for free silver, Francis A. Walker (1896b, pp. 217–19) gives an excellent description of the

> three classes of persons in the United States who have been wont to call themselves bimetallists. We have, first, the inhabitants of the silver-producing states. These citizens have what is called a particular interest, as distinct from a participation in the general interest. . . . Their interest in the maintenance of silver as a money metal has been of the same nature as the interest of Pennsylvanians in the duties on pig iron. . . . Although the silver-mining industry of the country is not large . . . it has yet been able to exert a high degree of power in our politics, partly because of our system of equal representation in the Senate, partly because of the eagerness and intensity with which the object has been pursued. The second of the three classes . . . consists of those who, without any particular interest in the production of silver, are yet, in their general economic views, in favor of superabundant and cheap money. Among the leaders of this element have been found the very men who, between 1868 and 1876, were foremost in advocating the greenback heresy [which, it is worth noting, is today's orthodoxy]. Beaten on

*The analysis was spelled out much earlier in Fisher (1894, pp. 527–37).

> the issue of greenback inflation, they have taken up the issue of silver inflation. . . . They are for depreciated silver, because, in their view, it is the next best thing (by which they mean what we would call the next worst thing) to greenbacks. Those who constitute the element now under consideration are not true bimetallists. What they really want is silver inflation [they are Schumpeter's "monetary monomaniacs"].
>
> The third element . . . comprises the convinced bimetallists of the country; men who believe, with Alexander Hamilton and the founders of the republic, that it is best to base the circulation upon both the precious metals. They are not inflationists, although . . . they strongly deprecate contraction.*

The persons who called themselves monometallists or hard-money men and favored a gold standard consisted of three parallel groups: those with interests in gold mining; deflationists, castigated by the free-silver forces, with some justice, as "Wall Street"; convinced monometallists, who interpreted the economic preeminence of Britain as testimony to the virtues of a gold standard and the move by many European countries in the 1870s from bimetallism to gold as testimony to the fragility of bimetallism.

The controversy was not restricted to the United States. It raged in Britain, France, and, indeed, throughout the world, producing, as Massimo Roccas remarks, "the liveliest theoretical disputes among economists and the sharpest economic policy debates in the 'civilized world' " (1987, p. 1). Elsewhere, also, the participants were divided into the same groups as in the United States, with one

*Francis A. Walker was a volunteer in the Civil War who was promoted to general after the war ended and had a distinguished career as a statistician, economist, and educational administrator.

difference: among advocates of bimetallism, the first group included not only silver-mining interests but, especially in Britain, persons involved in trade with India, which was on a silver standard with free coinage until 1893, and, everywhere, persons involved in trade with China, which was on a silver standard until the late 1930s. Traders with India and China favored bimetallism for the same reasons that exporters today favor fixed exchange rates—to reduce the inconvenience and risks accompanying a fluctuating exchange rate.

The distinctions between the groups are not ironclad. A clear example for the United States is the first and longtime chairman of the department of economics of the University of Chicago, James Laurence Laughlin. His 1886 book, *The History of Bimetallism in the United States,* was unquestionably a major scholarly contribution and was cited by both proponents and opponents of bimetallism. Yet Laughlin was also a highly active leader of the hard-money opposition to the free-silver movement. In that capacity, he was dogmatic and demagogic. Monetary scholars like Francis A. Walker and Irving Fisher almost surely shared his opposition to specific proposals of the populist advocates of free silver, yet they were apparently embarrassed by his dogmatism and by what they considered—in my view, correctly—his bad economics, since they went out of their way to dissociate their views from his.

An example for Great Britain is Sir Robert Giffen, immortalized by Alfred Marshall in the "Giffen paradox." Popular articles by Giffen on the subject, dating from 1879 to 1890, were republished in a book entitled *The Case Against Bimetallism* ([1892] 1896). Whatever the basis for his high repute may have been, the book provides ample evidence that it was not his command of monetary theory.*

Views about Actual Bimetallic Proposals

Most scholars who were persuaded that bimetallism is in principle preferable to monometallism opposed the particular practical proposals for bimetallism that were at the center of the political debate. They did so for two sets of reasons, the lure of still better reforms and practical considerations.

The Better versus the Good: W. Stanley Jevons ([1875] 1890, pp. 328–33) favored a tabular standard, under which the monetary unit, at least for long-term contracts, would be adjusted for changes in general prices—the system that has come to be called indexation.

Alfred Marshall, who also favored a tabular standard, regarded it as an impracticable ideal except for long-term contracts. He supported what F. Y. Edgeworth labeled symmetallism as a less extreme departure from a gold standard than a thoroughgoing tabular standard would be, yet preferable to bimetallism (Marshall 1926, pp. 12–15, 26–31).† A symmetallic standard is one in which the monetary unit would be a composite of two metals, "a unit of gold *and* so many units of silver—a linked bar on which a paper currency may be based" (Edgeworth 1895, p. 442).

*Evidence of Giffen's repute is the diplomacy with which F. Y. Edgeworth (1895, p. 435), one of the truly great economists of the time, prefaces his refutation of one of Giffen's fallacies: "An argument advanced by Mr. Giffen . . . is not likely to be open to dispute. It is with great diffidence that the following counter-reasoning is submitted."

†Francis A. Walker (1893, p. 175, n. 1) wrote: "Prof. Alfred Marshall, of Cambridge, easily the head of the English economists, has more than once told me that, as between bimetallism and gold monometallism, he is a bimetallist."

Under a bimetallic standard, the relative price of the two metals is fixed, but the relative quantities used as money are variable. Under a symmetallic standard, the relative quantities of the metals used as money are fixed and the relative price is variable; hence, there is no danger that a legal symmetallic standard will be converted into a de facto monometallic standard.

Léon Walras (1954, p. 361) favored a gold standard with a "silver regulator" managed by the monetary authorities so as to keep prices stable.

Irving Fisher (1913, p. 495) favored a "compensated dollar," or a system under which the gold equivalent of the dollar would be varied to keep a broad-based price index constant; that is, the weight in gold of the dollar would be changed "to compensate for the [change] in the purchasing power of each grain of gold."

Francis A. Walker opposed unilateral U.S. adoption of bimetallism but favored international bimetallism—that is, an agreement by a substantial number of countries to adopt a single legal gold-silver price ratio.* Essentially all the responsible supporters of bimetallism, even those in favor of its unilateral adoption by a single country, preferred international bimetallism. This sentiment was reflected in a series of international conferences on the subject, all of which ended in failure.

Practical Considerations: One important practical consideration was the proposed legal gold-silver price ratio. As Fisher pointed out, a range of legal ratios was consistent with the maintenance of a bimetallic currency.

*"Though a bimetallist, of the international type, to the very center of my being, I have ever considered the efforts made by this country, for itself alone, to rehabilitate silver as prejudicial equally to our own national interests and to the cause of true international bimetallism" (Walker 1896b, p. iv).

However, if different countries adopt different ratios, it is clear that only one can be effective. While I believe that 16 to 1 was feasible for the United States in 1873, I have argued in chapter 5 that by 1896 it was almost surely too late to undo the damage. And contemporary writers expressed similar views. Writing in 1896, Walker (1896b, pp. 212–13) says:

> While declining thus to discuss the actual ratio in any attempt to restore international bimetallism, I do not hesitate to say that all talk about taking the existing ratio of the market, say 30:1 as the ratio for the bimetallic mints, is simply silly. Silver has fallen to 30 for 1 of gold, because of demonetization. Remonetization, even by a weak league, would necessarily and instantly put it clear back and would hold it there against any but revolutionary forces. . . . The "factor of safety" will be smaller with the old ratio [15.5 to 1] than it would be with a new ratio somewhat more favorable to gold—say, 18 or 20:1. Yet, notwithstanding this, the "factor of safety" might still be sufficient . . . to enable [bimetallism] to do its beneficent work at the old ratio.

Walker apparently did not regard the United States alone as equivalent to "a weak league," since he opposed Bryan's proposal that the United States unilaterally adopt bimetallism at a 16 to 1 ratio. In his "Address on International Bimetallism," which he delivered a few days after the 1896 election, Walker referred to the defeat of Bryan as "the passing of a great storm" ([1896a] 1899, 1:251). In his 1896 book, *International Bimetallism,* Walker expressed the view that the United States "is not and has never been in a position to exert an equal effect [to France alone] upon the market for the money metals" (1896b, p. 220). As already noted, my own examination of the empirical evidence suggests that his "has never" was an overstatement, though his "is not" was probably correct.

Writing in 1888, one of the ablest of the British economists in favor of bimetallism, J. Shield Nicholson ([1888] 1895, pp. 270, 288), regarded the reestablishment of a ratio of 15.5 to 1 as entirely feasible if there was international agreement, agreeing in this respect with Walker. So far as I know, Nicholson did not express any view on the feasibility of unilateral adoption by Britain or the United States of a similar ratio.

Jevons is perhaps the best example of an economist who recognized the theoretical case for bimetallism yet vigorously opposed it on practical grounds. In a letter of 1868 to a supporter of bimetallism, he summarized his views (1884, p. 306; italics in original) by saying: "I must acknowledge that *in theory* you and the other defenders of what may be called *the alternative standard* are right. But in the *practical aspect* the subject looks very different, and I am inclined to hope for the extension of *the single gold standard*." The major practical considerations he cites in the letter (pp. 305–6) are these:

> I cannot see any prospect of a serious rise in the value of the precious metals. . . . The danger, therefore, that the value of gold would rise, and the burdens of nations become increased, is of an uncertain nature. . . .
>
> On the other hand, the conveniences of a single gold standard are of a tangible and certain nature. The weight of the money is decreased to the least possible amount, without the use of paper representative money. There is a simplicity and convenience about the system which has recommended it to the English during the half century which has passed since our new sovereigns were issued. The operation of our law of 1816 has, in fact, been so successful in most

> respects that I should despair altogether of the English people or Government ever being brought to adopt the double standard in place of it. I was glad, therefore, to see that the monetary convention had decided in favour of a single gold standard.*

Here and in other publications, Jevons places great emphasis on the inconvenience to wealthier countries of silver money because it weighs so much more than a quantity of gold of the same value. The argument presumes that a large fraction of transactions are conducted with coined money. This may have been true in his day, but it rapidly became less and less important with the wider use of token subsidiary coins, paper money, and deposits. Even in Jevons's day, it was in part true only because the Bank of England was prohibited from issuing notes of lower denomination than five pounds, a factor that was irrelevant in the United States.

In subsequent publications Jevons repeated these objections in ever stronger terms. In 1875, after the closing of the mints to silver in France and the adoption of the gold standard by Germany: "The price of silver has fallen in consequence of the German currency reforms, but it is by no means certain that it will fall further than it has already done. That any great rise will really happen in the purchasing power of gold [that is, a fall in the price level in terms of gold] is wholly a matter of speculation. . . . [A]s a mere

*Jevons's best and most concise statement of the theoretical case for bimetallism is in his *Money and the Mechanism of Exchange* ([1875] 1890, pp. 137–38). Fisher refers to this discussion in "The Mechanics of Bimetallism" (1894), in which he presents a much more thorough and definitive analysis. Fisher also notes that after his article was prepared he discovered that Walras "has covered nearly the same ground and expressed substantially the same conclusions" as a part of Fisher's article (1894, p. 529, n. 1).

guess, I should say that it is not likely to rise" ([1875] 1890, p. 143). In 1877 (1884, pp. 308, 309, 311; italics in original):

> In nothing is the English nation so conservative as in matters of currency. . . .
>
> [I]f the United States were to adopt the double standard, they would throw into confusion the monetary relations of the foremost commercial nations, while the universal bimetallism essential to the success of M. Cernuschi's schemes would be as far distant as ever. . . .*
>
> To say the least, it is quite open to argument that silver is now a metal less steady in value than gold. . . . Under these circumstances, it is probable that the double standard, or, as it ought to be called, the *alternative standard* will be really less steady in value than the gold standard alone.

Despite his deserved reputation as a pioneer in economic statistics, Jevons was almost consistently wrong in his empirical predictions. The price of silver in terms of gold fell drastically, the real price of gold rose (that is, the nominal price level fell), and, if anything, gold became more unstable in production than silver.†

Jevons's famous journalistic contemporary, Walter Bagehot, wrote a series of articles in *The Economist* in 1876 on the silver question. These were collected and published, shortly after Bagehot's death in 1877, in a monograph entitled *Depreciation of Silver.* The articles deal mainly with the problems raised for Britain's trade with India by the depreciation of silver—inevitably leading to a discussion of bimetallism, which Bagehot vigorously opposed. Although Bagehot's theoretical analysis is much

*Cernuschi was a well-known French bimetallist.

†Interestingly enough, Jevons's predictions in another field, the future role and availability of coal, were equally far from the mark (see Jevons 1865).

inferior to Jevons's, the practical considerations he cites in opposition to bimetallism duplicate Jevons's, including Jevons's erroneous predictions, in particular the prediction that the "fall" in the price of silver in 1876 was "only a momentary accident in a new and weak market, and not the permanent effect of lasting causes" (Bagehot [1877] 1891, 5:523). Like Jevons, Bagehot regards as a major consideration (5:613) the fact that "England has a currency now resting solely on the gold standard, which exactly suits her wants, which is known throughout the civilized world as hers, and which is most closely united to all her mercantile and banking habits. What motive, that an English Parliament could ever be got to understand, is there that would induce them to alter it?"*

I have quoted at length the practical considerations stressed by Jevons and Bagehot because, while these two were among the first to stress them, the same considerations undoubtedly played a major role in the opposition to or lukewarm support of bimetallism by almost all later British writers on the subject, including both Marshall and Edgeworth. Similarly, the very different practical circumstances of France and the United States explain why those countries produced the most vigorous support for bimetallism, not only by Schumpeter's "monetary monomaniacs" but also by respected scholars.

Gold versus Silver Monometallism

Britain's adoption of a monometallic gold standard in 1816, and its subsequent resumption of the convertibility

*Bagehot also expresses doubt that the French will demonetize silver, which they did very soon thereafter.

of legal tender into specie on the basis of gold on May 1, 1821, as a result of Peel's Act of 1819, was undoubtedly the key factor that made gold the world's dominant monetary metal (Feavearyear 1963, pp. 212–23). It had that effect partly because Britain's subsequent rise to economic preeminence in the world was attributed in considerable measure, rightly or wrongly, to its adoption of a strict gold standard, and partly because Britain's preeminence gave special importance to the exchange rates between sterling and other currencies.

Why did Britain adopt a monometallic standard instead of returning to its earlier bimetallism? And why gold instead of silver? In a recent paper, Angela Redish states: "The historical literature has typically explained the emergence of the gold standard as a matter of happenstance: the legislation of 1816 merely ratified the de facto gold standard that had existed in England since Newton's 'inadvertent' overvaluation of gold at the beginning of the eighteenth century" (1990, pp. 789–90). Redish disagrees, concluding (p. 805) that "England abandoned bimetallism in 1816 because a gold standard with a complementary token silver coinage offered the possibility of a medium of exchange with high and low denomination coins circulating concurrently. The gold standard succeeded because the new technology employed by the Mint was able to make [gold and token silver] coins that counterfeiters could not copy cheaply and because the Mint accepted the responsibility of guaranteeing the convertibility of the tokens."

The currency system Redish describes was indeed one consequence of the monetary reform. As Feavearyear (1963, p. 226) put it: "Peel's Act had left the pound upon a basis which approached more nearly to a completely automatic metallic standard than at any other time before or since. The seignorage and other mint charges had long been abolished. . . . [T]he introduction of improved machinery into the Mint, together with the growth of a more efficient organization for the detection of crime, was beginning to defeat the counterfeiter. Gold was more difficult to counterfeit than silver."

However, I believe that achieving a satisfactory silver token coinage would not have been a valid reason for returning to gold rather than silver even though it clearly was a consequence of that monetary reform and may have been a partial cause for its adoption. Under France's successful bimetallic system, high and low denomination full-bodied coins circulated simultaneously for seventy-five years, though the proportion between the two metals in circulation changed from time to time. Redish rejects the possibility that high and low denomination coins could long circulate concurrently because she implicitly regards the legal ratio as a knife-edge, requiring either frequent recoinage or changes in the nominal value of coins or shifts between alternate standards. But the experience of France indicates that there is a range of tolerance around the legal bimetallic ratio wide enough to absorb minor changes in the market ratio without difficulty. It also indicates that the adoption of a single legal ratio by one or more major financial powers has a significant stabilizing influence on the market ratio. The difficulty that Britain had in maintaining a dual standard earlier, and that the United States had then and later, arose because both countries set the legal ratio at a different level than France's, at a time when the French ratio dominated the market ratio.

Personally, I share Frank Fetter's judgment (1973, p. 16) that "With the hindsight of history, it is amazing that a decision of such importance for England [the adoption of a single gold standard], and by England's example for an entire world, should have been made without benefit of full analysis, and largely on the basis of details of small coin convenience, and not on larger issues of economic policy. Thus was formally established the gold standard which became effective with the resumption of cash payments in 1821 and survived for 93 years."*

Redish's explanation of why gold was adopted rather than silver echoes Jevons: under a silver standard, high-value coins would be excessively heavy and inconvenient. Gold could have been used for high-value transactions, but if gold coins were minted with a face value less than their market value, they would not have circulated at par. If the face value exceeded the market value, gold coins could be kept convertible into silver at their face value by limiting coinage to demand. Such overvalued gold coins would

*Resumption on gold in 1821 did not end the battle of the standards in Britain, any more than resumption on gold in 1879 ended the battle of the standards in the United States. "The most consistent and continuous attacks on the act of 1821 came from supporters of the silver standard or bimetallism" (Fetter 1973, p. 17). Fetter titles one subsection of his book on monetary orthodoxy "New Support for Bimetallism," with reference to reactions to the crisis of 1825; he titles another "Favorable Comments on Silver and Bimetallism" and writes (1965, pp. 124, 181): "The last serious Parliamentary move for a silver standard or bimetallism had been in 1835, but in the years between then and 1844 suggestions that silver should have a more permanent place in the monetary system came from many persons of widely diverse views on other aspects of monetary and banking policy." Later still, in the 1870s and 1880s, after the resumption on gold by the United States and the shift to gold by France, Germany, and other European countries had started a precipitous fall in the gold price of silver, "complications that fluctuations in the Indian exchange were creating for England, the pressure from the United States for bimetallism, and the domestic economic problems resulting from falling gold prices, led to serious consideration of the possibility of international bimetallism" (1973, p. 19). "A divided commission [appointed in 1887] recommended bimetallism, but the government did not push the proposal and the movement never got off the ground on the international political level" (Fetter 1973, p. 19).

have served the same function that overvalued silver coins and overvalued paper served then and later. They would, of course, have been subject to counterfeiting, but the return would be far less than from the counterfeiting of paper and, to judge from Feavearyear's comment, technically more difficult than the counterfeiting of silver, so it is hard to regard that as a decisive consideration.

Under either gold or silver, or for that matter under bimetallism, it is necessary to have small-denomination coins. Under a gold standard, full-bodied low-value coins would be excessively small. Redish argues that the British solved this problem by using overvalued silver coins whose convertibility at nominal value was guaranteed by the mint. That could also be done under a silver standard, and it was done under the U.S. legal bimetallic but de facto gold standard from 1837 to the Civil War.

Whatever may prove to be the merits of Redish's ingenious rationalization of the British action, it was certainly not a foregone conclusion at the time that resumption would be on gold rather than silver, though it does seem to have been taken for granted that resumption would be on a monometallic basis. For example, David Ricardo, in his pamphlet *The High Price of Bullion* ([1811] 1951, p. 65), wrote: "No permanent measure of value can be said to exist in any nation while the circulating medium consists of two metals, because they are constantly subject to vary in value with respect to each other. . . . Mr. Locke, Lord Liverpool, and many other writers, have ably considered this subject, and have all agreed, that the only remedy for the evils in the currency proceeding from this source, is the making one of the metals only the standard measure of value."

As regards gold versus silver, Ricardo, in his influential

pamphlet *Proposals for an Economical and Secure Currency,* favored silver, writing ([1816] 1951, p. 63):

> Much inconvenience arises from using two metals as the standard of our money; and it has long been a disputed point whether gold or silver should by law be made the principal or sole standard of money. In favour of gold, it may be said, that its greater value under a smaller bulk eminently qualifies it for the standard in an opulent country; but this very quality subjects it to greater variations of value during periods of war, or extensive commercial discredit, when it is often collected and hoarded, and may be urged as an argument against its use. The only objection to the use of silver, as the standard, is its bulk, which renders it unfit for the large payments required in a wealthy country; but this objection is entirely removed by the substituting of paper money as the general circulation medium of the country. Silver, too, is much more steady in its value, in consequence of its demand and supply being more regular; and as all foreign countries regulate the value of their money by the value of silver, there can be no doubt, that, on the whole, silver is preferable to gold as a standard, and should be permanently adopted for that purpose.

In subsequent testimony in 1819 before a committee of Parliament, Ricardo ([1819a] 1952, pp. 390–91; see also [1819b] 1952, p. 427) shifted to gold because "I have understood that machinery is particularly applicable to the silver mines, and may therefore very much conduce to an increased quantity of that metal and an alteration of its value, whilst the same cause is not likely to operate upon the value of gold."

Greater stability of value was a valid economic reason for favoring one metal over the other, but the technical prediction that induced Ricardo to decide that gold was likely to be more stable than silver proved erroneous. Silver production fell relative to that of gold until the discovery of the Comstock Lode in 1860, and machinery came to be at least as applicable to the mining of gold as to the mining of silver. However, the assertion that gold would have a more stable value than silver became a largely self-fulfilling prophecy once gold was chosen as the standard. Britain's choice led to drastic changes in the demand for gold and silver, both at the time and later, when other countries followed Britain's example. As a result, silver tended to replace gold in the French currency until the California and Australia gold discoveries, and the real price of gold was far less variable over the next century than the real price of silver was. However, if Britain had chosen silver on the expectation that its value would be more stable, that, too, would probably have become a self-fulfilling prophecy. Britain's choice of silver would have prevented the subsequent widespread demonetization of silver and, instead, would have led either to the demonetization of gold or to a continuation of effective bimetallism in at least some countries. Either result probably would have meant a more stable real price of silver than of gold and, if bimetallism had continued, very likely a more stable price level than under either of the monometallic standards.

It is fascinating to speculate on what might have been if Ricardo's technical adviser had informed him that "machinery is particularly apposite to" gold mines rather than silver mines—as, indeed, it ultimately turned out to be. With Ricardo's immense influence and prestige at the time the key decisions were being made, it is not at all fanciful to suppose that Britain would have resumed specie payments on silver instead of gold, transforming the subsequent economic history of the nineteenth century in major ways that we can only dimly see.

As it was, Britain's example, and subsequent rise to economic preeminence, proved decisive. It was a major factor leading first Germany and then the United States to adopt a gold standard. Happenstance or not, Britain's decision nearly two centuries ago to resume convertibility on the basis of gold is the fundamental source of the conventional view that gold is superior to silver as the basis for a monometallic standard.

Conclusion

Despite the continued presence among us of "monetary monomaniacs"—now mostly goldbugs—the near universal adoption of inconvertible paper standards throughout the world has rendered the discussion of specie standards, whether gold, silver, bimetallic, or symmetallic, of largely historical interest for the time being. That situation may change, but, regardless of what happens, it seems worth offering an antidote to the conventional view among monetary economists about bimetallism.* Far from being a thoroughly discredited fallacy, bimetallism has much to recommend it, on theoretical, practical, and historical grounds, as superior to monometallism, though not to symmetallism or to a tabular standard. Indeed, twentieth-century technological developments have undermined many of the practical considerations that were cited against bimetallism during the nineteenth century. In particular, the wider use of deposits and paper money has

* Two recent papers on bimetallism may be a sign that the situation is changing (Roccas 1987 and Dowd 1991).

rendered almost irrelevant Jevons's concern about the weight of silver, as well as the concern of many that a bimetallic standard might involve extensive recoinage from time to time. On the other hand, the reduction in the use of coins has undoubtedly weakened the hard-money myth that only specie is real money. That myth buttressed earlier popular support for a specie standard and still inspires the goldbugs around the world. When it was much stronger than it is today, the myth made it politically dangerous to depart from the unlimited convertibility of legal tender into specie, and it still has enough residual power to lead central banks around the world to continue carrying gold on their books at an artificial legal monetary price.

As a final note, we have here another striking example of the far-reaching but unintended effects of an event that is almost a matter of chance. In this case, the pebble that started an avalanche was Britain's decision to resume convertibility on the basis of gold. The economic history of the world ever since would have been very different if Britain had chosen instead to retain bimetallism or to resume convertibility on the basis of silver, though it is beyond our analytical ability to sketch in detail just how events would have evolved.

CHAPTER 7

FDR, Silver, and China

The U.S. silver purchase program that was initiated in 1933 by President Franklin Delano Roosevelt, under the authority of the Thomas amendment to the 1933 Farm Relief Bill, was the end product of a decade or more of political pressure by the silver lobby to "do something" for silver. The farm lobby supported silver purchases partly because it favored any measure that would produce inflation and thereby raise the prices of farm products—prices that had plummeted during the Great Depression. In addition, the farm lobby wanted to get the support of the silver lobby for other price inflation devices contained in the Farm Relief Bill. President Roosevelt supported silver purchases primarily to assure that congressmen from the silver and farm states would support other New Deal legislation.

The other inflation measures in the Farm Relief Bill had already demonstrated their capacity to produce inflation before any silver was purchased. However, the silver purchases did contribute to the growth in high-powered money that, from 1932 to 1937, supported an increase in the general price level of 14 percent, in wholesale prices of 32 percent, and in farm products of 79 percent.

The silver purchase program "did something" for silver by raising the price of the metal promptly and sharply, providing a large subsidy to producers of silver. However, the program also drove China—the only major country still on a silver standard in 1934—off silver, and it led other major users of silver for monetary purposes—notably Mexico and many Latin American countries—to reduce or eliminate the silver content of their minor coins. The program thereby assured the final and all but complete demonetization of silver.

The proponents of the silver purchase program had claimed benefits to China as one of its advantages. In fact, the program was a disaster for the Chinese republic, then ruled by Chiang Kai-shek. By virtue of being on a silver standard, China had been largely insulated against the worst effects of the early years of the Great Depression. But the U.S. silver policy imposed a major deflation on China in 1934–36, accompanied by troubled economic conditions, thereby undermining popular support for Chiang Kai-shek. More important, the policy denuded China of its monetary reserves and drove it off silver and onto a fiat paper standard. The war with Japan and the internal civil war between Chiang's Nationalist government and Mao Zedong's communists would undoubtedly have led to inflation in China in any event. However, the U.S. silver policy accelerated the onset of inflation and increased its magnitude, contributing to the hyperinflation of 1948–49. And, as Chang Kia-ngau wrote, while "many historical forces contributed to the collapse of the Nationalist government after World War II, . . . the direct and immediate cause which overshadowed all other factors was undoubtedly the inflation" (1958, p. 363). This sentiment is echoed by an American historian, C. Martin Wilbur, in his foreword to a slightly later book by a Chinese scholar on the Chinese inflation: "There seemed little doubt that China's wartime and postwar inflation was one of the prime factors which caused the downfall of the Nationalist government and the conquest of the mainland by the Chinese Communist Party" (Chou 1963, p. ix; see also Young 1965, p. 328). As a result, the U.S. silver purchase program must be regarded as having contributed, if perhaps only modestly, to the success of the communist revolution in China.

The Pressure for Silver

Like old soldiers, old causes never die; they only fade away. Supposedly interred by the defeat of Bryan in 1896, the silver issue repeatedly resurfaced.

Toward the end of World War I, "the government of India was having great difficulty in securing enough silver to provide for rupee circulation and for an adequate reserve behind the paper currency" (Leavens 1939, p. 145). The amount needed was greater than could be supplied out of current production. To accommodate Great Britain, the United States agreed to provide silver out of its ample monetary reserves. To authorize this sale and to accommodate the domestic silver bloc, the Pittman Act was passed in 1918. The act was named for Senator Key Pittman of Nevada, who was perhaps the most persistent advocate of "doing something for silver" from his first term as senator, beginning in 1913, to his death in 1940. To satisfy the silver bloc, the silver from the monetary reserves was to be replaced with purchases from domestic production, at a guaranteed price of $1.00 an ounce, when excess production became available.

The wartime inflation plus high wartime demand for silver, for both monetary and nonmonetary purposes, had raised the market price from 70 cents an ounce in 1914 to 97 cents in 1918 and to more than a dollar in 1919. "In 1920, the price dropped below a dollar an ounce. The Director of the Mint immediately began the purchase of silver bullion at the stipulated price of a dollar per fine ounce" (Leavens 1939, p. 147). All in all, the mint purchased some 200 million ounces of silver over the next three years at a price to American producers of $1.00 an ounce, while the market price was falling to less than 70 cents—a subsidy to the producers totaling roughly $16 million.

The pressure to "do something" for silver continued after the completion of the Pittman Act purchases, but it did not become vigorous again until 1930, when the Great Depression produced a sharp decline in the price of silver—from 58 cents an ounce in 1928 to 38 cents in 1930 and 25 cents in late 1932 and early 1933.

The silver bloc promptly revived all the earlier favorite remedies: calling an international conference, buying and stockpiling silver at a price above the market price, enacting the free and unlimited coinage of silver at 16 to 1. None came to fruition during the Hoover administration, but they promptly reemerged with the election of FDR.*

The explanation for the continued pressure is straightforward. As T. J. Kreps noted in a 1934 article: "Since silver is produced in the seven western states—Utah, Idaho, Arizona, Montana, Nevada, Colorado, and New Mexico—the silver senators control one-seventh of the votes in the Senate. This, under its rule of cloture, gives them a considerable strategic importance. Consequently

*For a detailed discussion of "proposals to do something for silver, 1923 to 1933," see the chapter so titled in Leavens (1939, pp. 224–35).

more than twenty bills on silver were recently pending in Congress. Tho the silver states have an aggregate population less than that of New Jersey, and tho the silver industry in 1929 employed less than 3,000 persons, the political leadership of the United States may soon find it expedient, in order to secure adequate political support for measures of far greater national importance, to 'do something for silver' " (p. 246).

New Deal Action for Silver

The Democratic platform on which Roosevelt was elected in 1932 pledged a "sound currency to be preserved at all hazards," but it went on to add "and an international monetary conference called on the invitation of our Government to consider the rehabilitation of silver and related questions." The Republican platform also favored an international conference but, in a separate plank, pledged to "continue to uphold the gold standard"—shades of difference that had persisted since the direct confrontation on the silver issue in 1896. In a campaign speech at Butte, Montana, the heart of silver country, Roosevelt declared that "silver must be restored as monetary metal, and the Democratic pledge on the subject must be kept" and that "he would call immediately after his inauguration an international monetary conference to consider the rehabilitation of silver" (*New York Times*, Sept. 20, 1932, p. 1).

The Democratic landslide in 1932 greatly strengthened the political power of the silver bloc, especially in the Senate. Before the election, the fourteen senators from the seven states producing the bulk of the silver were evenly divided: seven Republicans, seven Democrats. The Roosevelt sweep left only two Republicans versus twelve Democrats, and one of the Republicans, William E. Borah of Idaho, had long been a staunch supporter of silver. Some leaders of the silver bloc—like Borah, first elected in 1906, and Key Pittman, first elected in 1912—had, by virtue of seniority, become highly influential in the Senate. Similarly, the farm state allies of the silver bloc gained strength.

The first test in the Senate, on an amendment to adopt the free and unlimited coinage of silver at 16 to 1, was "rejected 44 to 33, but showed a gain of 15 votes since the time when the question had been voted on in January" by the lame-duck Congress (Leavens 1939, p. 245). Obviously the silver bloc was a potent political force, which the president could hardly ignore. And, as Roosevelt had made clear during the campaign, he had no intention of doing so.

The president's response was to support an amendment to a farm relief bill that was then being proposed by Senator Elmer Thomas, who was not from a silver state but nonetheless was "a sturdy inflationist" (Leavens 1939, pp. 245–46). As finally passed, on May 12, 1933, the Thomas amendment provided for an increase in Federal Reserve notes and deposits and U.S. notes, at the discretion of the president, in an amount ($3 billion) that would have nearly doubled the amount of high-powered money. In addition, the amendment authorized the president to reduce the gold content of the dollar and gave him sweeping powers with respect to silver—powers that would, for example, have enabled him to give immediate effect to Bryan's battle cry of free and unlimited coinage of silver at 16 to 1. These powers were "hardly used until December 21, 1933, when . . . President Roosevelt used the authority granted by the Thomas amendment to direct U.S. mints to receive all newly produced domestic silver offered to them up to December 31, 1937, at $64\frac{64}{99}$ cents an ounce (i.e., $0.6464 . . . an ounce)" (Friedman and Schwartz 1963, p.

483), at a time when the market price was 44 cents an ounce.* Roosevelt justified the bizarre purchase price by adopting the fiction that the Treasury was simply coining silver at the legally specified weight for the silver dollar—that is, at a monetary value of $1.2929 per ounce—but was charging 50 percent for seignorage. This device had the advantage that the subsidy to silver producers not only entailed no budgetary costs but actually yielded a budgetary income equal to the fictional seignorage. "Smoke and mirrors" in budgetary bookkeeping is not a recent invention.

In the meantime, the ill-fated World Economic Conference, called at the request of President Roosevelt to fulfill his campaign promise and, a couple of months later, summarily torpedoed by him, had come and gone.† About its only achievement was more smoke and mirrors: an agreement among silver-producing and silver-using countries to take measures to shore up the price of silver. This imposed no significant actions on any country other than the United States and simply provided the United States with the cover of an international agreement to do what it was going to do anyway—buy a limited amount of silver (for a full discussion, see Leavens 1939, pp. 248–51).

The climax came with the Silver Purchase Act, enacted by Congress in response to a message by President Roosevelt of May 22, 1934, and signed by him less than a month later, on June 19, 1934. The Silver Purchase Act "directed the Secretary of the Treasury to purchase silver at home

*A minor earlier effect of the Thomas amendment was its provision that for a limited time silver would be accepted at the artificial price of 50 cents an ounce in payment of governmental war debts. Some 20-odd million ounces were received under this provision earlier in the year.

†The conference opened in London on June 12, 1933, and closed on July 27, 1933.

and abroad until the market price reached $1.29+ an ounce, or until the monetary value of the silver stock held by the Treasury reached one-third of the monetary value of the gold stock. The Secretary was given wide discretion in carrying out that mandate" (Friedman and Schwartz 1963, p. 485).*

Purchases and, much later, sales under the 1934 and successor acts continued until late 1961, and the legal authority for purchases was not repealed until 1963. Yet, despite the massive acquisition of silver under the act, neither of its objectives—a price of $1.29+ an ounce and a 1 to 3 ratio of monetary silver to monetary gold—came close to being realized. The acquisitions—by purchase from domestic producers under the December 21, 1933, proclamation, by the "nationalization" of domestically held stocks of silver on August 9, 1934, and by purchases

*An excellent summary of the act by Paris (1938, pp. 54–55) follows:

Purposes

(1) To increase the price of silver

(2) To increase the monetary stock of silver to one-third the value of the monetary gold stock

(3) To issue silver certificates

Measures to be taken to achieve the purposes

(1) Secretary of the Treasury to purchase silver at home and abroad upon terms and conditions he believes in the public interest

(2) Purchases to cease when price reaches monetary value ($1.2929+ per fine ounce), or monetary silver stock equals one-third, in value, of monetary gold stock

(3) Price of silver situated in the United States on May 1, 1934, not to exceed $0.50 per fine ounce

(4) Silver to be sold when monetary silver stock exceeds one-third, in value, of monetary gold stock

(5) Silver certificates to be issued up to a face amount not less than the cost of the silver purchased

(6) Secretary of the Treasury may control import, export, and other transactions relating to silver

(7) President may "nationalize" silver

(8) Profit on purchase and sale of silver to be taxed 50 percent.

on the open market under the Silver Purchase Act—initially drove the price of silver from around 44 cents an ounce just prior to the December 1933 proclamation to a high of 81 cents an ounce on April 26, 1935. The price then fell to around 45 cents in early 1936 and did not rise appreciably until the inflation of World War II. By the end of the war the price had risen above the government's support price for domestically mined silver, so in 1946 an act was passed reducing seignorage to 30 percent, implying a support price of 90½ cents per ounce. The market price was pegged at this level by Treasury purchases and sales until 1961. After government intervention ended, the price finally rose above the legal monetary value, as silver participated in the postwar inflation. And then the price rose high enough to send even drastically undervalued minor silver coins to the melting pot or the numismatic market.

As to the second objective, the ratio of monetary silver to monetary gold never rose above 1 to 5 during the 1930s—a long way from the 1 to 3 objective. The massive additions to the gold stock that were produced by the increase in the legal monetary price of gold to $35 an ounce offset the effects of the massive silver purchases.

Domestic Effects

The silver legislation had only one significant domestic effect—the provision of a major subsidy, at taxpayer expense, to domestic producers of silver. They responded by greatly increasing their production, from 33 million ounces in 1934 to 70 million ounces in 1940. Economic growth would in any event have led to increased production of silver because much of it is a by-product of the mining of copper, lead, and zinc. However, the subsidized price stimulated the mining not only of silver but also of copper, lead, and zinc.

The silver bloc regarded the stimulation of silver production as a good thing in itself because it provided employment in the silver states. However, to get the support of other interests, notably the farm bloc, supporters of silver also argued that the purchase program would contribute to general inflation by increasing the money supply and would promote exports by increasing the purchasing power of countries using silver as money, notably, according to them, China and India.*

The Treasury paid for its silver purchases by printing silver certificates, and these did add to the money supply. However, there are many other ways to increase the money supply, and their actual monetary effect was simply that the silver certificates were printed instead of Federal Reserve notes. Put differently, nothing about the purchase program prevented the Federal Reserve from sterilizing the monetary effect of the silver purchases.

The effect on silver-using countries, as we shall shortly see, was precisely the opposite of what was claimed: great economic difficulty.

All in all, the major short-run domestic effect was simply that the taxpayers paid to have silver dug out of the ground, refined, coined, and shipped for storage in Washington and at other government depositories—a make-work program producing little if any useful output, if ever there was one. In the long run, even the domestic silver interests were harmed, because the effects on other countries destroyed what had been a major market for their output, namely, the use of silver for monetary purposes.

*China was still on a silver standard, but India no longer was. However, India had been until 1893, and Indian coinage had remained mostly silver.

As late as 1933, by which time China was the only populous country still on a silver standard, 43 percent of the total visible stock of silver and more than 30 percent of all the silver produced from 1493 to 1932 was in monetary use (Leavens 1939, p. 369). By 1979, coinage accounted for only 5 percent of total consumption of silver. Throughout most of the postwar period, industrial consumption of silver substantially exceeded new production plus silver scrap, the balance coming out of U.S. silver stocks and demonetized and melted silver coinage (see the following section).

The price of silver tells the same story. From 1670 B.C. to 1873, the year in which the United States and France demonetized silver, the yearly average price of gold never rose above 16 times the corresponding price of silver. The lowest recorded price ratio is a trifle below 9 in about 50 B.C. (Warren and Pearson 1933, p. 144.) Remarkably, the price ratio ranged between 9 and 16 for more than three millennia. From 1687, when continuous annual estimates begin, to 1873—years when silver was unquestionably the dominant monetary metal—the range is much narrower, between 14 and 16.* The situation changed drastically after 1873. From then to 1929, the ratio varied between 15 and 40 and was mostly in the high 30s, except for a few years during and just after World War I. The drastic fall in the price of silver during the Depression raised the ratio to 76 in 1933. The silver purchase program lowered the ratio temporarily to 54 in 1935, but then it rose to an all-time high of over 100 in 1940 and 1941. It fell to a low of 18 in 1970 because the United States pegged the price of gold at $35 an ounce, while inflation was pushing up the price of silver along with the prices of other commodities. After the price of gold was set

*The narrow range of the relative price of gold and silver does not mean that the purchasing power of either gold or silver was constant.

free in 1971, the ratio rose again, fluctuating considerably. Currently it is around 75 to 1.

Many forces other than the silver purchase program affected the use and price of silver during those troubled decades, notably the change in the character of monetary systems around the world, ending in the adoption of fiat money standards after 1971. Yet there is little doubt that the initial rise in the price of silver occasioned by the purchase program played a significant role in reducing the monetary demand for silver, which ultimately drove its price below the level that would otherwise have prevailed.

Nonetheless, as Figure 1 shows, in a long view the silver purchase program shows up as only a minor bubble. The figure plots the price of silver, adjusted for changes in the general level of prices, from 1800 to 1989.* At 1982

Figure 1

Real Price of Silver, 1800–1989 (in 1982 dollars)

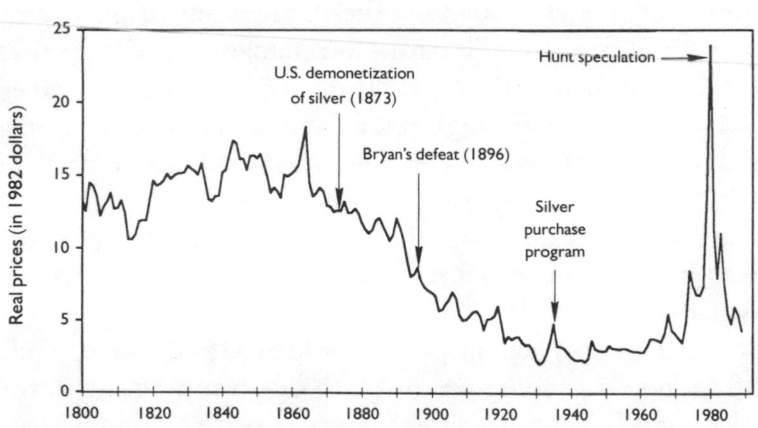

*A continuous price series was obtained by linking the deflator in Friedman and Schwartz (1982) to the Department of Commerce GNP deflator from 1976

prices, the real price of silver ranged between $10 and $18 from 1800 to 1873, when the demonetization of silver in the United States and other countries started the price on its long slide. The slide turned into a rout in the early 1890s, when first the repeal of silver purchase legislation and then the defeat of Bryan ended any realistic chance that silver would be remonetized. The 1934 silver purchase program stopped the rout, but only temporarily. The price decline did not really end until the 1960s, when the increasing use of silver in photography and other industries came to the rescue. The ill-fated speculation on silver by the Hunt brothers, who lost much of their fabulous fortune in the venture, drove the price to historically unprecedented levels, which averaged nearly $25 over the full year but reached a much higher peak during it. Silver then declined to the earlier levels.

Effects on Other Countries

The high price the United States offered for silver affected many other countries. Although silver had lost out to gold in the 1870s as the major monetary metal, centuries of silver dominance left many countries with a large silver coinage. After the shift to gold, the face value of the silver coins was set above the market value of the silver they contained; they were token coins. But as the United States drove up the price of silver, that situation changed, and coins in many countries became more valuable as metal

to 1986 and to wholesale prices as reported from 1800 to 1867 in the report of the U.S. Commission on the Role of Gold (1982). The price of silver in New York was pieced together from Warren and Pearson (1933), *Historical Statistics,* and Jastram (1981).

than as money and so were consigned to the melting pot.

The same phenomenon had occurred in the United States during the greenback inflation of the Civil War, which caused an acute shortage of minor coins and a resort to postage stamps—"shinplasters"—as a substitute. The nickname stuck even after the post office started to produce stamps without mucilage to satisfy the demand for their use as fractional currency. Later, fractional paper currency supplemented stamps. The phenomenon occurred again in the United States after World War II, when inflation drove the price of silver above its legal monetary value. This time, preparations were made in advance by reducing the amount of silver in coins. While today's dimes, quarters, and half-dollars may have a silver sheen, they are really copper coins with a thin coating of nickel.

In 1935 and 1936, as the price of silver rose higher and higher, one country after another changed the silver content of its coins. "The Silver coinage debasement campaign to keep coins from the melting pot was world-wide. Central America, South America, Europe, Asia and even Africa participated" (Paris 1938, p. 72).

Mexico was a special case. As the largest producer of silver, it benefited from the higher prices. But, also, much of its money supply consisted of silver coins. Toward the end of April 1935, the value of the silver peso as metal rose above its value as money. "[I]n order to prevent the peso from being shipped to the United States either as a coin or in melted-down form, President Cardenas proclaimed a bank holiday on April 27. Then he ordered all coins to be exchanged for paper currency, and prohibited the export of silver money. . . . [A] year and a half later, when silver prices had fallen, these orders were revoked and silver coinage was restored" (Paris 1938, p. 71). Nonetheless, Mexico had permanently converted its monetary system to a managed paper standard. The short-term benefit from the higher price of silver may have outweighed the immediate harm from the bank holiday and the accompanying monetary developments. However, over the long term, this immediate gain was almost surely more than offset by the loss of a major source of demand for silver and by the lasting monetary effects of being forced to adopt a managed paper standard.

The Effect on China

I single out China for special attention because it was the only major country that was on a silver standard in 1933, when U.S. action to raise the price of silver began.* As a result, the U.S. silver purchase program had more far-reaching effects on China than on any other country. Although China did not produce any significant amount of silver, it had accumulated a large stock of the metal as a result of its use as money. Only India had a larger silver stock. (Like China, India had long been on a silver standard, but, unlike China, it had gone off silver in 1893 and had adopted a gold standard in 1899.)

The silver standard was a blessing for China in the early years of the Great Depression. The countries it traded with were on a gold standard, and prices in those countries fell drastically after 1929, including the price of silver. With China on a silver standard, the fall in the price

*Because of its close economic ties to China, Hong Kong was also on a silver standard, and so also were Ethiopia (then Abyssinia) and Persia (now Iran) (Leavens 1939, p. 369).

To describe China as on a silver standard is a simplification. "Copper . . . is used for an even larger proportion of the business done in China [than silver]. . . . These copper coins . . . circulate on the basis of their value as metal. They constitute the medium of exchange and of account for the common people" (Kreps 1934, pp. 251–52). However, essentially all of the wholesale trade and foreign trade was conducted on the basis of silver.

of silver was equivalent to a depreciation of the exchange rate of its currency with respect to gold-standard currencies; it gave China the equivalent of a floating exchange rate. For example, in 1929 the Chinese dollar was valued on the foreign exchange market at 36 U.S. cents; in the next two years the price of silver in terms of gold fell more than 40 percent, making the Chinese dollar worth only 21 cents. Since U.S. wholesale prices fell by only 26 percent, China could command higher prices in terms of its own currency for its exports, despite their lower price in terms of gold. Imports, of course, were also more expensive. The net result was that while exports from China fell, they fell much less than either world exports or Chinese imports. In 1930 and 1931, China had a balance-of-payments surplus reflected in net imports of gold and silver. Internally, it experienced a mild inflation and a mild boom while the rest of the world was suffering from drastic deflation.*

The departure of Britain, India, Japan, and other countries from the gold standard in 1931 eroded the advantage conferred on China by a floating exchange rate. These countries' currencies depreciated vis-à-vis the U.S. dollar, which meant that the Chinese dollar appreciated in terms of the pound sterling, the rupee, and the yen, while continuing to depreciate vis-à-vis the U.S. dollar—to 19 cents at the end of 1932. For the first time China began to feel the effects of the world depression, though sheltered somewhat by the continued decline in the price of silver in terms of the U.S. dollar, the limited monetization of its economy, and the large-scale use of copper coins by the general

*For an excellent discussion of the impact that China's being on the equivalent of a floating exchange rate had on prices in China, see Wignall (1978a, pp. 33–43; 1978b, p. 39). The articles are unsigned in the original source. I have attributed authorship on the basis of a personal letter of April 18, 1990, from John Greenwood, founder and editor of the *Asian Monetary Monitor*.

populace. The Chinese balance of payments deteriorated sharply, and in 1932 China had to export gold and silver to pay for the excess of imports over exports. Internally, wholesale prices peaked in 1931 and then fell sharply, and economic conditions deteriorated, in the judgment of most contemporary observers (Salter 1934, p. 6; Wignall 1978b, pp. 36, 37).

The adverse effect on China of the departure of Britain and other countries from the gold standard in 1931 was reinforced by the Japanese occupation of Manchuria in September 1931. At the time, China was governed by the Kuomingtang, under Chiang Kai-shek, although regional warlords ruled some areas and the communists were leading a rebellion. "Chiang Kai-shek's response to the Manchurian occupation was indicative of China's weakness. The reality was accepted and no resistance offered. The Kuomintang leader concentrated instead on building up his army to meet the inevitable Japanese aggression. A strong army was also required to suppress the Communists and the regional power bases of the remaining warlords. These military demands were a crucial reason for the growing budgetary deficits of the Kuomintang. The debilitating effect of a long background of deficit financing was a prime factor in China's subsequent hyperinflation" (Greenwood and Wood 1977a, p. 27.)* Nonetheless, Chiang had considerable success in unifying the country. "The regional powerbases of the warlords were undermined, while by 1934 the Communists were driven back to the northwestern mountain retreat of Yenan" (Greenwood and Wood 1977a, p. 27).

The temporary advantage in foreign trade that China

*This article and two others by Greenwood and Wood are unsigned in the original source. I have attributed authorship on the basis of a personal letter of April 18, 1990, from John Greenwood, founder and editor of the *Asian Monetary Monitor*.

had gained by its silver standard was not just eroded, but was eliminated and converted into a major disadvantage when the United States, too, went off gold in 1933. The Chinese dollar appreciated further with respect to the pound, the yen, and the rupee and, for the first time, with respect to the U.S. dollar, from 19 cents at the end of 1932 to 33 cents at the end of 1933—almost all the way back to the 1929 level. True, prices in terms of the dollar and other currencies were rising, offsetting some of the effects of the appreciation of the Chinese dollar. But the U.S. price of silver rose much more sharply than prices in general, so that only a small part of the appreciation was offset. As a result, Chinese exports fell sharply, by 58 percent compared to 1930, and exports of precious metals continued. While most of the rest of the world was beginning to recover from the Great Depression, China was, according to contemporary observers, entering into the severest phase of its internal depression.*

The adverse effect on China of the U.S. departure from gold was strongly reinforced by the U.S. action to "do something" for silver, which was a major factor in the near doubling of the price of silver during 1933 and its more than tripling at its peak in April 1935. At that point the Chinese dollar was valued on the market at 41 cents. The price of silver subsequently declined, as noted earlier, but by then the harm to China had been done. China went off the silver standard on October 14, 1934, by raising the export duty on silver and imposing an adjustable "equalization charge." It went onto "what was essentially a paper

*The data in this and the preceding two paragraphs are taken from Salter (1934, pp. 15–19). However, see the Appendix to this chapter for different interpretations by Brandt and Sargent (1989), Rawski (1989), and P. H. K. Chang (1988).

standard" (Wignall 1978b, p. 38), though an official statement that China was leaving the silver standard was postponed until November 3, 1935, when the government announced a sweeping currency reform.

Had silver been simply a commodity in China, the rise in the price of silver would have been a welcome windfall, enabling China to dispose of its large stock of silver on highly favorable terms. But because silver was China's money, the rise in the price of silver had produced a major deflation, which in turn had led to severely troubled economic conditions. "Imports declined while exports became increasingly uncompetitive. Industrial production drew to a halt with the low level of activity in the economy, unemployment rose and prices slumped. The effect of the deflation on agriculture is clear from the fall of the price index of agricultural produce from 100 in 1926 to 57 in 1933. This represented an appalling decline in income, and hence purchasing power, for those living by cultivation of the land" (Greenwood and Wood 1977a, p. 32).* According to Arthur N. Young, who served as a financial adviser to China from 1929 to 1947, "China passed from moderate prosperity to deep depression" (1971, p. 209).

An adverse effect of the U.S. silver policy on China was neither unpredictable nor unpredicted. In a February 1934 report, Sir Arthur Salter, who had been "invited by the Chinese Government to become for a few months an official adviser to the National Economic Council," wrote: "There are great dangers and difficulties in any departure from the present silver basis of the Chinese dollar. Without that, however, China can only escape the injury of further

*See the chapter Appendix for alternative interpretations of the events set in motion by the U.S. silver purchase program.

deflation if silver ceases to rise substantially in relation to the foreign currencies and to the world prices of commodities. The principal factor is the U.S.'s silver policy. It seems important, therefore, that China (whose real interest in silver is overwhelmingly greater than that of any other country) should make her position clear to the Government of that country" (Salter 1934, unnumbered prefatory page, pp. 108–9). Note that this was after much of the damage had already been done. In a subsequent editorial of September 3, 1934, based largely on Salter's report, the *New York Times* wrote: "One of the odd aspects of our silver policy is that it was originally advocated precisely to help the 'silver-using' countries and to 'restore the buying power of the Far East.' . . . The only important country on the silver standard, however, is China, and those who are intimately acquainted with the Chinese situation are practically unanimous in holding that raising the price of silver can only be injurious to that country." The *Times* editorial concluded by noting that the American silver policy might "have the ironic result of driving the only important remaining silver country on to the gold standard."* In fact, the policy drove China onto a paper standard.

In March 1934, the U.S. Treasury sent Professor James Harvey Rogers of Yale University to China to report on the effect that higher silver prices would have there. Like Salter, Rogers reported that the effect would be highly adverse, going so far as to write to Secretary of the Treasury Henry Morgenthau in October, after most of the damage had been done, that "to proceed with this new policy [bidding up the

*Salter had served as a *New York Times* correspondent covering the London World Economic Conference in 1933, and he continued to write special articles for the *Times* thereafter. The *Times* reports him as having given several speeches in New York in late 1934, so it is not inconceivable that he wrote the editorial from which I have quoted.

silver price]—before giving the Chinese government an opportunity to adjust to the resulting monetary disturbances—seems to me to border very closely on international irresponsibility" (Young 1971, p. 205).

The effect on Chinese internal prices of the departure from the silver standard was prompt but, until 1937, moderate. According to annual averages for Shanghai, wholesale prices, which had fallen by 23 percent from 1931 to 1934, fell another 1 percent from 1934 to 1935 and then rose 24 percent in the next two years. The situation changed drastically, however, when Japan invaded China in the summer of 1937. "Government expenditure soared skyward to meet the cost of suppressing the Japanese invasion, and later to finance the civil war against the Communists" (Greenwood and Wood 1977a, p. 25). No doubt government expenditures would have soared even if the United States had not driven up the price of silver, and China would sooner or later have left the silver standard and gone on a paper standard. But the U.S. action assured that the paper standard and inflation came sooner, not later. Chiang's position was directly weakened by the loss of the silver reserves that could have financed at least the initial expansion of government spending, thereby postponing the need to engage in inflationary monetary creation. He was weakened indirectly by the severely disturbed economic conditions to which the U.S. action contributed and which undermined popular support for the Nationalist regime.* If the United States had not driven

*Some idea of how important this effect might have been can be gained from data on the export of silver and the government's budget. From 1932 to 1936, roughly 900 million yuan of silver (valued at the legal Chinese price) was exported and, from 1932 to 1938, nearly 1,400 million (Leavens 1939, p. 303). Indirect evidence suggests that while much of the silver came from privately held stocks, as much as half may have come from monetary reserves held by

up the U.S. dollar price of silver, China would have left the silver standard later—perhaps several years later—than it actually did and under better economic and political conditions. The future course of events would have been altered. The ultimate hyperinflation might not have been prevented, but at least it would have been postponed, giving the Nationalist government more time to recover from wartime disasters and to repel the communist threat.

From 1937 on, U.S. silver policy had no further effects on China (though other U.S. policies undoubtedly did). The damage caused by the U.S. government's myopic concentration on the narrow short-time self-interest of a small but politically potent group had been done. However, the aftershock was still to come.

The Chinese Hyperinflation

The Japanese invasion of China launched the Nationalist government on a frantic arms program, financed primarily

---

the government directly or in government-owned banks as reserves against deposits and paper currency. In 1936, the year before the Japanese invasion but when the Nationalist government was already desperately trying to build up its military strength, government borrowing was 276 million yuan, and a substantial fraction of that was for the refinancing of maturing debt (Rawski 1989, p. 15; Brandt and Sargent 1989, p. 43). So even the directly held government silver would have financed several years of such deficits. Moreover, had the silver been available, it would have made for a healthier monetary situation, with prices more stable, at least for a time. Hence, the deficits generated by military expansion would have been less and the capacity to engage in noninflationary borrowing much greater. All in all, it seems not unreasonable to suppose that the onset of inflationary monetary expansion could have been postponed by at least a year and possibly by two years or more.

Of course, some of the silver exported must be regarded as purchasing goods and services used by the government. But much or most of it presumably went toward accumulating foreign assets on private account to replace domestic assets.

by the printing of money. The issue of notes multiplied nearly 300-fold from 1937 to 1945, or on the average by 100 percent a year, starting at 27 percent from 1937 to 1938 and ending at 224 percent in the final year of the war. Prices rose even faster, to nearly 1,600 times their initial level, or an average of more than 150 percent a year.* Clearly that was a major inflation. Yet the price rise "had been kept from reaching hyperinflationary levels by the flow of U.S. aid to the KMT government, by the entry of America in the Pacific War, and the sharp decline in the flow of refugees from Japanese occupied territory. In the weeks preceding victory over Japan commodity prices had actually slumped in anticipation of allied victory over Japan and the resumption of foreign supplies" (Greenwood and Wood 1977b, p. 32).

The initial prospects after the Japanese surrender looked favorable. A truce was reached between the Nationalists and the communists. However, "neither side was really interested in a united front when the main struggle was for domestic control. . . . [A]rmed clashes became more serious and civil war was renewed . . . by the end of 1947. . . . A mammoth war spread over thousands of miles and involving millions of men on both sides. . . . By the end of 1947 the communists occupied Hopei and Shansi, and by the end of 1948 they had scored a decisive victory on the plains of the Hwai River near Suchow. In January 1949, the Nationalist commander, General Tu Yu-ming, surrendered with the best part of the surviving Nationalist army . . . Chiang Kai-shek resigned in February, and fled

*Data on note issue from Yang (1985, p. 35), on wholesale price index from Huang (1948, p. 564). I am indebted to Liu Na for translating the titles and headings of the tables in Yang from Chinese to English.

with the last of the gold reserves (about three million ounces) to Taiwan" (Greenwood and Wood 1977b, pp. 33, 44).

There is little doubt that bureaucracy, corruption, and bad financial management, which led to the collapse of the money market and a true hyperinflation, were major factors contributing to the defeat of the Nationalists. In a final desperate measure, "on the 22nd of August, 1948, Chiang Kai-shek announced an official reform of the currency. . . . Under the terms of the reform a 'Gold Yuan' was created. . . . Prices were frozen, and all private holdings of gold, silver, and foreign exchange were to be surrendered within three months" at terms that amounted to outright confiscation. Only force might produce results. But in the process "the authorities forfeited the respect of the lingering few who had not already abandoned their wider sense of social responsibility" (Greenwood and Wood 1977b, pp. 40–41). By November, with the black market raging, the government admitted defeat. All in all, linking together the "gold yuan" and the earlier currency, prices in Nationalist territory in April 1949—by which time power had effectively changed hands—were more than 54 million times their level in December 1946. This was an average rate of rise of nearly 90 percent a *month*—far above the 50 percent a month that Phillip Cagan adopted, in his now classic study of hyperinflation, as separating hyperinflation from other inflationary episodes (1956, p. 25).

The hyperinflation not only helped sweep the communists into power. Oncc the warfare was over, the communists were able to eliminate the hyperinflation, and that unquestionably helped to cement them in power (Greenwood and Wood 1978).

Conclusion

It is impossible to assess with any precision the role that the U.S. silver purchase program played in bringing the communists to power in China. There is little doubt that the wartime inflation and, even more, the postwar hyperinflation undermined confidence in the Nationalist government so severely that "the accession of the communists to power in October 1949 did not provoke mass hysteria amongst China's business and financial community." But that can hardly be attributed solely or even largely to the aftereffects of the silver purchase program. "The prevailing attitude [when the communists came to power] was that nothing could be worse than the previous regime's incompetence and corruption" (Greenwood and Wood 1978).

With or without the silver purchase program, the war with Japan and the internal civil war would have led to inflation, and incompetence and corruption would still have existed. However, in the absence of the silver purchase program, the Nationalists would probably have had an extra year or two during which inflation would have been low. The existence of a silver standard would have been one check on inflation, the availability of silver would have been another, and the absence of an earlier major deflation still another. No doubt the same ultimate scenario would have unrolled, but it would not have done so in the same time span; it would have taken longer. The odds for avoiding catastrophe would have been a little better—better for China, and better for the United States.

Appendix to Chapter 7

Alternative Interpretations of China's Departure from Silver

The discussion in this chapter of the China episode is an expanded version of Anna Schwartz's and my discussion in our *Monetary History* (1963, pp. 489–91) and offers essentially the same interpretation of the episode. That interpretation has recently been questioned by Loren Brandt and Thomas Sargent and by P. H. Kevin Chang on the basis of two more recent sets of statistical estimates.

We had taken it for granted that the export of silver (particularly in 1934 and 1935) produced a decline in China's stock of money that spread the deflation from internationally traded goods to the general price level. We also had regarded the depressed economic conditions reported by contemporary observers as largely a consequence of the monetary deflation.

There is no disagreement that the rise in the price of silver produced a severe deflation. The question is, how? And was the higher price of silver really a catastrophe for China, as we maintained, or a boon?

Estimates of gross domestic product by K. C. Yeh (1964) indicate that real income in China fell appreciably from 1933 to 1934, primarily because of bad agricultural harvests, but was not otherwise particularly depressed between 1932 and 1936 (see Brandt and Sargent 1989, table

5, p. 46). Estimates of the Chinese money supply by Thomas Rawski (1989, pp. 312–400) indicate that an increase in bank notes and bank deposits more than offset the decline in specie as a result of silver exports, so that the total quantity of money rose, not only prior to 1931 but also from 1931 on (see Rawski 1989, table C16, p. 394). Taken at face value, these two sets of estimates are inconsistent with our interpretation of the episode as a monetary deflation.

Loren Brandt and Thomas Sargent (1989) regard this additional evidence as suggesting that the episode was one of "free banking" on a specie standard in which the higher real price of silver meant that a smaller physical stock of silver was necessary to support the same total stock of money in nominal units. The price deflation, they suggest, was produced by the "law of one price," that is, arbitrage between international and domestic prices, rather than by monetary contraction. And prices, they conjecture, were sufficiently flexible to insulate the real economy from the price deflation produced by the "law of one price." The higher value of silver was simply a boon to holders of silver, and to benefit from that boon they exported the amount no longer needed to support the money stock.

They conclude that "the U.S. silver purchase program did not set off a chain of bad economic events which eventually forced China off silver and onto a fiat standard. The U.S. silver purchase program undoubtedly did help cause the fall in the Chinese price level. . . . But the evidence points against any massive disruptions in real economic activity as having resulted from the price level fall. . . . The Chinese monetary system was driven off silver by its government, which wanted to increase its share of [the boon from the higher price of silver] . . . and which also perhaps foresaw that in coming years it would be easier to issue debt with low rates of returns if it could prevent competition from banks offering high-yielding low-denomination assets in the form of bank notes convertible into silver" (p. 49).

Evidence on foreign trade—which incidentally rests on a firmer statistical basis than Yeh's and Rawski's estimates—sharply contradicts this highly imaginative and theoretically attractive interpretation. If the deflation had negligible real effects, it should not on that account have had any effect on exports or imports in real terms, though both would go down in nominal terms. On the contrary, with the rest of the world in general expanding from 1933 on, both exports and imports might have been expected to increase in real terms. Add now the effect of the "boon" to the holders of silver. The unanticipated increase in wealth would induce them to spend more on both foreign and domestic goods and services. Extra spending on foreign items would increase real imports, and extra spending on domestic items would reduce real exports, the difference being financed by the export of now redundant silver.

The actual pattern was the opposite. Both nominal imports and nominal exports fell, but imports fell much more. Expressed in real terms (adjusting by a wholesale price index), imports fell every year from 1931 to 1935, and particularly sharply from 1933 to 1935, the years of the heavy export of silver. Exports in real terms actually rose from 1932 to 1933, apparently benefiting from recovery elsewhere and low real prices in China. They fell slightly from 1933 to 1934 and rose slightly from 1934 to 1935 (based on data in Chang 1988, table 4, p. 103). This pattern is entirely consistent with the monetary deflation interpretation but the opposite of that required by the Brandt-Sargent interpretation. Real imports began to fall when Britain went off gold in 1931, falling most sharply when the United States went off gold in 1933 and began its silver purchase program. Real exports fluctuated up and down, reflecting the low real prices in China produced by a failure of internal prices to respond fully to the change in external prices expressed in terms of silver.

Examined more closely, neither new set of estimates constitutes a real challenge to the monetary interpretation. Both Schwartz and I and the contemporary observers may well have overestimated the real effects of the nominal deflation. "Money illusion" tends to produce such an overestimate, as was noted by Alfred Marshall many years ago. In *Monetary History* we report that such an overestimate occurred with respect to the 1873–79 U.S. depression. Nonetheless, I find it hard to dismiss entirely the judgments of contemporary observers on the basis of the necessarily imperfect and incomplete aggregate statistics that underlie Yeh's estimates.* In addition, it stretches credibility to

*Several examples of contemporary observations about the effect of declining prices on the economy were referred to earlier (Salter 1934, Young 1971, Rogers as cited by Young 1971). Another, somewhat later observation is contained in T'ang (1936). Referring to the period after the abandonment of the gold standard by Britain in 1931, he wrote: "Falling prices greatly aggravated conditions, as farmers and manufacturers found their income steadily decreasing, while such expenditures as interest on loans, taxes, etc., remained high, and rent, wages, etc., declined more slowly than prices. The conditions of workers in steady employment on fixed incomes improved through the fall in prices, but great numbers of wage-earners had been thrown out of employment by the crisis, more than cancelling the benefit to those who retained their positions. The economic situation steadily worsened" (p. 51).

With respect to conditions a few years later, T'ang wrote: "The effect of the slump upon industry in 1932/3 was registered by a great increase in unemployment. . . . In 1934 conditions became still worse. The fall in prices had first affected manufacturers and land-owning farmers, while farm labourers, and such other workers who remained in employment, were aided by lower living costs. But wages both for farm and factory labour sank as economic conditions worsened, and suffering extended further and further" (p. 60).

Still another example of a contemporary observation, though published much later, is Young (1971, pp. 208–11, 220–23).

suppose that prices in China were sufficiently flexible so that a major deflation would have a negligible effect on real magnitudes.

Rawski's conclusion that the money supply rose despite the export of silver is equally questionable. He constructs two alternative monetary totals, embodying different estimates of the amount of monetary silver. Both increase from 1931 to 1935—by 23 percent and 20 percent—thanks exclusively to a sharp increase in deposits in "domestic modern banks" and "foreign banks." It is highly questionable whether such deposits were relevant to domestic nonfinancial activity. Modern domestic and foreign banks were concentrated in Shanghai and served primarily the transactions activities and liquidity desires of the Shanghai financial community, domestic and international. Their lack of relevance to domestic nonfinancial activity is documented by Rawski's estimates of the ratio of currency outside of banks to the total money supply. Currency declines from 47 percent or 55 percent of the total in 1931 to only 33 percent or 41 percent of the total in 1935. Even the initial ratios are hardly credible for so underdeveloped a country as China, and the even lower final ratios are literally incredible.* By contrast, throughout the period form 1931 to 1935, currency outside banks was around 80 percent of totals that exclude the deposits of modern and foreign banks. That is much more credible for a country at China's stage of economic and financial development.†

*Such a low ratio was not reached in the United States until after the Civil War, by which time real income per capita in the United States was about ten times as large as estimated real income per capita in China in 1933. Such a low ratio was not reached in France until 1952 (Saint Marc 1983, pp. 38–39)!

†Some percentages for underdeveloped countries for 1988, based on IMF estimates, are 60 for India, 62 for Syria and Mexico, 65 for Chad, 68 for Zaire and Nepal, 74 for Yemen Arab Republic, 78 for Central African Republic.

The narrower totals, which include specie plus bank notes plus deposits in native banks, fell by 11 percent and 9 percent from 1931 to 1935, and by 13 percent and 11 percent from 1933 to 1935—so the severe decline came after the United States departed from gold and started on its silver purchase program.* I conclude that the money supply relevant to domestic nonfinancial economic activities did behave as Schwartz and I assumed.

P. H. Kevin Chang (1988), in a detailed analysis of the same period, also rejects Brandt and Sargent's explanation, on different though related grounds, namely, that "it fails to explain the sudden increase in silver exports occurring in 1934 and 1935, . . . the timing of the Chinese deflation does not correspond to the pattern of Chinese silver exports" (pp. 73–74). He rejects our interpretation both because he erroneously believes that it is contradicted by the new estimates that Brandt and Sargent rely on and because "we overlook the true cause of the silver outflow from China" (p. 69).

Chang argues that "America's determination to support silver prices and China's strong aversion to deflation and silver export [which Chang regards as greatly overdone], clearly pointed to an eventual suspension of the silver standard . . . [which] led those holding silver within China to seek to export it," reinforcing the government's concerns and leading to the eventual departure from silver (p. 43).

Chang's explanation of the time pattern of silver exports seems convincing. The speculative response to the

*The decline in the smaller total may be an overestimate because Rawski does not allow for a probable decline in the silver reserve held behind bank notes. But even making the maximum possible allowance for such a decline serves to produce only a negligible increase from 1931 to 1935 and leaves a decrease of 3 percent and 2 percent from 1932 to 1935.

widespread fears of the effect of the U.S. determination to raise the price of silver may well have been the trigger for the government's decision to embargo exports of silver and subsequently to establish a fiat standard. The effects that we emphasized in *Monetary History* would have led to the same result, but they might well have taken a longer time to produce that result.

The differences among the interpretations are important for a full understanding of events in China between 1931 and 1936. But it is worth emphasizing that all three interpretations agree that (1) the rise in the U.S. price of silver produced a sharp deflation in China; (2) large amounts of silver were exported, both legally and via smuggling after the government embargoed exports; (3) contemporary observers saw the deflation as accompanied by severely depressed economic conditions—whether because of money illusion or because their firsthand information was more reliable than the later highly aggregated, partial, and inexact statistical data; (4) the deflation, whether solely nominal or accompanied by declines in real magnitudes, produced widespread uncertainty and discontent; (5) these phenomena led, by one route or another, to the departure of China from a silver standard and its replacement by a fiat standard; (6) the monetary "reform" established institutional arrangements that contributed to the hyperinflation.

It follows that the different interpretations of the events from 1932 to 1936 are all consistent with the conclusion that the U.S. silver purchase program was responsible for the hyperinflation's occurring earlier and being more severe than it would have if the price of silver had not risen sharply. In that way the silver purchase program contributed to the ultimate triumph of communism in China.

CHAPTER 8

The Cause and Cure of Inflation

> There is no subtler, no surer means of overturning the existing basis of society than to debauch the currency. The process engages all the hidden forces of economic law on the side of destruction, and does it in a manner which not one man in a million is able to diagnose.
>
> —JOHN MAYNARD KEYNES (1920, p. 236)

The Chinese hyperinflation is a striking example of Keynes's dictum. If the Chiang Kai-shek regime had been able to avoid inflation or keep it to single- or even low double-digit rates, whether by better management of its finances and its monetary policy or because of a different silver policy of the United States in the 1930s, the odds are high that China today would be a wholly different society.

War and revolution have been the progenitors of most hyperinflations. The earliest episodes in the West are the U.S. Revolution, with its Continental currency, and the French Revolution, with its *assignats*—both paper currencies that ultimately became nearly worthless.

The many earlier inflations included no hyperinflations for one simple reason. So long as money consisted of specie (whether gold, silver, copper, iron, or tin) inflation was produced either by new discoveries or technological innovations that reduced the cost of extraction or by debasement of the currency—the substitution of "base" metals for "precious" metals. New discoveries or innovations necessarily led to modest rates of growth in the quantity of money—producing nothing like the double-digit rates of inflation *per month* that are characteristic of hyperinflations. In the case of debasement, no matter how "base" the metal, it still cost something to produce, and that cost set a limit to the quantity of money. As Forrest Capie points out in a fascinating paper (1986, p. 117), it took a century for the inflation in Rome, which contributed to the decline and fall of the empire, to raise the price level "from a base of 100 in 200 AD to 5000 . . . —in other words a rate of between 3 and 4 percent per annum compound." The limit was set by the relative price of silver, the initial money metal, and copper, the ultimate money metal. The implication is that the silver-copper price ratio was of the order of 50 to 1—roughly the same market ratio as in 1960. (Since then, silver has risen sharply in price relative to copper, so the ratio is now much higher.)

Inflation in the range to which we have become accustomed, let alone in the hyperinflationary range, became feasible only after paper money came into wide use. The nominal quantity of paper money can be multiplied indefinitely at a negligible cost; it is necessary only to print higher numbers on the same pieces of paper.

The first recorded "true currency," according to Lien-sheng Yang, author of *Money and Credit in China*—which is subtitled *A Short History* and covers more than two millennia—"appeared in Szechuan [China] . . . during the early part of the eleventh century" (1952, p. 52). It lasted for more than a century but eventually succumbed to the fatal temptation of inflationary overissue, "primarily," writes Yang, "to meet military expenditures." He records a number of additional paper money issues during the next five centuries in different parts of China and under various dynasties, each going through the same cycle of a period of initial stability, moderate and then substantial overissue, and eventual abandonment. There is no further record of extensive paper money issues in China until the nineteenth century.

Paper money came into wide use in the West only in the eighteenth century. It began, so I believe, with John Law's "Mississippi Bubble" of 1719–20, when, as the *Encyclopaedia Britannica* (1970) puts it, "the excessive issue of bank notes stimulated galloping inflation with commodity prices more than doubled" (see also Hamilton 1936)—a pale precursor of the million-, billion-, and trillionfold multiplication of prices in subsequent true hyperinflations.

Until recent decades, all the hyperinflations that I know of were the product of war or revolution. But that is no longer the case. Bolivia, Brazil, Argentina, Israel have all had hyperinflations in peacetime—hyperinflations that are still continuing, as I write, in Brazil and Argentina. And there may well be others that I am not aware of. The reason, as we shall see, is because war and revolution are no longer the only, or even the primary, reasons why governments resort to the printing press to finance their activities.

Whatever its proximate source, inflation is a disease, a dangerous and sometimes fatal disease, a disease that, if not checked in time, can destroy a society, as it did in China. The hyperinflations in Russia and Germany after World War I prepared the ground for communism in the one country and nazism in the other. When inflation in Brazil reached 100 percent a year in 1954, it brought military government. More extreme inflations also brought military government to Chile and Argentina by contributing to the overthrow of Salvador Allende in Chile in 1973 and of Isabel Perón in Argentina in 1976. Repeated inflations in Brazil and Argentina in the 1980s have led to repeated unsuccessful "reforms," the replacement of governments, flights of capital, and heightened economic instability.

No government willingly accepts the responsibility for producing inflation even in moderate degree, let alone at hyperinflationary rates. Government officials always find some excuse—greedy businessmen, grasping trade unions, spendthrift consumers, Arab sheikhs, bad weather, or anything else that seems remotely plausible. No doubt businessmen are greedy, trade unions are grasping, consumers are spendthrifts, Arab sheikhs have raised the price of oil, and the weather is often bad. Any of these can produce high prices for individual items; they cannot produce rising prices for goods in general. They can cause temporary ups and downs in the rate of inflation. But they cannot produce continuing inflation, for a very simple reason: not one of the alleged culprits possesses a printing press on which it can legally turn out those pieces of paper we carry in our pockets and call money; none can legally authorize a bookkeeper to make entries on ledgers that are the equivalent of those pieces of paper.

Inflation is not a capitalist phenomenon. Yugoslavia, a communist country, has experienced one of the most rapid rates of inflation of any country in Europe; Switzerland, a bastion of capitalism, one of the lowest. Neither is inflation a communist phenomenon. China had little inflation under Mao; the Soviet Union had little for decades, though it is now (1991) in the midst of rapid inflation; Italy, the United Kingdom, Japan, the United States—all largely capitalist—have experienced substantial inflation, most recently in the 1970s. In the modern world, inflation is a printing-press phenomenon.

The recognition that *substantial inflation is always and everywhere a monetary phenomenon* is only the beginning of an understanding of the cause and cure of inflation. The more basic questions are: Why do governments increase the quantity of money too rapidly? Why do they produce inflation when they understand its potential for harm?

The Proximate Cause of Inflation

Before turning to those questions, it is worth dwelling a while on the proposition that inflation is a monetary phenomenon. Despite the importance of that proposition, despite the extensive historical evidence to support it, it is still widely denied—in large part because of the smoke screen with which governments try to conceal their own responsibility for inflation.

If the quantity of goods and services available for purchase—output, for short—were to increase as rapidly as the quantity of money, prices would tend to be stable. Prices might even fall gradually as higher incomes led people to want to hold a larger fraction of their wealth in the form of money. Inflation occurs when the quantity of money rises appreciably more rapidly than output, and the more rapid the rise in the quantity of money per unit of output, the greater the rate of inflation. There is probably no other proposition in economics that is as well established as this one.

Output is limited by the physical and human resources

available and by the degree of knowledge and capacity for using those resources. At best, output can grow only somewhat slowly. Over the past century, output in the United States grew at the average rate of about 3 percent a year. Even at the height of Japan's most rapid growth after World War II, its output never grew at much above 10 percent a year. The quantity of commodity money is subject to similar physical limits, though it has at times grown more rapidly than output in general, as the examples of the flood of precious metals from the New World in the sixteenth and seventeenth centuries and of gold in the nineteenth century illustrate. The modern forms of money—paper and bookkeeping entries—are subject to no such physical limits.

During the German hyperinflation after World War I, hand-to-hand money increased at the *average* rate of more than 300 percent a *month* for more than a year, and so did prices. During the Hungarian hyperinflation after World War II, hand-to-hand money increased at the *average* rate of more than 12,000 percent a *month* for a year, and prices at the even higher rate of nearly 20,000 percent a month (see Cagan 1956, p. 26).

During the moderate inflation in the United States from 1969 to 1979, the quantity of money increased at the average rate of 9 percent a year and prices at the average rate of 7 percent a year. The difference of 2 percentage points reflects the 2.8 percent average rate of growth of output over the same decade.

As these examples show, what happens to the quantity of money tends to dwarf what happens to output; hence our reference to inflation as a *monetary* phenomenon, without adding any qualification about output. These examples also show that the rate of monetary growth does not have a precise one-to-one correspondence to the rate of inflation. However, I know no example in history of a substantial inflation lasting for more than a brief time that was not accompanied by a roughly corresponding rapid increase in the quantity of money; and no example of a rapid increase in the quantity of money that was not accompanied by a roughly corresponding substantial inflation.

A few charts (Figures 1–5) illustrate the universality of this relation. The solid line on each chart is the quantity of money per unit of output for the country in question, year by year for the various periods. The other line is a price index—either a deflator or a consumer price index.* To make the two series comparable, both have been expressed as percentages of their average values for the period as a whole. Moreover, the vertical scale is logarithmic; that is, equal distances record equal percentage changes. The reason is straightforward. What matters for prices is the percentage change, not the absolute change. A $1.00 increase in price is a far more drastic change for an item initially priced at $1.00 than it is for an item initially priced at $100; the price of the $100 item would have to double to $200 to

*For the United States and the United Kingdom, the price index is the deflator implicit in computing real national income; for Germany, Japan, and Brazil, it is consumer prices. For all the countries except Brazil, money is defined as the counterpart of the total designated M2 in the United States; for Brazil, money is defined as the counterpart of the total designated M1 in the United States, since that is the only total for which data were available through 1989. For the U.S. and the U.K., output is real national income; for the other countries, real gross national product. For the U.S. and the U.K., the data come from Friedman and Schwartz (1982, tables 4.8 and 4.9), extrapolated after 1975 by official data. For the other countries, the data come from various issues of *International Financial Statistics,* published annually by the International Monetary Fund, and, for Brazil, also from the 1989 annual report of the Central Bank of Brazil.

undergo a comparable change. The scales on the various charts are not identical, but they are comparable, in the sense that the same slope corresponds to the same rate of inflation.*

The two lines in each chart necessarily have the same average level, but there is nothing in the arithmetic that requires the two lines to be the same for any single year or to have the same pattern over time. For example, one line could rise from beginning to end, the other fall. Yet in every chart—for different periods, different countries, and vastly different monetary and economic policies—the two lines, while not identical, seldom deviate much from each other and clearly have the same pattern. That is hardly pure coincidence.

Figures 1 and 2, for the United States and Britain, cover a full century, in order to show how persistent the relation is despite vast changes in circumstances. (Chapter 3 covers the earlier part of this period in greater detail.) Until 1931, both countries were on a gold standard (except for Britain, from 1915 to 1925) and were linked by a fixed exchange rate, which explains why the patterns for the two countries are so similar before World War II. For both countries, also, the years of the two world wars stand out sharply, displaying rapid monetary growth. There is an interesting difference about the two world wars, though: in the first war, the price rise roughly parallels the rise in money; in the second, the price rise is slower and more spread out and does not match the money rise until the end of the 1950s. The difference is partly a statistical illusion; in World War II,

*This is achieved by making the ratio of the vertical to the horizontal scale the same in all the charts.

Figure 1

A Century of Money and Prices in the United States, 1891–1990

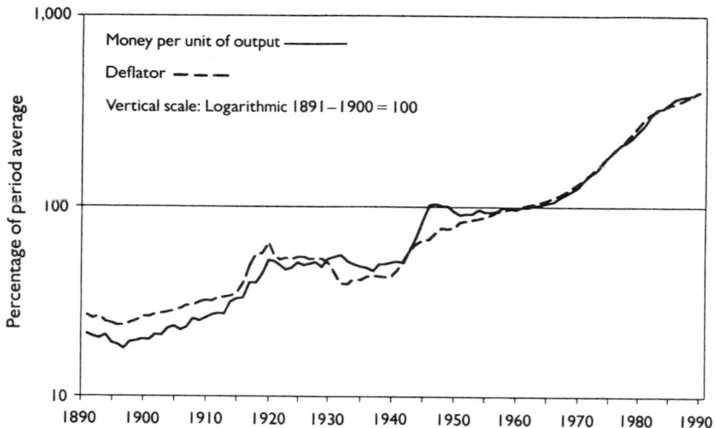

the price rise was suppressed and spread out by a far greater reliance on price controls and rationing.

Before World War I and in the period between the two wars, prices were relatively stable, except for the sharp drop in prices in the United States during the Great Depression. The period after World War II is very different, displaying peacetime rates of rising prices that rival or even exceed the rates experienced during the war. Moreover, the money and price-level lines hug each other much more closely after the war than before (perhaps simply because the data have become more accurate).

All told, in the United States, prices in 1990 were fifteen times their initial level in 1891; in Britain, fifty times. The divergence between the two countries came mostly during and after World War II, when the gold-standard link was no longer there to tie prices in the two countries together. The rate of inflation during the first half of the century

Figure 2

A Century of Money and Prices in the United Kingdom, 1891–1990

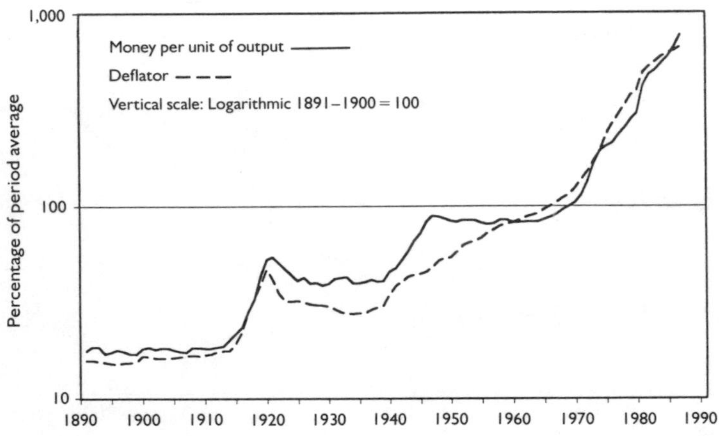

(1891–1940) averaged under 1 percent a year in the United States, 1.6 percent in Britain. During the second half it quadrupled in both countries, averaging 4 percent in the United States, 6.4 percent in Britain.

The charts for Germany and Japan (Figures 3 and 4) cover a shorter period, the three decades from 1961 to 1990. In both countries, money rose more rapidly than prices: in Germany, 4.8 percent a year for money versus 2.7 percent for prices; in Japan, 7 percent for money versus 5.7 percent for prices. The rapid growth in output and in financial activities in both countries led to a greater demand for real money balances per unit of output (a decline in velocity). The same phenomenon had occurred in the United States at an earlier date, as can be seen in Figure 1. Although both Japan and Germany are correctly regarded as countries with relatively low inflation, in both countries

Figure 3

Three Decades of Money and Prices in Germany, 1961–1990

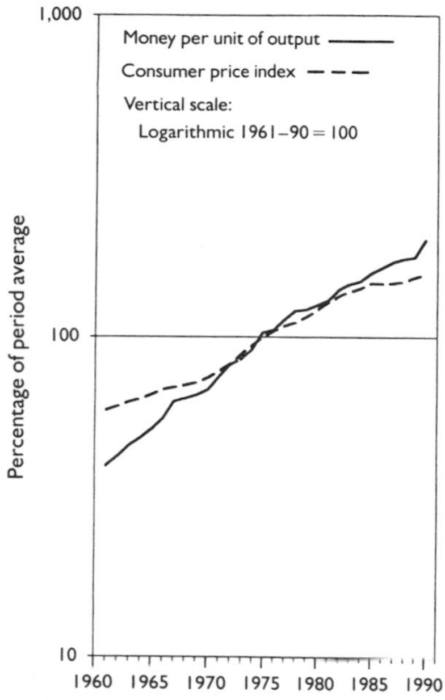

inflation was decidedly higher than it had been before World War II in gold-standard countries.

The chart for Brazil (Figure 5) covers an even shorter period, the quarter century from 1965 to 1989, because of data limitations. It tells a story of hyperinflation, with the price level at the end nearly 6 million times the level at the beginning—an average rate of inflation of 86.5 percent a year. Oh, the power of compound interest! As the chart shows, the inflation accelerated during the period; in the final years, the rate of inflation per month was running higher than the average annual rate for the period as a whole. And the end may not yet be in sight. We do not have money and output data for 1990, but we do have an

Figure 4

Three Decades of Money and Prices in Japan, 1961–1990

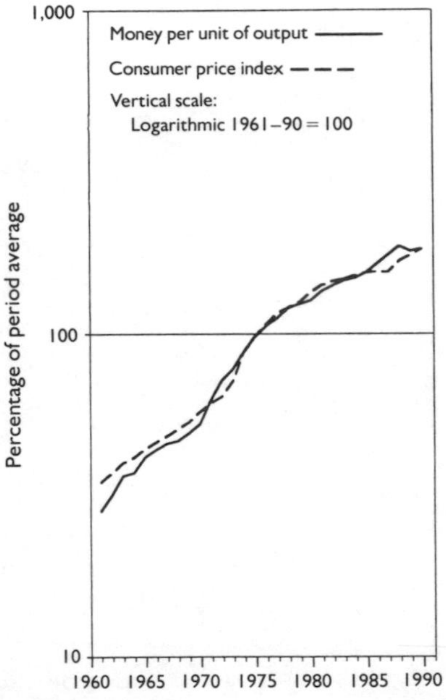

estimate that prices multiplied thirtyfold between 1989 and 1990. To date, repeated so-called monetary reforms directed at ending the hyperinflation have all ended in failure. However, sooner or later one will succeed. No country can continue to operate at Brazil's hyperinflationary rates without abandoning its national currency and adopting a substitute.

As the charts show, money and prices clearly move together. But that leaves open the question of which causes which. Do prices go up because the quantity of money increases, or vice versa? A large number of historical episodes make it crystal clear which is cause and which is effect.

Figure 5

A Quarter Century of Inflation in Brazil, 1965–1989

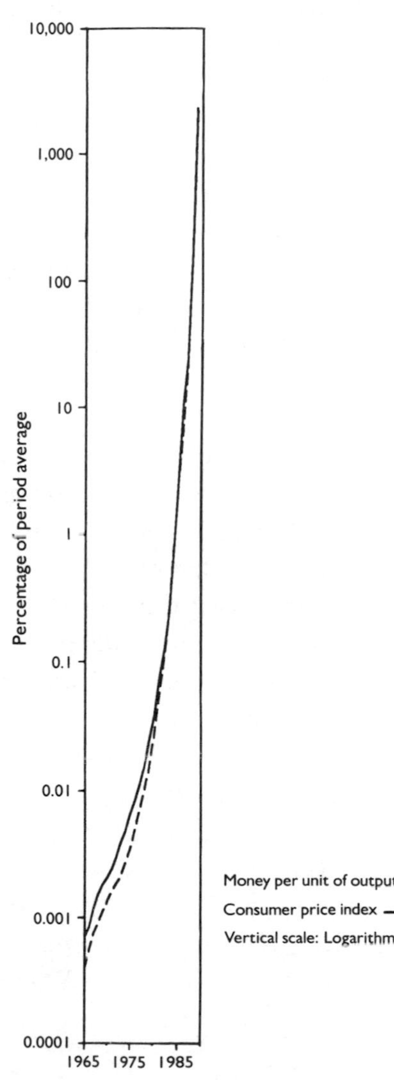

One dramatic example comes from the American Civil War. The South financed the war largely through the printing press, in the process producing an inflation that averaged 10 percent a month from October 1861 to March 1864. In an attempt to stem the inflation, the Confederacy enacted a monetary reform: "In May, 1864, the currency reform took hold, and the stock of money was reduced. Dramatically, the general price index dropped . . . in spite of invading Union armies, the impending military defeat, the reduction in foreign trade, the disorganized government, and the low morale of the Confederate army. Reducing the stock of money had a more significant effect on prices than these powerful forces" (Lerner 1956, p. 172). Such examples can be multiplied manyfold. In substantial inflations, money is the cause (or proximate cause), the rise in prices the effect.

The charts and this conclusion dispose of many widely held explanations of inflation. Labor unions are a favorite whipping boy. They are accused of using their monopoly power to force up wages, which drive up costs, which drive up prices. Then how is it that the charts for Japan, where unions are of minor importance, and for Brazil, where they exist only at the sufferance and under the close control of the government, show the same relation between prices and money as do the charts for the United Kingdom, where unions are stronger than in any of the other nations, and for Germany and the United States, where unions have considerable strength? Unions may provide useful services for their members, and they may also do a great deal of harm, by limiting employment opportunities for others. But they do not produce inflation. Wage increases in excess of increases in productivity are a result of inflation, rather than a cause.

Similarly, businessmen do not cause inflation. Businessmen are surely no more greedy in countries that have experienced much inflation than they are in countries that have experienced little, no more greedy at one period than another. How, then, can inflation be so much greater in some places and at some times than in other places and at other times?

Another favorite explanation of inflation, particularly among government officials seeking to shift blame, is that it is imported from abroad. That explanation was often correct when the currencies of the major countries were linked through a gold standard, as we saw in chapter 3. Inflation was then an international phenomenon because many countries used the same commodity as money and anything that made the quantity of that commodity money grow more rapidly affected them all. But the explanation clearly is not correct for recent years. If it were, how could the rates of inflation be so different in different countries? Japan and the United Kingdom experienced inflation at the rate of 30 percent or more a year in the early 1970s, when inflation in the United States was around 10 percent and in Germany under 5 percent. Inflation is a worldwide phenomenon in the sense that it occurs in many countries at the same time—just as high government spending and large government deficits are worldwide phenomena. But inflation is not an international phenomenon in the sense that each country separately lacks the ability to control its own inflation—just as high government spending and large government deficits are not produced by forces outside each country's control.

Low productivity is another favorite explanation for inflation. Yet consider Brazil. During the 1960s and 1970s it experienced one of the most rapid rates of growth in output in the world, and also one of the highest rates of inflation. Nothing is more important for the long-run economic welfare of a country than to improve productivity. If productivity grows at 3.5 percent a year, output doubles in twenty years; at 5 percent a year, in fourteen years—quite a difference. But productivity is a bit player in the inflation story; money is at center stage.

What about the Arab sheikhs and OPEC? They have imposed heavy costs on most of the world. The sharp rise in the price of oil in the 1970s lowered the quantity of goods and services that was available for people to use because everyone had to export more abroad to pay for oil. This reduction in output raised the price level. But that was a once-for-all effect. It did not produce any longer-lasting effect on the rate of inflation. In the five years after the 1973 oil shock, inflation in both Germany and Japan declined, in Germany from about 7 percent a year to less than 5 percent, in Japan from over 30 percent to less than 5 percent. In the United States, inflation peaked a year after the oil shock at about 12 percent, declined to 5 percent in 1976, and then rose to over 13 percent in 1979. How can these very different experiences be explained by an oil shock that was common to all countries? Germany and Japan are 100 percent dependent on imported oil, yet they did better at cutting inflation than did either the United States, which is only 50 percent dependent on imported oil, or the United Kingdom, which has become a major producer of oil.

We return to our basic proposition. Inflation is primarily a *monetary phenomenon* that is produced by a more rapid increase in the quantity of money than in output. The behavior of the quantity of money is the senior partner, the behavior of output the junior partner. Many phenomena can produce temporary fluctuations in the rate of inflation, but they can have lasting effects only insofar as they affect the rate of monetary growth.

Why the Excessive Monetary Growth?

The proposition that inflation is a monetary phenomenon is important, yet it is only the beginning of an answer to the cause of and cure for inflation. It is important because it guides the search for basic causes and limits possible cures. But it is only the beginning of an answer because the deeper question is why excessive monetary growth occurs.

Whatever may have been true for money linked to silver or gold, with today's paper money it is governments and governments alone that can produce excessive monetary growth, and hence inflation.

In the United States, the accelerated monetary growth from the mid-1960s to the end of the 1970s—the most recent period of accelerating inflation—occurred for three related reasons: first, the rapid growth in government spending; second, the government's full-employment policy; third, a mistaken policy pursued by the Federal Reserve System.

Higher government spending will not lead to more rapid monetary growth and inflation *if* the additional spending is financed either by taxes or by borrowing from the public. In both cases, the government has more to spend, the public less. However, taxes are politically unpopular. While many of us may welcome additional government spending, few of us welcome additional taxes. Government borrowing from the public is also politically unpopular, generating an outcry against the growing government debt and diverting private savings from investment to the financing of the government deficit.

The only other way to finance higher government spending is by increasing the quantity of money. The U.S. government can do that by having the U.S. Treasury, one branch of the government, sell bonds to the Federal

Reserve System, another branch of the government.* The Federal Reserve pays for the bonds either with freshly printed Federal Reserve notes or by entering on its books a deposit to the credit of the U.S. Treasury. The Treasury can then pay the government's bills either with the cash or with checks drawn on the Treasury's account at the Fed. When this additional high-powered money is deposited in commercial banks by its initial recipients, the money serves as reserves for the banks and as the basis for a much larger addition to the quantity of money.

Legally, the Treasury is limited in the volume of bonds it can sell directly to the Fed. But the limit is easily evaded: the Treasury sells bonds to the public; the Fed buys bonds

*There is much confusion about whether the Federal Reserve System is a branch of the government or a private enterprise. That confusion has sparked a host of "crank" conspiracy literature.

The Board of Governors of the Federal Reserve System is composed of seven members, all appointed by the president with the aid and advice of the Senate. It clearly is a branch of the government.

The confusion arises because the twelve Federal Reserve banks are federally chartered corporations, each with stockholders, directors, and a president. The stockholders of each bank are the member banks of its district, and they select six of its nine directors. The remaining three directors are appointed by the Board of Governors. Each member bank is required to purchase an amount of stock equal to 3 percent of its capital and surplus. So, nominally, the Federal Reserve banks are privately owned.

However, dividends paid on the stock are limited to 6 percent. Any additional income in excess of costs is turned over to the U.S. Treasury (nearly $20 billion in 1989). The Board of Directors of each district bank names the managing officials of the bank. However, the Board of Governors has a veto power and in practice has often played the major role in naming the presidents of the district banks.

Finally, the most important policy body in the system, other than the Board of Governors itself, is the Open Market Committee, which has as members the seven governors plus the twelve bank presidents. However, only five of the presidents have a vote at any time, so that the Board of Governors is guaranteed ultimate control.

In short, the system is in practice a branch of the government, despite the smoke screen of nominally private ownership of the district banks.

from the public. The effect is the same as that of a direct sale, except for the commission collected by the intermediaries—their payment for providing the smoke screen.

Financing government spending by increasing the quantity of money is often the most politically attractive method, to both the president and the members of Congress. They can increase government spending, and provide "goodies" for their supporters and constituents, without having to propose or vote for new taxes to pay for spending and without having to borrow from the public.

A second source of higher monetary growth in the United States was the attempt to produce full employment. The objective, as for so many government programs, is admirable, but the results have not been. Full employment is a much more complex and ambiguous concept than it appears to be on the surface.

Moreover, there is an asymmetry that imparts a bias to government policy in the direction of adopting unduly ambitious targets of full employment. Any measure that can be represented as adding to employment is politically attractive. Any measure that can be represented as adding to unemployment is politically unattractive.

The relation of employment to inflation is twofold. First, government spending can be represented as adding to employment, government taxes as adding to unemployment by reducing private spending. Hence, the full-employment policy reinforces the tendency for the government to increase spending without increasing taxes, or even while lowering taxes, and to finance any resulting deficit by increasing the quantity of money. Second, the Federal Reserve System can increase the quantity of money in ways other than the financing of government spending. One way it can do so is by buying outstanding government bonds and paying for them with newly created high-powered money. That enables the banks to make a larger volume of private loans, which can also be represented as adding to employment. The pressure to promote full employment has given the Fed's monetary policy the same inflationary bias as it has given the government's fiscal policy.

These policies have not succeeded in producing full employment, but they have produced inflation. As Prime Minister James Callaghan put it in a courageous talk to a British Labour party conference in September 1976: "We used to think that you could just spend your way out of a recession and increase employment by cutting taxes and boosting government spending. I tell you, in all candour, that that option no longer exists; and that insofar as it ever did exist, it only worked by injecting bigger doses of inflation into the economy followed by higher levels of unemployment as the next step. That is the history of the past twenty years."

The third source of higher monetary growth in the United States was a mistaken policy of the Federal Reserve System. The Fed has the power to control the quantity of money, and it gives lip service to that objective. But it acts a little like Demetrius, in Shakespeare's *A Midsummer Night's Dream,* when he shuns Helena, who is in love with him, to pursue Hermia, who loves another. The Fed has given its heart not to controlling the quantity of money, which it can do, but to controlling interest rates, something it does not have the power to do. The result has been failure on both fronts: wide swings in both money and interest rates. These swings, too, have had an inflationary bias. With memories of its disastrous mistake between 1929 and 1933, when it permitted the quantity of money to decline by a third and thereby turned a severe recession into a disastrous depression, the Fed has been much quicker to correct a swing toward a low rate of monetary growth than to correct a swing toward a high rate of monetary growth.

The financial public, too, believes that the Fed can control interest rates, and that belief has spread to the Treasury and Congress. As a result, every recession brings calls from the Treasury, the White House, Congress, and Wall Street for the Fed to "bring down interest rates." Counterbalancing pleas, at times of expansion, for the Fed to raise interest rates are notable by their absence.

The end result of higher government spending, the full-employment policy, and the Fed's obsession with interest rates has been a roller coaster along a rising path ever since the end of World War II—though perhaps it stalled somewhat in the 1980s (see chapter 10 for some reason for optimism). Inflation has risen and then fallen. Until 1980, each rise carried inflation to a level higher than the preceding peak had been. Each fall left inflation above its preceding trough. All the time, government spending was rising as a fraction of income; government tax receipts, too, were rising as a fraction of income, but not quite as fast as spending, and so the deficit, too, rose as a fraction of income.

These developments are not unique to the United States or to recent decades. Since time immemorial, sovereigns—whether kings, emperors, or parliaments—have been tempted to resort to increasing the quantity of money as a means of acquiring resources to wage wars, to construct monuments, or for other purposes. They have often succumbed to the temptation. Whenever they have, inflation has followed close behind.

Government Revenue from Inflation

Financing government spending by increasing the quantity of money looks like magic, like getting something for nothing. To take a simple example, the government builds a road, paying for it in newly printed Federal Reserve notes. It looks as if everybody is better off. The workers who built the road get their pay and can buy food, clothing, and housing, nobody has paid higher taxes, and yet there is now a road where there was none before. Who has really paid for it?

The answer is that all holders of money have paid for the road. The extra money that is printed raises prices when it is used to induce the workers to build the road instead of to engage in some other productive activity. Those higher prices are maintained as the extra money circulates in the spending stream from the workers to the sellers of what they buy, from those sellers to others, and so on. The higher prices mean that the money people have in their pockets or in safe-deposit boxes or on deposit at banks will now buy less than it would have before. In order to have on hand an amount of money with which they can buy as much as before, they will have to refrain from spending all their income and use part of it to add to their money balances. As we saw in chapter 2, the extra money printed is equivalent to a tax on money balances. The newly printed Federal Reserve notes are in effect receipts for taxes paid.

The physical counterpart to these taxes is the goods and services that could have been produced with the resources that built the road. The people who spent less than their income in order to maintain the purchasing power of their money balances have given up these goods and services in order that the government could get the resources to build the road.

Inflation may also yield revenue indirectly by automatically raising effective tax rates. Until 1985, as personal dollar incomes went up with inflation, the income was pushed into higher and higher brackets and was taxed at higher rates. Such "bracket creep" was greatly reduced by the Federal Tax Act of 1981, which provided that personal income tax brackets be indexed for inflation beginning in 1985, but some of the effect remains because indexation has not been extended to all elements of the personal income tax structure. In a similar way, corporate income is artificially inflated by inadequate allowances for depreciation and other costs. On the average, prior to the mid-1980s, if income rose by 10 percent simply to match a 10 percent inflation, federal tax revenue tended to go up by more than 15 percent—so that the taxpayer had to run faster and faster to stay in the same place. That process enabled the president, Congress, governors, and state legislatures to pose as tax cutters when all they had done was to keep taxes from going up as much as they otherwise would have. Each year there was talk of cutting taxes. Yet there has been no reduction in taxes. On the contrary, taxes, correctly measured, have gone up—at the federal level, from 22 percent of national income in 1964 to 26 percent in 1978 and 28 percent in 1989, despite the Reagan tax cuts in 1981 and the Tax Reform Act of 1986; at the state and local level, from 11 percent in 1964 to 12 percent in 1978 and 14 percent in 1989.*

A third way that inflation yields revenue to the government is by paying off—or repudiating, if you will—part of

*By correctly measured, I mean the inclusion of the so-called deficit as a hidden tax. The figures cited are for government expenditures as a fraction of national income, a better measure of the tax burden than the total called "taxes." A better measure, but still too low because it does not include spending mandated by government but omitted from the budget figures.

the government's debt. Government borrows in dollars and pays back in dollars. However, thanks to inflation, the dollars it pays back buy less than the dollars it borrowed do. That would not be a net gain to the government if in the interim it had paid a high enough interest rate on the debt to compensate the lender for inflation. For the most part, it has not done so. Savings bonds are the clearest example. Suppose you had bought a savings bond in December 1968, had held it until December 1978, and then had cashed it in. You would have paid $37.50 in 1968 for a ten-year bond with a face value of $50 and would have received $64.74 in 1978, when you cashed it in (because the government raised the interest rate in the interim to make some allowance for inflation). But by 1978 it took $70 to buy as much as $37.50 would have bought in 1968. Yet not only would you have gotten back only $64.74; you would also have had to pay income tax on the $27.24 difference between what you received and what you paid—in effect, you would have ended up paying for the dubious privilege of lending money to your government.

You would have done better in the 1980s, after inflation was reduced and the Treasury adjusted the interest rate so that it more fully reflected inflation. Suppose you bought a Series EE U.S. Savings Bond in May 1981, held it until May 1991, and then cashed it in. You would have paid $25 in 1981 for a ten-year bond with a face value of $50 and would have received $56.92 on cashing it in. By 1991 it took about $41.38 to buy as much as $25 would have bought in 1981. So you would have received $15.54 in purchasing power as interest, an apparent real rate of return of 3.24 percent a year. However, that would not have been a clear gain because of the income tax due on the $31.92 difference between what you received and what you paid. Depending on your income level, the tax would have eaten up between one-third and two-thirds of the meager real return. All in all, you would have earned between 1 percent and 2 percent a year in real terms for letting the government use your money for ten years. Hardly a princely return, but certainly better than ending up in the red.

Although the federal government has run large deficits year after year and its debt in terms of dollars has gone up, because of inflation the debt has gone up far less in terms of purchasing power, and for a time it actually fell as a percentage of the national income. In the decade from 1968 through 1980, when inflation was accelerating, the federal government had a cumulative deficit of more than $340 billion, yet the debt amounted to 32 percent of national income in 1968, 25 percent in 1980. In the years from 1981 through 1989, when inflation was coming down, the cumulative deficit totaled more than $1,400 billion and the debt climbed to 45 percent of the national income.*

The Cure for Inflation

The cure for inflation is simple to state but hard to implement. Just as an excessive increase in the quantity of money is the one and only important cause of inflation, so a reduction in the rate of monetary growth is the one and only cure for inflation. The problem is not one of knowing what to do. That is easy enough—government must increase the quantity of money less rapidly. The problem is to have the political will to take the necessary measures. Once the inflationary disease is in an advanced state, the cure takes a long time and has painful side effects.

*The figures usually cited for the debt are misleading because they include debt owed by federal agencies and the Federal Reserve System. For example, in June 1990, the gross debt was $3,233 trillion and the net debt $2,207 trillion, a third less.

Two medical analogies illustrate the nature of the problem. One analogy is about a young man who had Buerger's disease, a disease that interrupts the blood supply and can lead to gangrene. The young man was losing his fingers and toes. The cure was simple to state: stop smoking. But the young man did not have the will to do so; his addiction to tobacco was too great. His disease was in one sense curable, in another not.

A more instructive analogy is one between inflation and alcoholism. When the alcoholic starts drinking, the good effects come first; the bad effects come only the next morning, when he wakes up with a hangover—and often cannot resist easing the hangover by taking "the hair of the dog that bit him."

The parallel with inflation is exact. When a country starts on an inflationary episode, the initial effects seem good. The increased quantity of money enables whoever has access to it—nowadays, primarily governments—to spend more without anybody else having to spend less. Jobs become more plentiful, business is brisk, almost everybody is happy—at first. Those are the good effects. But then the increased spending starts to raise prices. Workers find that their wages, even if higher in dollars, will buy less; businesses find that their costs have risen, so that the higher sales are not as profitable as had been anticipated, unless prices can be raised even faster. The bad effects are emerging: higher prices, less buoyant demand, inflation combined with stagnation. As with the alcoholic, the temptation is to increase the quantity of money still faster, which produces the kind of roller coaster the United States has been on. In both cases, it takes a larger and larger amount, of alcohol or of money, to give the alcoholic or the economy the same "kick."

The parallel between alcoholism and inflation carries over to the cure. The cure for alcoholism is simple to state: stop drinking. But the cure is hard to take because this time the bad effects come first, the good effects later. The alcoholic who goes on the wagon suffers severe withdrawal pains before emerging in the happy state of no longer having that almost irresistible desire for another drink. So also with inflation. The initial side effects of a slower rate of monetary growth are painful: lower economic growth and temporarily higher unemployment without, for a time, much reduction in inflation. The benefits begin to appear only after one or two years or so, in the form of lower inflation, a healthier economy, the potential for rapid noninflationary growth.

The 1980s provide a clear example of this sequence. In 1980 the Federal Reserve stepped hard on the monetary brakes. The result was a severe recession and then a sharp decline in inflation. In late 1982 the Fed changed course and increased monetary growth. The economy picked up shortly afterward and embarked on its longest post–World War II expansion. The bad effects came first, the good ones later. And the country benefited greatly from taking the cure.

The painful side effects are one reason why the alcoholic and the inflationary nation both find it difficult to end their addictions. But another reason, at least in the earlier stages of the disease, may be even more important: the absence of a real desire to end the addiction. The drinker enjoys his liquor; he finds it hard to admit, even to himself, that he really is an alcoholic, and he is not sure he wants to take the cure. The inflationary nation is in the same position. It is tempting to believe that inflation is a temporary and mild matter, produced by unusual or extraneous circumstances, and that it will go away of its own accord—something that never happens.

Moreover, many of us are not unhappy about inflation. Naturally, we would like to see the prices of the things we *buy* go down, or at least stop going up. But we are glad to see the prices of the things we *sell* go up—whether it is goods we produce, our labor services, or houses or other items that we own. We saw in chapters 3 and 5 how the desire for inflation animated the populists and generated support for free silver. More recently, farmers have complained about inflation but have congregated in Washington to lobby for higher prices for their own products. Most of us do the same in one way or another. That is why our inflation binge lasted so long, from the early 1960s to the early 1980s, and why inflation remains a continued threat.

One reason inflation is so destructive is because some people benefit greatly and others suffer; society is divided into winners and losers. The winners regard the good things that happen to them as the natural result of their own foresight, prudence, and initiative. They regard the bad things—the rise in the prices of the things they buy—as the fault of forces outside their control. Almost all of us will say that we are against inflation; what we generally mean is that we are against the bad things about it that have happened to us.

For example, almost every person who owned a home during the 1960s and 1970s benefited from inflation. The value of the home rose sharply. If the owner had a mortgage, the interest rate was generally below the rate of inflation. As a result, the payments called interest, as well as those called principal, in effect paid off the mortgage. To take a simple case, suppose that both the interest rate and the inflation rate were 7 percent in one year. If a homeowner had a $10,000 mortgage on which he paid only the interest, a year later the mortgage would correspond to the same buying power as $9,300 would have a year earlier. In real terms, he would owe $700 less—just the amount he paid as interest. In real terms, he would have paid nothing for the use of the $10,000. (Indeed, because the interest was deductible in computing his income tax, he would actually have benefited—would have been paid for borrowing.) This effect became apparent to homeowners as their equity in their houses went up rapidly. The counterpart was the loss to the small savers who provided the funds that enabled savings and loan associations, mutual savings banks, and other institutions to finance mortgage loans. The small savers had no good alternative because the government limited narrowly the maximum interest rate that such institutions could pay to their depositors—supposedly to protect the depositors. The loss ultimately showed up on the national level in the collapse of the savings and loan industry and the accompanying burden on taxpayers.

Just as higher government spending can contribute to excessive monetary growth, so lower government spending can contribute to reduced monetary growth. Here, too, we tend to be schizophrenic. We would all like to see government spending go down, provided it is not spending that benefits us. We would all like to see deficits reduced, provided it is through taxes imposed on others.

As inflation accelerates, sooner or later it does so much damage to the fabric of society, creates so much injustice and suffering, that a genuine public will develops to do something about it—as we saw happen in the United States in 1980. The level of inflation at which that may occur depends critically on the country in question and its history. In Germany, the will to do something came at a low level of inflation because of Germany's terrible experiences after World Wars I and II; the will came at a much higher level of inflation in the United Kingdom, Japan, and the United States.

Side Effects of a Cure

Before the United States took the cure, and again more recently, we were told over and over again that the real alternatives we face are more inflation *or* higher unemployment, that we must reconcile ourselves to indefinitely slower growth and higher unemployment in order to cure inflation and keep it low. Yet over the 1960s and 1970s the growth of the U.S. economy slowed, the average level of unemployment rose, and at the same time the rate of inflation moved higher and higher. We had both more inflation and more unemployment. Other countries have had the same experience. How could that be?

The answer is that slow growth and high unemployment are not *cures* for inflation. They are *side effects* of a successful cure—as we found out in 1980–83. Many policies that impede economic growth and add to unemployment may at the same time increase the rate of inflation. That has been true of some of the policies the United States has adopted—sporadic price and wage controls, increased government intervention in business, accompanied by higher and higher government spending and a rapid increase in the quantity of money.

Another medical example will perhaps make clear the difference between a cure and a side effect. You have acute appendicitis. Your physician recommends an appendectomy but warns that after the operation you will be confined to bed for an interval. You refuse the operation but take to your bed for the indicated interval as a less painful cure. Silly, yes, but faithful in every detail to the confusion between unemployment as a side effect and as a cure.

The side effects of a cure for inflation are painful, so it is important to understand why they occur and to seek means to mitigate them. The basic reason why the side effects occur is because variable rates of monetary growth introduce "static" into the information transmitted by the price system. This static is translated into inappropriate responses by the economic actors, and it takes time to overcome those responses.

Consider, first, what happens when inflationary monetary growth starts. A seller of goods or labor or other services cannot distinguish the higher spending financed by the newly created money from any other spending. Retail merchants, for example, find that they are selling more goods at their former prices. The initial reaction is to order more goods from the wholesaler, who in turn orders more goods from the manufacturer, and so on down the line. *If* the demand for the goods had increased at the expense of some other segment of demand—say at the expense of government spending rather than as a result of inflationary monetary growth—the increased flow of orders for one set of goods would be accompanied by a decreased flow for another. Some prices would tend to rise, others to fall; but there would be no reason for prices *on the average* to change.

The situation is wholly different when the increased demand has its origin in newly created money. The demand for most goods and services can then go up simultaneously. There is more total spending (in dollars). However, the retail merchants do not know this. They proceed as just outlined, initially holding the selling price constant, content to sell more until, as they believe, they will be able to restock. But now the increased flow of orders down the retail channel is not offset by a decreasing flow down the government channel. As the increased flow of orders generates a greater demand for labor and materials to produce more, the initial reaction of the workers and the producers of materials will be similar to that of the retailers—to work longer and produce more, and also to charge more, in the belief that the demand for what they have been providing has gone up. But this time there is no offset, no declines in demand roughly matching the increases in demand, no declines in prices matching the increases. This situation will not at first be obvious. In a dynamic world, demands are always shifting, with some prices going up, some going down. The general signal of increasing demand will be confused with the specific signals reflecting changes in relative demands. That is why the initial side effect of faster monetary growth is an appearance of prosperity and greater employment. But sooner or later the signal will get through the static generated by the changed rate of monetary growth.

As it does, workers, manufacturers, retailers all discover that they have been fooled. They have reacted to higher demand for the small number of things they individually sell in the mistaken belief that the higher demand was special to them and hence would not much affect the prices of the many things they buy. When they discover their mistake, they raise wages and prices still higher—not only to respond to higher demand but also to allow for the rises in the prices of the things they buy. The economy is off on a price-wage spiral that is itself an effect of inflation, not a cause. If monetary growth does not speed up further, the initial stimulus to employment and output will be replaced by the opposite; both will tend to go down in response to the higher wages and prices. A hangover will succeed the initial euphoria.

It takes time for these reactions to occur. As stated at

the end of chapter 2, over the past century and more in the United States, the United Kingdom, and some other Western countries, roughly six to nine months have elapsed on the average before increased monetary growth has worked its way through the economy and produced increased economic growth and employment. Another twelve to eighteen months have elapsed before the increased monetary growth has affected the price level appreciably and inflation has occurred or speeded up. The time delays have been that long for these countries because, wartime aside, the countries were mostly spared widely varying rates of monetary growth and inflation. Wholesale prices in the United Kingdom averaged roughly the same on the eve of World War II as they did two hundred years earlier, and in the United States as they did one hundred years earlier. The post–World War II inflation was a new phenomenon for these countries. They had experienced many ups and downs but not a long movement in the same direction.

Many countries in South America have had a less happy heritage. They experience much shorter time delays—amounting at most to a few months. If the United States had not cured (at least for a time, and we hope for a long time) its recent propensity to indulge in widely varying rates of inflation, the time delays would have shortened here as well. So far they seem not to have done so.

The sequence of events that follows a slowing of monetary growth is the same as that just outlined, except in the opposite direction. The initial reduction in spending is interpreted as a reduction in demand for specific products, which after an interval leads to a reduction in output and employment. After another interval, inflation slows, in turn accompanied by an expansion in employment and output. The alcoholic is through the worst of the withdrawal pains and on the road to contented abstinence.

All these adjustments are set in motion by *changes* in the rates of monetary growth and inflation. If monetary growth was high but steady, so that, let us say, prices tended to rise year after year by 10 percent, the economy would adjust to it. Everybody would come to anticipate a 10 percent inflation. Wages would rise by 10 percent a year more than they otherwise would; interest rates would be 10 percentage points higher than otherwise, in order to compensate the lender for inflation; tax rates would be adjusted for inflation; and so on and on.

Such an inflation would do no great harm, but neither would it serve any function. It would simply introduce unnecessary complexities in economic arrangements. More important, such a situation, if it ever developed, would probably not be stable. If it were politically profitable and feasible to generate a 10 percent inflation, the temptation would be great, when and if inflation ever settled there, to make the inflation 11 or 12 or 15 percent. Zero inflation is a politically feasible objective; a 10 percent inflation is not. That is the verdict of experience.

Mitigating the Side Effects

I do not know of any example of any inflation that has been ended without an interim period of slow economic growth and higher than usual unemployment. That is the basis in experience for the judgment that there is no way to avoid these side effects of a cure for inflation.

However, it is possible to mitigate the side effects, to make them milder.

The most important mitigating device is to slow inflation *gradually but steadily* by a policy announced in advance and then adhered to, so that it becomes credible. That is feasible for moderate inflations. It is not feasible for major inflations, let alone hyperinflations. In such cases, only a shock treatment is feasible; the patient is too ill to support a long-drawn-out cure.

The reason for gradualness and advance announcement is to give people time to readjust their arrangements, and to induce them to do so. Many people enter into long-term contracts—for employment, to lend or borrow money, to engage in production or construction—on the basis of *anticipations* about the likely rate of inflation. These long-term contracts make it difficult to reduce inflation rapidly, because trying to do so will impose heavy costs on many people. Given time, the contracts will be completed or renewed or renegotiated, and they can then be adjusted to the new situation. However, the economic advantage of gradualness is partly or wholly offset by a political disadvantage. A crisis may generate the political will to support a shock treatment. But the political will may disintegrate during a long-drawn-out adjustment.

One other device that has proved effective in mitigating the adverse side effects of curing inflation is the inclusion in longer-term contracts of an automatic adjustment for inflation, or what is known as an escalator clause. The most common example is the cost-of-living adjustment clause that is included in many wage contracts. Such a contract specifies that the hourly wage shall increase by, say, 2 percent plus the rate of inflation or plus a fraction of the rate of inflation. In that way, if inflation is low, the wage increase in dollars is low; if inflation is high, the wage increase in dollars is high. But in either case the wage has the same purchasing power.

Another example concerns contracts for the rental of property. Instead of stating the rent as a fixed number of dollars, the contract may specify that the rent shall be adjusted from year to year by the rate of inflation. Rental contracts for retail stores often specify the rent as a percentage of the gross receipts of the store. Such contracts have no explicit escalator clause, but there is an implicit one, since the store's receipts will tend to rise with inflation.

Still another example is a contract for a loan. A loan is typically for a fixed dollar sum for a fixed period at a fixed annual rate of interest, say, $1,000 for one year at 10 percent. An alternative is to specify the rate of interest not at 10 percent but at, say, 4 percent plus the rate of inflation, so that if inflation turns out to be 5 percent, the interest rate will be 9 percent, and if inflation turns out to be 10 percent, the interest rate will be 14 percent. A roughly equivalent alternative is to specify the amount to be repaid not as a fixed number of dollars but as a number of dollars adjusted for inflation. In our simple example, the borrower would owe $1,000 increased by the rate of inflation plus interest at 4 percent. If inflation turned out to be 5 percent, the amount owed would be $1,050 plus interest at 4 percent; if inflation was 10 percent, $1,100 plus the interest.

Except for wage contracts, escalator clauses have not been common in the United States. However, they began to spread during the 1970s and early 1980s, especially in the form of variable-interest mortgages. And they have been common in almost all countries that have experienced both high and variable rates of inflation over any extended period.

Escalator clauses reduce the time delay between the slowing of monetary growth and the subsequent adjustment of wages and prices. In that way they shorten the transition period and reduce the interim side effects. However, escalator clauses are far from a panacea. It is impossible to escalate *all* contracts (consider, for example, paper money) and it is costly to escalate any. A major advantage of using money is precisely the ability to carry on transactions cheaply and efficiently. Escalator clauses reduce this advantage. It is far better to have no inflation and no escalator clauses.

There is one exception with regard to escalator clauses. They are a desirable permanent measure in the federal government sector. Social Security and other retirement benefits, the salaries of federal employees, including the salaries of members of Congress, and many other items of government spending are now automatically adjusted for inflation. However, there are two glaring and inexcusable gaps: some tax items, such as capital gains and interest payments, and government borrowing. Adjusting the personal and corporate tax structure for inflation—so that a 10 percent price rise would raise taxes in dollars by 10 percent and not, as it does now, by something between 10 and 15 percent on the average—would eliminate the imposition of higher taxes without their having been voted on. It would end such "taxation without representation." By so doing, it would reduce the government's revenue from inflation and hence its incentive to inflate.

The case for inflation-proofing government borrowing is equally strong. The U.S. government itself produced the inflation that made the purchase of long-term government bonds such a poor investment in recent decades. Fairness and honesty toward citizens on the part of their government require the introduction of escalator clauses into long-term government borrowing.

Price and wage controls are sometimes proposed as a cure for inflation. Recently, as it has become clear that such controls are not a cure, they have been urged as a device for mitigating the side effects of a cure. It is claimed that they would serve this function by persuading the public that the government was serious in attacking inflation; that in turn would lower the anticipations of future inflation that are built into long-term contracts.

Price and wage controls are counterproductive for this purpose. They distort the price structure, reducing the efficiency with which the system works. The resulting lower output adds to the adverse side effects of a cure for inflation, rather than reducing them. Price and wage controls waste labor, both because of the distortions in the price structure and because of the immense amount of labor that goes into constructing, enforcing, and evading the controls. These effects are the same whether controls are compulsory or are labeled voluntary.

In practice, price and wage controls have almost always been used as a substitute for monetary and fiscal restraint, rather than as a complement to them. This experience has led participants in the market to regard the imposition of price and wage controls as a signal that inflation is heading up, not down. It has therefore led to the raising of inflationary expectations rather than their lowering.

Price and wage controls often seem to be effective for a brief period right after they are imposed. Quoted prices, the prices that enter into index numbers, are kept down because there are so many indirect ways of raising prices and wages—lowering the quality of items produced, eliminating services, promoting workers, and so on. But then, as the easy ways of avoiding the controls are exhausted, distortions accumulate, the pressures suppressed by the controls reach the boiling point, the adverse effects get worse and worse, and the whole program breaks down. The end result is more inflation, not less. In light of the experience of forty centuries, only the short time perspective of politicians and voters can explain the repeated resort to price and wage controls (Schuettinger and Butler 1979).

Institutional Reform to Promote Price Stability

The repeated ups and downs in the price level have generated a vast literature offering and analyzing proposals for institutional reform designed to promote price stability. My own suggestions have centered on means of assuring that the quantity of money will grow at a relatively constant rate.*

Recently, Robert Hetzel has made an ingenious proposal that may be more feasible politically than my own earlier proposals for structural change, yet that promises to be highly effective in restraining the inflationary bias that infects government. He proposes that

> the Treasury be required through legislation to divide its issue of bonds at each maturity into a standard bond and an indexed bond. Interest and principal payments on the indexed bond would be linked to a price index. The Treasury would be required to issue the two forms of bonds in equal amounts.
>
> The market yield on the standard bond, which makes

*My earliest systematic statement is in *A Program for Monetary Stability* (1960). My most recent is in "Monetary Policy for the 1980s" (1984).

> payments in current dollars, is the sum of a real (inflation-adjusted) yield and the rate of inflation expected by investors. The market yield on the indexed bond, which pays interest in dollars of constant purchasing power, in contrast, would simply be a real yield. The difference in yields on the two kinds of bonds would measure the inflation investors expect over the life of the bonds. (1991, p. A14)

In explaining his proposal, Hetzel notes:

> The long lag between monetary policy actions and inflation means that it is difficult to associate particular policy actions with the rate of inflation. Changes in expected inflation registered in changes in the difference in yields between standard and indexed bonds would provide an immediate and continuous assessment by the market of the expected effects on inflation of current monetary policy actions (or inactions).
>
> A market measure of expected inflation would constitute a useful restraint on inflationary policy. Fed behavior judged inflationary by the market would produce an immediate rise in yield on standard bonds and an increase in the difference between the yields on the standard and indexed bonds. Holders of standard bonds, but not indexed bonds, would suffer a capital loss. Indeed, all creditors receiving payment in dollars in the future would feel threatened. The ease of associating increases in expected inflation with particular monetary policy actions will encourage creditors to exert a pressure that would counteract political pressures to trade off price stability for short-term output gains. (1991, p. A14)

Equally important, a market measure of expected inflation would make it possible to monitor the Federal Reserve's behavior currently and to hold it accountable. That is difficult at present because of the "long lag" Hetzel refers to between the Fed's actions and the market reaction. Also, the market measure would provide the Fed itself with information to guide its course that it now lacks.

An extension of Hetzel's proposal would be the enactment of legislation to require the Federal Reserve to keep the difference between the two interest rates less than a specified amount, say, 3 percentage points. That would provide a congressional guide for monetary policy far more specific than anything in the current law. There have been recent proposals for legislation requiring the Fed to aim at zero inflation. The objective is desirable, but such a requirement cannot be effectively monitored or enforced—again because of the "long lag," which would visit the sins (or the reverse) of the current monetary authorities on their successors. That problem does not arise with a requirement based on the difference between the two interest rates.

Any such requirement should be accompanied by definite sanctions—such as removal from office or a reduction in compensation—for failure to conform.

A Case Study

Japan's recent experience is almost a textbook illustration of how to cure inflation. Before 1973, Japan had been following a monetary policy of pegging the exchange rate of the yen in terms of the dollar. In 1971, following President Nixon's closing of the gold window and the floating of the dollar, there developed strong upward pressure on the yen. To counter the pressure, the Japanese central bank bought dollars with newly created money, which added to the money supply. In principle the Japanese could have sterilized the additions to the money supply by selling yen-denominated obligations, but they did not do so. As a result, the quantity of money began growing at higher and higher rates. By mid-1973 it was growing at more than 25 percent a year.* As Figure 6 shows, inflation did not respond until about two years later. But in early 1973 it started to rise rapidly, and by 1975 it was proceeding at a rate of more than 20 percent a year.

This dramatic rise in inflation produced a fundamental change in monetary policy. Emphasis shifted from the external value of the yen—the exchange rate—to its internal value—inflation. Monetary growth was reduced sharply,

Figure 6

Effect of Change in Japanese Monetary Policy on Inflation Two Years Later

(Quarterly data: 1960.1–1990.4)

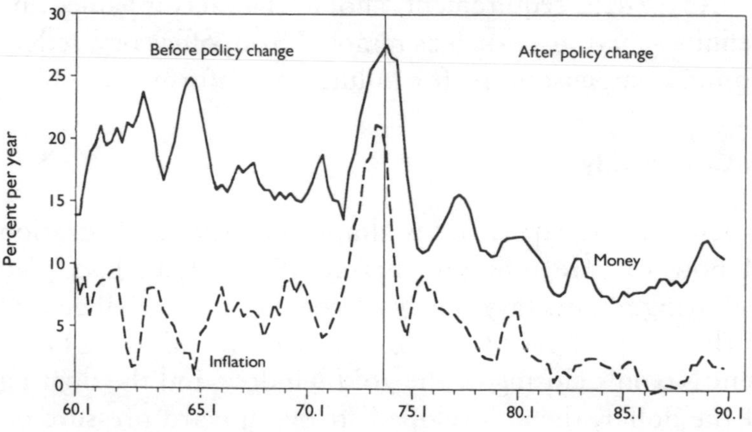

Note: Dates for money are two years earlier than dates for inflation.

*I am indebted to Yoshio Suzuki for detailed up-to-date data for Japan.

from more than 25 percent a year to between 10 percent and 15 percent. It was kept there, with minor exceptions, for five years. (Because of Japan's high rate of economic growth at the time, monetary growth in this range was consistent with roughly stable prices. The comparable rate for the United States is 3 percent to 5 percent.)

About eighteen months after monetary growth started to decline, inflation followed suit, but it took two and a half years before the inflation rate fell below double digits. Inflation held roughly constant for about two years, despite a mild upturn in monetary growth, and then started moving rapidly toward zero in response to a new decline in monetary growth.

The numbers on inflation in the chart are for the deflator, that is, a price index for output as a whole. The outlook for wholesale prices was even better. They actually declined after mid-1977. The postwar shift of workers in Japan from low-productivity sectors to high-productivity sectors, such as automobiles and electronics, has meant that the prices of services have risen sharply relative to the prices of commodities. As a result, consumer prices have risen relative to wholesale prices.

Two things are worth noting in Figure 6. First, monetary growth was not only higher but also much more variable before the policy change than after. Second, with a two-year lag, inflation tended to mimic even the minor wiggles in monetary growth after the policy change. Like money growth, inflation was both lower and less variable after the policy change. Although not shown in the chart, output was also less variable after the policy change than before.

Japan did not escape the side effects of its cure. It experienced lower growth in output and higher unemployment after the slowing of monetary growth, particularly during 1974, before inflation had started to respond appreciably to the slower monetary growth. The low point was reached at the end of 1974. Output then began to recover and grew thereafter, more modestly than in the boom years of the 1960s but at a highly respectable rate nonetheless—more than 5 percent a year. As the chart shows, after 1983 monetary growth started to creep up and so also, after 1985, did inflation.

Price and wage controls were not imposed at any time during the tapering down of inflation. And the tapering down occurred at the same time that Japan was adjusting to higher prices for crude oil.

Conclusions

Five simple truths embody most of what we know about inflation:

1. Inflation is a monetary phenomenon arising from a more rapid increase in the quantity of money than in output (though, of course, the reasons for the increase in money may be various).
2. In today's world, government determines—or can determine—the quantity of money.
3. There is only one cure for inflation, a slower rate of increase in the quantity of money.
4. It takes time (measured in years, not months) for inflation to develop; it takes time for inflation to be cured.
5. Unpleasant side effects of the cure are unavoidable.

The United States has embarked on raising its monetary growth five times between 1960 and 1990. Each time the higher monetary growth has been followed first by economic expansion and later by inflation. Each time the authorities have slowed monetary growth in order to stem inflation. Lower monetary growth has been followed by an inflationary recession. Later still, inflation has declined and the economy has improved. So far, the sequence is identical with Japan's experience from 1971 to 1975. Unfortunately, until the 1980s the United States did not display the patience Japan did in continuing the monetary restraint long enough. Instead, our government overreacted to the recession by accelerating monetary growth, setting off on another round of inflation, and condemning the country to higher inflation plus higher unemployment. Finally, in the 1980s, the United States began to display some persistence. When more rapid monetary growth in late 1982 was followed by economic expansion, the Fed exercised monetary restraint in 1987, well before inflation could reach its prior peak, though not before it had risen appreciably above the low point reached in the mid-1980s. Once again the Fed is seeking to exercise the restraint required to reduce inflation permanently to low levels—and again we have experienced, as I write (July 1991), an inflationary recession, which seems to have ended, or to be on the verge of ending, though inflation has not yet come down appreciably.

We have been misled by a false dichotomy: inflation or unemployment. That option is an illusion. The real option is whether we have higher unemployment as a result of higher inflation or as a temporary side effect of a cure for inflation.

CHAPTER 9

*Chile and Israel: Identical Policies, Opposite Outcomes**

Chile in 1979 and Israel in 1985 adopted identical monetary policy measures for the same purpose. The result was a disaster for Chile, an outstanding success for Israel. The two episodes provide a striking example of how the same monetary action can lead to very different results, depending on circumstances. The episodes also serve to clarify the fundamental difference between two superficially similar monetary standards: pegged exchange rates and a unified currency.

Chile

When General Augusto Pinochet overthrew the government of Salvador Allende, which had been in power in

*I am indebted to Dan Gressel and Arnold Harberger for information on the Chile episode and to Haim Barkai and Michael Bruno for information on the Israel episode.

Chile since November 1970, and replaced it with a military junta in September 1973, he inherited a battered economy and an inflation of more than 500 percent a year. During the initial stage of the Pinochet regime, military officers were given the responsibility for economic policy, and the inflation increased still further—the direct consequence of financing a large deficit by the creation of money.*

In 1974, Pinochet realized that radical measures were necessary to curb the inflation. Accordingly, he decided to adopt a drastic reform program—one that had been developed by a group of economists who came to be dubbed the "Chicago boys" because almost all of them had done graduate work at the University of Chicago. In 1975, he appointed some of these economists to his cabinet. They cut government spending and employment sharply, reprivatized enterprises that had been taken over by the Allende government, and removed controls on prices, wages, imports, and exports. These changes permitted a drastic reduction in money creation. Inflation promptly slowed. As measured by the deflator implicit in calculating real gross domestic product (GDP), inflation fell from 694 percent in

*Pinochet took office in September 1973, and the peak rate of inflation in consumer prices, as measured from the same month a year earlier, was reached in April 1974.

In the simplest terms, government spending in 1973 amounted to 44 percent of gross domestic product (GDP), and explicit tax receipts amounted to 20 percent of GDP, leaving a deficit of 24 percent of national income. By this time the ability of the government to borrow from the public or from abroad had essentially disappeared, and the only recourse for financing the deficit was the creation of money. In addition, the public had learned during the inflation how to economize on government-created money, so that the outstanding stock of money had declined to a small fraction of GDP, something like 3 percent or 4 percent of GDP. To finance a deficit of 24 percent of national income by a tax on the stock of money thus required a tax of 600 percent to 800 percent, and the deflator in 1974 was about 700 percent higher than in 1973.

1974 to half that (342 percent) in 1975 and to less than 46 percent in 1979. After a difficult transitional year, during which real income fell by 13 percent, the economy boomed. Real growth averaged 7.5 percent a year from 1975 to 1980. Foreign exchange rates fluctuated until June 1979, with the Chilean peso permitted to depreciate in response to the higher rate of inflation in Chile than in the United States and other industrialized countries.

In June 1979, the Ministry of Finance took the fateful decision to which I referred in the first paragraph: it decided to peg the Chilean peso to the U.S. dollar, that is, to specify a fixed rate at which the Chilean central bank would stand ready to exchange pesos for U.S. dollars and U.S. dollars for pesos. The government took this step in the hope of cementing the gains that had already been made in reducing inflation and of facilitating further reduction.

The basis for such a hope is a familiar one: committing Chile to a fixed exchange rate would provide external discipline that would inhibit the excessive creation of money. As long as Chile kept its commitment, it gave up any independent control over the quantity of money, which would have to be whatever was necessary to keep prices in Chile compatible with prices in the United States (to state the requirement in somewhat oversimplified terms). For two years the hope was fulfilled. In 1980 inflation fell to 29 percent, in 1981 to 12 percent, while output grew by 8 percent in 1980, 6 percent in 1981 (see Figure 1). Maintenance of the fixed exchange rate was facilitated by, and no doubt also contributed to, a very large inflow of capital from abroad, especially in 1981 (Harberger 1984, table 1).

Unfortunately for Chile, not long after it pegged the

Figure 1

Chile: Year-to-Year Percentage Change in Real Income and Deflator, 1977–1986

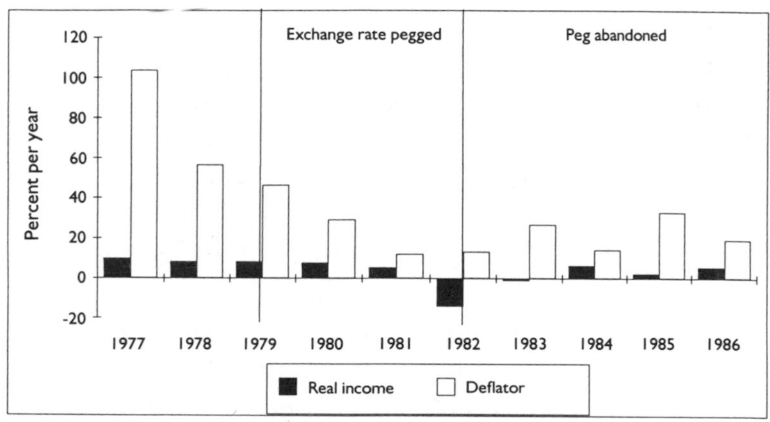

SOURCE: Banco Central de Chile, 1986.

exchange rate, the United States adopted a severely restrictive monetary policy in order to stem the inflation of the 1970s. The U.S. inflation peaked in 1980 and then decelerated sharply, accompanied by a severe recession that lasted until late 1982. The U.S. change in policy was accompanied by a major appreciation in the foreign exchange value of the U.S. dollar—by 18 percent from 1980 to 1981, another 13 percent from 1981 to 1982, and a further 23 percent from 1982 to 1985. If Chile had continued to let the exchange rate fluctuate, it could have offset the appreciation in the U.S. dollar by letting the Chilean peso depreciate vis-à-vis the U.S. dollar while remaining fairly stable vis-à-vis other major currencies. As it was, that option was ruled out. Chile was forced to let its currency match the appreciation of the U.S. dollar against other foreign currencies. To add to Chile's problems, the dollar price of oil more than doubled from 1979 to 1981, and the dollar price of copper, Chile's major export, fell, by more than 25 percent from 1980 to 1981 and by nearly 40 percent from 1980 to 1982.

The combined effect of the appreciation of the U.S. dollar, the doubling of the price of oil, and the near halving of the price of copper was disastrous for the Chilean economy. At prior peso prices and wages, Chilean goods became much more expensive to countries other than the United States in terms of their own currencies, and these countries' goods, other than oil, became cheaper in pesos. In addition, the recession in the United States reduced the demand for Chilean goods. To limit any drain on its foreign exchange reserves, the Central Bank of Chile adopted a restrictive monetary policy. In order for economic growth to have continued, nominal prices and wages would have had to decline drastically, and they were not sufficiently flexible to do so.* Indeed, they continued to rise, propelled partly by backward-looking indexation. As a result, Chile was thrown into a major recession, far more severe than the recession in the United States: real output fell by 14 percent in 1982 and another 1 percent in 1983 (see Figure 1).

*In addition, as Harberger emphasizes, the change in the terms of trade and a sharp reduction in the inflow of capital required a reduction in real wages for full adjustment, and that was prevented by a legal limitation. However, the reduction in the inflow of capital was, at least in part, itself a result of the pegging of the Chilean peso and the appreciation of the dollar. The pegging of the currency undoubtedly encouraged the heavy inflow of capital in 1980 and 1981. The appreciation of the dollar had the opposite effect, by making capital investment in Chile less attractive to non-dollar foreign investors. In addition, its effect on the Chilean balance of payments and the domestic economic situation raised fears of a devaluation against the dollar, which discouraged dollar investors.

The political and economic pressure forced the resignation in 1982 of Sergio de Castro, the minister of finance who had made the decision to peg the exchange rate. The peg was abandoned in August 1982 and the peso permitted to depreciate in terms of the U.S. dollar. The adverse effects continued into 1983, but by 1984 the economy was growing again, at an annual rate of 6 percent.

Even if Chile had not pegged the peso to the dollar, it nonetheless would have experienced a recession, in company with much of the rest of the world and because of the changes in the prices of oil and copper. However, the recession would have been far less severe. Chile paid a high price for its experiment of pegging the peso.

Israel

Chile pegged its currency to the U.S. dollar after the country had successfully reduced inflation from high triple digits to low double digits. It did so as what it hoped would be the final step in curbing the inflation.

Israel pegged its currency to the U.S. dollar as part of an initial reform designed to curb inflation. Israel's inflation was at an annual rate of about 500 percent in the second quarter of 1985, just prior to the implementation of this 1985 economic stabilization program. The main features of the program were: "a 20% devaluation of the shekel vis-à-vis the dollar and the pegging of a new rate at this level; a substantial reduction in the budget deficit involving mainly a cut in subsidies. A temporary wage and price freeze was to function as the income policies complement" (Barkai 1990a, pp. 147–48). The muscle to enforce the policy was a "very tight monetary policy . . . [which] did what it was expected to do: to act as a stopgap and allow the restrictive fiscal policy . . . to come into its own, and correspondingly, allow fiscal absorption to sustain the downward pressure on liquidity" (Barkai 1990a, p. 151). In these respects, the Israeli reform closely paralleled the initial steps taken by Chile to curb its hyperinflation in 1975.

The major difference was that the Israeli reform included the pegging of the currency and a temporary freeze on wages and prices, steps intended to add credibility to the government's intention to bring down inflation and thereby ease the transition to a lower rate of inflation. The reform was spectacularly successful. Inflation fell from an annual rate of 500 percent in the second quarter of 1985 to a rate of 18 percent in the first two quarters of 1986 and 20 percent for 1986 as a whole. Inflation has since remained around 15 percent to 20 percent (Barkai 1987; Bruno and Meridor 1990).* There was a significant, though only moderately severe, economic slowdown in reaction to the reform. The slowdown was brief and was followed by a rapid recovery in 1986–87. Then, however, there was a delayed reaction in the form of a more severe recession lasting two years (Bruno and Meridor 1990).

Pegging the shekel to the dollar contributed to the success of Israel's reform because two of the developments that had doomed the Chilean peg were, by happy chance for Israel, reversed. The dollar peaked in foreign exchange value in early 1985 and then depreciated from 1985 to 1990 by about as much as it had appreciated from 1980 to 1985.

*In another article, Barkai (1990b) compares the reforms undertaken at about the same time in Israel, Argentina, and Brazil. Israel's was a success; the other two were failures, slowing inflation only briefly. He attributes the difference to Israel's enforcement of a tight monetary policy and a reduction in the government deficit, contrasted with the failure to do so in the other two countries.

In addition, the price of oil, which peaked in terms of dollars in 1981 and fell gradually until 1985, plummeted in 1985. The depreciation of the dollar meant that the shekel, too, depreciated vis-à-vis other currencies, encouraging exports and discouraging imports and so contributing to a reduction in an adverse balance of payments. In addition, Israel, as an oil importer, was able to benefit fully from the fall in the dollar price of oil.

Israel retained the peg to the dollar for only thirteen months. In August 1986, the shekel was pegged instead to a basket of currencies of Israel's major trading partners, followed by devaluations at irregular intervals to offset the difference between the roughly 20 percent inflation in Israel and the lower inflation of its trading partners.* However, the thirteen months during which the shekel was pegged to the dollar was also the period of the most rapid depreciation of the dollar. By August 1986, the dollar had already depreciated by 32 percent from its peak value in early 1985.†

Never underestimate the role of luck in the fate of individuals or of nations.

Why Is Pegging an Unreliable Policy?‡

The examples of Chile and Israel help to illustrate the difference between two superficially similar but basically very different exchange rate arrangements.

One such arrangement is a unified currency: the dollar

*The shekel was devalued in January 1987, December 1988, January 1989, June 1989, and September 1990, by 12, 5, 8, 4, and 10 percent, respectively.
†Based on the Federal Reserve Board's "weighted-average exchange value of U.S. dollar against the currencies of 10 industrial countries."
‡This section draws heavily on Friedman (1989).

in the fifty states of the United States and Panama; the pound sterling in Scotland, England, and Wales and, at an earlier date, Ireland as well.

A slightly more complex example is the Hong Kong dollar. Before 1972 it was unified with the pound sterling by means of a currency board that stood ready to convert Hong Kong dollars into pounds at a fixed rate, keeping in reserve an amount of sterling equal to the sterling value of the outstanding Hong Kong dollar currency.* Since the currency reform of 1983, the Hong Kong dollar has been unified with the U.S. dollar through a similar currency board mechanism.

Likewise, under the pre–World War I gold standard, the pound, the dollar, the franc, the mark were simply different names for specified fixed amounts of gold, and so they constituted a unified currency area.

The key feature of a unified currency area is that it has at most one central bank with the power to create money—"at most" because no central bank is needed with a pure commodity currency. The U.S. Federal Reserve System has twelve regional banks, but there is only one central authority (the Open Market Investment Committee) that can create money. Scotland and Wales do not have central banks. When Hong Kong unified its currency with the dollar, it left open the possibility of giving the currency board central-bank powers, and, before the Tiananmen Square episode in China, the Hong Kong authorities were contemplating the introduction of changes that would in effect have converted the currency board into a central bank. One of the few good effects from what

*Such a currency board was the standard arrangement for British colonies during the heyday of the British Empire.

happened in China has been the derailment of that project.

With a unified currency, the maintenance of fixed rates of exchange between the different parts of the currency area is strictly automatic. No monetary or other authority need intervene. One dollar in New York is one dollar in San Francisco, one pound in Scotland is one pound in Wales, plus or minus perhaps the cost of shipping currency or arranging book transfers—just as under the late-nineteenth-century gold standard the rate of exchange between the dollar and the pound varied from $4.8865 only by the cost of shipping gold (yielding the so-called gold points). Similarly, 7.8 Hong Kong dollars is essentially just another name for 1 U.S. dollar, plus or minus a minor amount for transactions costs. It requires no financial operations by the Hong Kong currency board to keep it there, other than to live up to its obligation to give 7.8 Hong Kong dollars for 1 U.S. dollar, and conversely. And it can always do so because it holds a volume of U.S. dollar assets equal to the dollar value of the Hong Kong currency outstanding.

An alternative arrangement is the one adopted by Chile and Israel: exchange rates between national currencies pegged at agreed values, the values to be maintained by the separate national central banks by altering ("coordinating" is the favorite term) domestic monetary policy appropriately.

Many proponents of a common European currency regard a system of pegged exchange rates, such as the current European Monetary System (EMS), as a step toward a unified currency. I believe that such a view is a serious mistake. In my opinion, a system of pegged exchange rates among national currencies is worse than either of the extremes, a truly unified currency or national currencies linked by freely floating exchange rates. Under current conditions, national central banks will not be permitted to shape their policies with an eye solely to keeping the exchange rates of their currencies at the agreed level. Pressure to use monetary policy for domestic purposes will from time to time be irresistible. And when that occurs, the exchange system becomes unstable.

The contrast between the behavior of Chile and that of Hong Kong is a somewhat blurred example of this phenomenon. The central bank of Chile understandably was unwilling or unable to undertake the drastic deflationary measures that would have been necessary to maintain the pegged rate of the peso in 1982. Similarly, Israel has had repeated devaluations since it pegged the shekel to the dollar in 1985 and to a basket of currencies in 1986. Hong Kong, on the other hand, had no such recourse after it unified its currency with the U.S. dollar in 1983. It adjusted to the further appreciation of its currency vis-à-vis non-U.S. currencies by permitting prices and wages to adjust. The example is blurred because most of the appreciation of the U.S. dollar occurred before Hong Kong unified its currency with the U.S. dollar.

Pegged exchange rates can be maintained for a time by governmentally arranged capital flows, by foreign exchange controls, or by restrictions on international trade. But there is ample evidence by now that these are at best temporary expedients and generally lead to the conversion of minor problems into major crises.

That was certainly the experience under Bretton Woods before 1971. Exchange rate changes were numerous and often massive. The system worked only so long as the United States followed a moderately noninflationary policy and remained passive with respect to capital movements and exchange controls imposed by other countries.

It has been equally true of the succession of monetary arrangements in the Common Market: the European Payments Union, the "snake," the current EMS. None of these arrangements has been able to avoid exchange crises and exchange rate changes, and several have simply broken down. The EMS has been working reasonably well because Germany has been willing to play the role that the United States played under Bretton Woods, of pursuing a moderately noninflationary policy and tolerating capital movements and foreign exchange controls imposed by other member countries. I suspect that EMS, too, will break down if Germany ever becomes unwilling to follow those policies, as it well may as a result of the unification of East and West Germany.

Many observers give the EMS credit for enabling its members, notably France, to reduce inflation in recent years. No doubt the French anti-inflationary policy did gain greater credibility from France's membership in the EMS, that is, from its tie to the relatively stable German mark. However, the decline in inflation was a worldwide phenomenon that was by no means limited to members of the EMS.

In my view, the explanation for the worldwide decline in inflation is linked to the end of Bretton Woods. That led to the adoption of a world monetary system that has no historical precedent. For the first time in the history of the world, so far as I know, all major currencies are pure fiat currencies—not as a temporary response to a crisis, as often occurred in the past in individual countries, but as a permanent system expected to last. The countries of the world have been sailing uncharted seas. It is understandable that in the first decade of that voyage all sorts of things might happen, and, in particular, a worldwide outburst of inflation did occur. That worldwide outburst of inflation discredited the simpleminded idea that there was any long-term trade-off between inflation and unemployment, reduced the fiscal benefits from inflation, and increased the public's aversion to inflation. It became politically profitable for countries to follow policies consistent with a sharp reduction in inflation. That occurred in the EMS, but it also occurred in Japan, in Britain, in the United States, and throughout much of the world, apart from the basket-case countries. (For a fuller discussion, see chapter 10.)

In 1987, Britain followed the example of Chile and Israel for a few months when the then chancellor of the exchequer, Nigel Lawson, tried to peg the pound to the West German mark at three marks to the pound, at a time when the pound was tending to appreciate relative to the mark. The result was a sharp rise in monetary growth that brought the attempt to an untimely end and left a legacy of inflation and high interest rates.

Britain tried again in 1990, when it decided to join the EMS, in effect pegging its currency to the German mark, though with a broad range of ±6 percent around the designated central value. Britain's inflation rate was high when it joined the EMS—around 13 percent—compared with the rates of Germany, France, Japan, and the United States, though far lower than the rate prevailing in Israel when it adopted its monetary reform program. Britain was animated by the same motive in joining the EMS as Chile and Israel had been in pegging their currencies to the U.S. dollar—to give greater credibility to an announced anti-inflation policy. As in the latter two cases, the outcome in Britain is likely to depend on the future behavior of the currency to which it has pegged its own currency. If the mark were to behave as the U.S. dollar did after 1985, the British, like the Israelis, might regard the move as a great success. However, given the past behavior of the mark, such an outcome seems highly unlikely—though it cannot be ruled out, in view of the heavy fiscal burden Germany has assumed to promote the revival of the former East German territory. If, on the other hand, Germany continues to keep inflation low and the mark remains strong vis-à-vis other major currencies, the British are more likely to suffer the fate of Chile, in a milder form. Milder because there is little chance that the mark will appreciate against the dollar and the yen to anything like the extent that the dollar appreciated against the mark, the pound, and the yen from 1980 to 1985. However, if even a mild appreciation of the mark occurs, I conjecture that Britain will drop the peg or will adopt a new central rate.

There is much talk of establishing a single currency for the Common Market. Current proposals call for a staged movement toward an ultimate unified currency and a single central bank. The intermediate stages would retain separate central banks to administer pegged rates.

A truly unified currency makes a great deal of sense. But to achieve it where it doesn't exist—as in Europe today—requires the elimination of all central banks, if the unified currency is a pure commodity currency, or of all except one, if the unified currency is a fiat or partly fiat currency.

In Europe, the obvious choice for a single central bank would be the Bundesbank, which has been the dominant bank in the EMS. But that would require either the elimination of the Bank of England, the Bank of France, the Bank of Italy, and so on or their conversion into administrative branches of the Bundesbank. A possible alternative is the Bank for International Settlements, which would require the elimination of the Bundesbank as well. It is hard to regard any of these possibilities as serious options.

It seems to me an utter mirage to hope that a system of national central banks linked by pegged and managed exchange rates can prove a way station to a truly unified currency. It will be no easier to abolish the central banks after such a system is in operation than before it starts. And the prospect of a consortium of central banks operating as a unit, mimicking a single central bank, strikes me as equally farfetched.

Some four decades ago (in 1950), I spent some months as a consultant to the U.S. Marshall Plan agency, analyzing the plan for the Schuman Coal and Steel Community, the precursor to the Common Market. I concluded then that true economic unification in Europe, defined as a single relatively free market, was possible only in conjunction with a system of freely floating exchange rates. (I ruled out a unified currency on political grounds, if memory serves.)

Experience since then has only strengthened my confidence in that conclusion, while also making me far more skeptical that a system of freely floating exchange rates is politically feasible. Central banks will meddle—always, of course, with the best of intentions. Nonetheless, even dirty floating exchange rates seem to me preferable to pegged rates, though not necessarily to a unified currency.

CHAPTER 10

Monetary Policy in a Fiat World

We saw in chapter 2 that a world monetary system has emerged that has no historical precedent: a system in which every major currency in the world is, directly or indirectly, on an irredeemable paper money standard—directly, if the exchange rate of the currency is flexible though possibly manipulated; indirectly, if the currency is unified with another fiat-based currency (for example, since 1983, the Hong Kong dollar). The ultimate consequences of this development are shrouded in uncertainty.

The system has emerged by bits and pieces since World War I. From then until 1971, much of the world was effectively on a dollar standard, while the United States, though ostensibly on a gold standard (except for a brief interval in 1933–34), actually was on a fiat standard combined with a government program for pegging the price of gold. The Bretton Woods agreement in the main simply ratified that situation, despite the lip service it paid to the role of gold and its provisions for changes in exchange rates.

In the United States, the gradual change in the monetary role of gold was marked by two major milestones: (1) prohibition of the private ownership of gold in 1933 and (2) the elimination of gold reserve requirements for Federal Reserve deposits in 1965 and Federal Reserve notes in 1968. President Nixon's closing of the gold window in 1971, which removed both the formal link between gold and the dollar and the pretense that the United States was on a gold standard, simply set the seal on an ongoing process. Stocks of gold listed on the books of central banks are a relic of a bygone era, though a slim possibility remains that at some future date they will again become more than that. The 1974 removal of the prohibition against private ownership of gold in the United States was, somewhat paradoxically, a tribute to the end of gold's monetary role.

President Nixon's action was precipitated by an inflationary surge in the United States in the 1960s. In turn, the end of the arrangements entered into at Bretton Woods helped to produce a continuation and acceleration of inflation during the 1970s, in both the United States and much of the rest of the world.

Irregular and highly variable inflation has stimulated interest in monetary reform. Inflation brought into sharp focus the poor performance of the monetary authorities, reinforcing and giving greater credence to the conclusions about prior policy that various scholars had reached (including Anna Schwartz and me in our *Monetary History*).

In addition, inflation in the United States produced a rise in nominal interest rates that converted the government's control, via Regulation Q, of the interest rates that banks could pay from a minor to a serious impediment to the effective clearing of credit markets. One response was the invention of money-market mutual funds as a way to enable small savers to benefit from high market interest rates. The money-market funds proved an entering wedge to financial innovation that forced the prompt relaxation and subsequent abandonment of control over the interest rates that banks could pay, as well as the loosening of other regulations that restricted the activities of banks and other financial institutions. Such deregulation as has occurred came too late and has been too limited to prevent a sharp reduction in the role of banks, as traditionally defined, in the U.S. financial system as a whole. Such banks now account for a far smaller share of the credit market than they did earlier. Their place has been taken by such non-banks as Sears Roebuck, American Express, Merrill Lynch, and so on.

One particularly notable effect of the inflation and subsequent deregulation was the savings and loan crisis, which is imposing an extremely heavy cost on the federal insurance of deposits at savings and loans, and hence on taxpayers, and is threatening the solvency of the Federal Deposit Insurance Corporation.*

*For the first thirty years after the FDIC and the FSLIC were instituted, failures were few and far between, either of commercial banks or of savings and loan institutions. While depositors had nothing to lose from excessive risk taking by banks, equity owners did. Hence, so long as there was a substantial equity cushion, the owners (or, for mutual institutions, the managers) had ample incentives to avoid excessive risk.

The accelerating inflation of the 1970s produced a rise in interest rates that undermined the net worth of both banks and savings and loan institutions, all of which borrowed on demand and loaned on time. Savings and loan institutions were particularly vulnerable because their assets consisted primarily of mortgage loans at fixed rates for long periods. Once net worth is eliminated, banks have an incentive to engage in risky activities: it's a "heads, the bank wins, tails, the taxpayers lose" proposition. Hence, the late 1970s produced a substantial rise in commercial bank failures and a catastrophic jump in savings and loan failures.

Had monetary growth been restrained from 1970 on, the accelerating

Irregular inflation and high and variable interest rates have produced similar developments in other countries. As a result, there is pressure for deregulation throughout the world.

It is worth stressing how little precedent there is for the present situation. Throughout recorded history, as noted in chapters 2 and 8, commodity money has been the rule. So long as money was predominantly coin or bullion, very rapid inflation was not physically feasible. The extent of debasement was limited by the ratio of the value of a given physical quantity of the precious metal to the base metal used as alloy. It took the invention and widespread use of paper money to make technically feasible the kind of rapid inflations that have occurred in more recent times.

In evaluating past experience with such episodes, Irving Fisher wrote in 1911: "Irredeemable paper money has almost invariably proved a curse to the country employing it" (1929, p. 131). Experience since Fisher wrote certainly conforms to his generalization. That period has seen the most extensive series of paper money disasters in history: the hyperinflations that followed World War I and World War II; the rapid inflations and hyperinflations in many South American and other countries around the world, particularly in many of the less-developed countries; and most recently, of course, the worldwide inflationary experience of the 1970s.

The end of specie standards and the emergence of a world monetary system in which every country, in Fisher's

inflation would have been avoided, and the number of annual bank and savings and loan failures would still be in single digits, despite the defects in the insurance arrangements.

terms, has an "irredeemable paper money" have produced two very different streams of economic literature, one stream scientific and the other popular. The scientific literature deals with monetary reform and the government's role in providing what economists call outside money, in other words, money that is not a promise to pay but is simply money—full-bodied gold coins under a gold standard, paper money and deposits at the Federal Reserve under the current U.S. standard. The popular literature is alarmist and hard-money, essentially all of it based on the proposition that Fisher's generalization will continue to hold and that the world is inevitably condemned to runaway inflation unless and until the leading nations once again adopt commodity standards.

Interestingly enough, there has been little intersection between these two streams. In my opinion, the scientific literature has largely evaded the question raised by the popular literature: Have the conditions that produced the current unprecedented monetary system been accompanied by developments that change the likelihood that the system will go the way of all the earlier paper standards? The rest of this chapter offers some tentative and preliminary observations on this question.

Inflation, as pointed out in chapter 8, has always been an attractive alternative source of revenue, since it enables governments in effect to impose taxation without anyone's voting for it, and, in Keynes's words, "in a manner which not one man in a million is able to diagnose" (1920, p. 236). However, the existence of a commodity standard widely supported by the public served as a check on inflation. Certainly public opinion is the primary reason why hyperinflations, and even very rapid inflations, have been relatively rare in the more advanced countries. In periods of peace and in the absence of widespread civil disturbance, the public has been able to impose pressure on governments to keep money convertible or, if convertibility has been suspended, to return to a situation in which it is once again convertible.

The key challenge that now faces us in reforming our monetary and fiscal institutions is to find a substitute for convertibility into specie that will serve the same function: maintaining pressure on the government to refrain from its resort to inflation as a source of revenue. To put it another way, we must find a nominal anchor for the price level to replace the physical limit on a monetary commodity.

It is not possible to say whether Fisher's 1911 generalization that "irredeemable paper money has almost invariably proved a curse to the country employing it" will hold true in coming decades. The recent experiences of such countries as Argentina, Bolivia, Brazil, Chile, Mexico, and Israel support Fisher's generalization. However, they all are less highly developed countries, and they may have more in common with the kind of country Fisher had in mind than they do with the more advanced countries of today. The experience of those more advanced countries—Japan, the United States, and the members of the Common Market—gives grounds for greater optimism. The pressures on governments to obtain resources for government use without levying explicit taxes are as strong today in these countries as they were earlier. However, counterpressures have developed that reduce the political attractiveness of paper money inflation. The information revolution has greatly reduced the cost of acquiring information and has enabled expectations to respond more promptly and accurately to economic disturbances, including changes in government policy. As a result, both the public at large and the financial markets have become far more sensitive to inflation and more sophisticated about it than in earlier times.

As chapter 8 points out, inflation provides governments with resources in three ways: first, issues of government money constitute an implicit inflation tax on base money holdings; second, inflation may produce an unvoted increase in explicit taxes as a result of the failure to adjust for inflation at least some of the components of the income tax base, or income tax brackets; third, inflation reduces the real value of outstanding debt issued at interest rates that do not include sufficient allowance for future inflation. Recent economic, political, and financial developments have greatly eroded the potency of all three sources of revenue.

With respect to the first, the figures for the United States suggest the trend. Base, or high-powered, money remained remarkably constant at about 10 percent of national income from the middle of the nineteenth century to the Great Depression. It then rose sharply, to a peak of about 25 percent in 1946. Since then the ratio of base money to national income has been declining, and in 1990 was about 7 percent. For a modern society in which government taxes and spending have mounted to between 30 percent and 50 percent—occasionally even more—of the national income, this component is perhaps the least important of the three. Even if inflation did not reduce the ratio of the base to national income (which it unquestionably would do), a 10 percent annual increase in the base would currently yield as revenue to the U.S. government only about seven-tenths of 1 percent of national income. Further financial innovation is likely to reduce still further the ratio of base money to national income, even aside from the effect of inflation, making this source of revenue still less potent. I believe that the same tendencies have been present in many other countries, so that this source of revenue has become less important for them as well.

The second component of revenue—bracket creep—has very likely been far more important than the first. That certainly was true in the United States in recent decades. Inflation subjected low- and moderate-income persons to levels of personal income tax that could never have been voted for explicitly.

One result of bracket creep was political pressure that led to the indexation of the personal income tax schedule for inflation, which has largely though not wholly eliminated this source of revenue.* I do not know what the situation is in other countries, but I suspect that wherever there has been substantial inflation there has also been substantial indexation of the personal tax structure.

The third component has also been extremely important. At the end of World War II, the funded U.S. federal debt amounted to 106 percent of a year's national income. By 1967 the debt was down to about 32 percent of national income, despite repeated deficits in the official federal budget. Since then it has risen as deficits have continued and increased, but, even so, to only about 46 percent currently. Real growth partly accounts for the decline in the deficit ratio, but inflation has been the major explanation. Inflation converted the positive nominal interest rates at which the debt had been issued into negative real rates *ex post* (see Figure 1 in chapter 2).

*The most important residual effects of inflation on the personal income tax arise from the failure to adjust capital gains and interest rates for inflation. Nominal capital gains and nominal interest receipts are subject to tax, not the nominal values of real capital gains and real interest receipts. There are also residual effects on the corporate income tax.

Developments in the financial markets have sharply eroded this source of revenue. Market pressures have made it difficult for governments to issue long-term debt at low nominal rates. One result in the United States was a sharp reduction in the average term to maturity of the federal debt during the inflation of the 1970s—from nine years and one month for the marketable interest-bearing public debt in 1946 to as low as two years and seven months in 1976. After fluctuating only slightly above that level during the rest of the 1970s and the early 1980s, the average maturity has risen as inflation has come down, reaching six years and one month in 1990. Except under wartime conditions, it is far more difficult to convert positive nominal interest rates on short-term debt into *ex post* negative real rates by unanticipated inflation than it is to do so for long-term debt. Moreover, it is less profitable to do so for short-term debt than it is for long-term debt. Several decades of historically high and variable inflation have made it far more difficult to produce unanticipated inflation of any magnitude for any substantial period than it was even a decade or two ago, when the public's perceptions still reflected the effect of a relatively stable price level over long periods.

In the United Kingdom, the government now issues bonds adjusted for inflation. For such bonds, there is no way that the government can benefit from *ex post* negative real interest rates. There has long been support in the United States for the Treasury to issue similar securities, but so far it has been unwilling to do so. However, pressure to issue purchasing-power securities would undoubtedly intensify if inflation in the United States again became high and variable.

Perhaps several decades of a relatively stable long-run price level would again lull asset holders into regarding nominal interest rates as equivalent to real interest rates. But that is certainly not the case today.

To summarize, inflation has become less attractive as a political option. Given a voting public very sensitive to inflation, it may currently be politically profitable to establish monetary arrangements that will make the present irredeemable paper standard an exception to Fisher's generalization.

Recent experience provides some support for that view. The inflationary episode of the 1970s was severe by the standards that had become accepted in the United States, the United Kingdom, Japan, and other advanced countries during the nineteenth and most of the twentieth century (though it was mild by comparison with the experience of many other countries of the world). It was sufficiently severe to generate political pressures that led to policies of disinflation throughout the Western world, policies of restraining monetary growth and of accepting substantial temporary unemployment in order to avoid continued inflation.

Inflation has come down in the United States from double digits to low single digits, and there is widespread support for the Federal Reserve's repeatedly stated intention to reduce inflation still further from the 3 percent to 5 percent level that has prevailed from 1983 on.

As we saw in chapter 8, Japan offers perhaps the most impressive example. In the early 1970s, inflation in Japan reached levels well over 20 percent. The government and the Bank of Japan reacted promptly and effectively, bringing down sharply the rate of monetary growth. They have continued to maintain a relatively steady rate of monetary growth. As a result, not only has inflation been brought down to low levels, but also Japan has escaped the sharp ups and downs in inflation that have plagued many other countries.

Germany offers an example of a rather different kind, an example of how experience can alter the political attractiveness of the inflation option. Throughout the post–World War II period, Germany has tended to have lower inflation than the United Kingdom, the United States, and most other Western countries. The reason clearly seems to be the long-term effects of the post–World War I hyperinflation, reinforced by the post–World War II experience of suppressed inflation, which incapacitated the monetary system and forced a resort to barter.

Similarly, the United Kingdom succeeded for a time in sharply reducing inflation after having experienced double-digit inflation and despite an accompanying rise in unemployment. That has also been true for France and other countries in the Common Market that have linked their currencies through the European Monetary Union.

The apparent decline in the political profitability of inflation is a source of promise, but it is far from a guarantee that Fisher's generalization is obsolete. Governments often act under short-run pressures in ways that have strongly adverse long-run consequences. Israel in the early 1980s offers a conspicuous example. It continued to resort to inflation under conditions that made inflation a poor source of revenue; indeed, in the particular circumstances of Israel, the inflation may have been a drain on government resources rather than a source of revenue. However, in 1985, as we saw in the preceding chapter, Israel, too, took strong steps to end inflation.

Nonetheless, it remains an open question whether the temptation to use fiat money as a source of revenue will lead to a situation that will ultimately force a return to a commodity standard—perhaps a gold standard of one kind or another. The promising alternative is that over the coming decades the advanced countries will succeed in developing monetary and fiscal institutions and arrangements that will provide an effective check on the propensity to inflate and that will again give a large part of the world a relatively stable price level over a long period of time.

The final answer will come only as history unfolds over the next decades. What that answer will be depends critically on our success in learning from historical episodes such as those that have been examined in this book. Such a learning process has been under way for centuries, ever since the first appearance of systematic analyses of money and monetary institutions. It has entered a new and urgent stage as the world ventures into hitherto unexplored terrain.

CHAPTER 11

An Epilogue

We have covered a wide range of space and time in the course of our explorations—from classical Rome and Greece to modern Israel and Chile, with all sorts of stops in between. Although we have explored only a few episodes in detail, we have touched indirectly on many others.

I trust that my readers have been impressed, as I have been after nearly half a century of close study of monetary phenomena, with the universal role that money plays, the wide applicability of a few relatively simple propositions about money, and yet the difficulty that the public at large and even the monetary authorities have in understanding and applying those propositions. Georges Clemenceau, the prime minister of France at the end of World War I and one of the architects of the Treaty of Versailles, once remarked: "War is much too serious a matter to be entrusted to the military." I have often paraphrased him by saying that money is much too serious a matter to be left to the central bankers.

Money is so crucial an element in the economy, yet also largely an invisible one, that even what appear to be insignificant changes in the monetary structure can have far-reaching and unanticipated effects. Leaving out a single line from a law, as in the Coinage Act of 1873, can bedevil—indeed, come close to shaping—a nation's politics and economy for decades. Inventors in Scotland and miners in South Africa can write finis to the political career of a rising star in the United States. Appeasing a small group of influential legislators in the United States can have an effect on whether China ends up as a communist state. The same monetary decision made by two different countries can have opposite results because the decisions are made six years apart—a disaster in one case, a triumph in the other. A change in the monetary regime can set the world sailing on uncharted monetary seas for more than a decade of instability and turbulence before matters start to settle down, but still without any agreed on and trustworthy map to the future course of the monetary voyage. And the litany could be extended far beyond the episodes touched on in this book.

Perhaps the single most important and most thoroughly documented yet obstinately rejected proposition is that "inflation is always and everywhere a monetary phenomenon."* That proposition has been known by some scholars and men of affairs for hundreds, if not thousands, of years. Yet it has not prevented governmental authorities from yielding to the temptation to mulct their subjects by debasing their money—taxation without representation—while vigorously denying that they are doing anything of the kind and attributing the resulting inflation to all sorts of other devils incarnate.

*I believe I first published the statement in these words in Friedman (1963), which was reprinted in Friedman (1968, p. 39).

Nor is this ancient history. One need go back no further than the 1970s in the United States and other advanced countries. Yielding to that temptation is the source of the current desperate straits of Argentina, Brazil, Nicaragua, and a number of other Latin American states. The most recent full-fledged hyperinflation was in Bolivia, which fortunately has now reformed its monetary system, though not without paying a high price in lost production, misery, and lowered living standards. And I suspect that the world will see more episodes of both high inflation and full-fledged hyperinflation within the next few decades.

Rapid increases in the quantity of money produce inflation. Sharp decreases produce depression. That is an equally well documented proposition. It is not directly documented in this book, though some episodes of it are referred to: the 1873–79 depression in the United States, the depressed years of the early 1890s, the great contraction of 1929–33 that brought Franklin Delano Roosevelt to the White House and set the stage for the silver purchase program of the 1930s.

Why are these and similarly well documented propositions about money so often neglected in shaping policy? One reason is the contrast between the way things appear to the individual and the way they are to the community. If you go to the market to buy some strawberries, you will be able to buy as many as you wish at the posted price, subject only to the dealer's stock. To you, the price is fixed, the quantity variable. But suppose everyone suddenly got a yen for strawberries. For the community at large, the total amount of strawberries available at a given time is a fixed amount. A sudden increase in the quantity demanded at the initial price could be met only by a rise in price sufficient to reduce the quantity demanded to the amount available. For the community at large, the quantity is fixed, the price variable—just the opposite of what is true for the individual.

Such a contrast is true of most things. In the area of money that we have been dealing with, you as an individual can hold any amount of cash you wish, subject only to the level of your wealth. But at any time there is a fixed total amount of cash, determined primarily by the Federal Reserve if cash is defined as the base, or by the Fed and the banks if cash is defined more broadly. You can hold more only if someone else is holding less, yet there is nothing in your personal situation to make you aware of that.

To you as an individual, an increase in income is a good thing, whether its ultimate source is your own enhanced productivity or the government's printing of money. Yet to the community at large the two sources are very different: the first is a boon, while the second may be a curse, as it was in the helicopter fable of chapter 2.

It is natural for individuals to generalize from their personal experiencc, to believe that what is true for them is true for the community. I believe that that confusion is at the bottom of most widely held economic fallacies—whether about money, as in the example just discussed, or about other economic or social phenomena.

It is human, also, to personalize both the good and the bad, to attribute anything bad that happens to the evil intent of someone else. However, good intentions are at least as likely to be frustrated by misunderstanding as by an unseen devil. The antidote is to be found in explanation, not recrimination.

The importance of a correct understanding of economic relations in general and of monetary matters in particular is vividly brought out by a statement made two centuries ago by Pierre S. du Pont, a deputy from Nemours to the French National Assembly. Speaking on a proposal to issue additional *assignats*—the fiat money of the French Revolution—he said: "Gentlemen, it is a disagreeable custom to which one is too easily led by the harshness of the discussions, to assume evil intentions. It is necessary to be gracious as to intentions; one should believe them good, and apparently they are; but we do not have to be gracious at all to inconsistent logic or to absurd reasoning. Bad logicians have committed more involuntary crimes than bad men have done intentionally [September 25, 1790]" (quoted from Friedman 1977, p. 471).

References

Bagehot, Walter. *Lombard Street*. London: H. S. King, 1873.

———. *Some Articles on the Depreciation of Silver and on Topics Connected With It*. London: H. S. King & Co., 1877. Reprinted in *The Works of Walter Bagehot,* vol. 5, edited by Forrest Morgan. Hartford, Conn.: The Travelers Insurance Co., 1891.

Banco Central de Chile, Dirección de Estudios. *Indicadores económicos y sociales 1960–1985*. Santiago, Chile: Central Bank of Chile, 1986.

Barkai, Haim. "Israel's Attempt at Economic Stabilization." *Jerusalem Quarterly,* Summer 1987, pp. 3–20.

———. "The Role of Monetary Policy in Israel's Stabilization Effort." In *Transcript of the Symposium on American-Israel Economic Relations* (held June 5–7, 1988). New York: American Israel Economic Corporation, 1990. (a)

———. "The Role of Monetary Policy in Israel's 1985 Stabilization Effort." Working Paper WP/90/29. Washington: International Monetary Fund, April 1990. (b)

Barnes, James A. "Myths of the Bryan Campaign." *Mississippi Valley Historical Review* 34 (December 1947): 367–400.

Barnett, Paul S. "The Crime of 1873 Re-examined." *Agricultural History* 38 (July 1964): 178–81.

Brandt, Loren, and Sargent, Thomas J. "Interpreting New

Evidence about China and U.S. Silver Purchases." *Journal of Monetary Economics* 23 (1989): 31–51.

Bruno, Michael, and Meridor, Leora (Rubin). "The Costly Transition from Stabilization to Sustainable Growth: Israel's Case." Discussion Paper 90.01. Jerusalem: Bank of Israel, January 1990.

Bryan, William Jennings. *The First Battle*. Chicago: W. B. Conkey Co., 1896.

Cagan, Phillip. "The Monetary Dynamics of Hyperinflation." In *Studies in the Quantity Theory of Money*, edited by Milton Friedman. Chicago: University of Chicago Press, 1956.

Capie, Forrest. "Conditions in Which Very Rapid Inflation Has Appeared." In *The National Bureau Method, International Capital Mobility and Other Essays*, edited by Karl Brunner and Allan H. Meltzer. Carnegie-Rochester Conference Series on Public Policy, vol. 24. Amsterdam: North-Holland, 1986.

Carothers, Neil. *Fractional Money*. New York: Wiley & Sons; London: Chapman & Hall, Ltd., 1930.

Chang, Kia-ngau. *The Inflationary Spiral*. Cambridge: Technology Press of Massachusetts Institute of Technology; New York: Wiley; and London: Chapman & Hall, Ltd., 1958.

Chang, P. H. Kevin. "Commodity Price Shocks and International Finance." Ph.D. dissertation. Massachusetts Institute of Technology, 1988.

Chou, Shun-hsin. *The Chinese Inflation, 1937–1949*. Foreword by C. Martin Wilbur. New York and London: Columbia University Press, 1963.

Commager, Henry. "William Jennings Bryan, 1860–1925." In *There Were Giants in the Land*. Introduction by Henry Morgenthau, Jr. New York and Toronto: Farrar & Rinehart, 1942.

Culbertson, John M. *Macroeconomic Theory and Stabilization Policy*. New York: McGraw-Hill, 1968.

Deane, Phyllis. "New Estimates of Gross National Product for the United Kingdom, 1830–1914." *The Review of Income and Wealth* 14 (June 1968): 95–112.

Dowd, Kevin. "The Mechanics of the Bimetallic Standard." Unpublished Discussion Paper. Nottingham, England: University of Nottingham, April 1991.

Drake, Louis S. "Reconstruction of a Bimetallic Price Level." *Explorations in Economic History* 22 (April 1985): 194–219.

Edgeworth, Francis Y. "Thoughts on Monetary Reform." *Economic Journal* 5 (September 1895): 434–51.

Encyclopaedia Britannica, 11th ed. (1910). S.v. "Gold."

Encyclopaedia Britannica, 1970 ed. S.v. "Panic."

Feavearyear, Albert. *The Pound Sterling.* 2d ed., revised by E. Victor Morgan. Oxford: The Clarendon Press, 1963.

Fetter, Frank W. *Development of British Monetary Orthodoxy, 1797–1875.* Cambridge: Harvard University Press, 1965.

———. "Monetary Policy." In *Monetary and Financial Policy,* by Frank W. Fetter and Derek Gregory. [Dublin]: Irish University Press, 1973.

Fisher, Irving. "The Mechanics of Bimetallism." *Economic Journal* 4 (September 1894): 527–37.

———. *Appreciation and Interest.* American Economic Association Monograph, 1st ser., vol. 11, no. 4. Cambridge, Mass.: American Economic Association, 1896.

———. *The Purchasing Power of Money.* New York: Macmillan, 1911. 2d ed. New York: Macmillan, 1913. New ed. New York: Macmillan, 1929.

Friedman, Milton. *A Program for Monetary Stability.* New York: Fordham University Press, 1960.

———. *Inflation: Causes and Consequences.* Bombay: Asia Publishing House, 1963. Reprinted in Milton Friedman, *Dollars and Deficits.* Englewood Cliffs, N.J.: Prentice-Hall, 1968.

———. *The Quantity Theory of Money and Other Essays.* Chicago: Aldine, 1969.

———. "Money." *Encyclopaedia Britannica,* 15th ed. (1974).

———. "Nobel Lecture: Inflation and Unemployment." *Journal of Political Economy* 85 (June 1977): 451–72.

———. "Monetary Policy for the 1980s." In *To Promote Prosperity: U.S. Domestic Policy in the Mid-1980s,* edited by John H. Moore. Stanford, Calif.: Hoover Institution Press, 1984.

———. "The Resource Cost of Irredeemable Paper Money." *Journal of Political Economy* 94, part 1 (June 1986): 642–47.

———. "Quantity Theory of Money." In *The New Palgrave: A Dictionary of Economics,* vol. 4, edited by John Eatwell, Murray Milgate, and Peter Newman. New York: Stockton Press, and London: Macmillan, 1987.

———. "The Case for Floating Rates." *Financial Times* (London), December 18, 1989.

Friedman, Milton, and Schwartz, Anna J. *A Monetary History of the United States, 1867–1960.* Princeton: Princeton University Press, 1963.

——— and ———. *Monetary Statistics of the United States.* New York: Columbia University Press, 1970.

——— and ———. *Monetary Trends in the United States and the United Kingdom.* Chicago: University of Chicago Press, 1982.

Froman, Lewis A. "Bimetallism Reconsidered in the Light of Recent Developments." *American Economic Review* 26 (March 1936): 53–61.

Furness, William Henry. *The Island of Stone Money: Uap and The Carolines.* Philadelphia and London: J. B. Lippincott Co., 1910.

Giffen, Sir Robert. *The Case Against Bimetallism.* London: G. Bell & Son, 1892. 4th ed. London: George Bell & Sons, 1896.

Greenwood, John G., and Wood, Christopher J. R. "The Chinese Hyperinflation: Part 1. Monetary and Fiscal Origins of the Inflation, 1932–45." *Asian Monetary Monitor* 1, no. 1 (September–October 1977): 25–39. (a)

——— and ———. "The Chinese Hyperinflation: Part 2. The Crisis of Hyperinflation, 1945–49." *Asian Monetary Monitor* 1, no. 2 (November–December 1977): 32–45. (b)

——— and ———. "The Chinese Hyperinflation: Part 3. Price Stabilization after the 1949 Revolution." *Asian Monetary Monitor* 2, no. 1 (January–February 1978): 27–34.

Hamilton, Alexander. Treasury Report on the Establishment of a Mint, January 28, 1791. Reprinted in *Documentary History of Banking and Currency in the United States,* vol. 1, edited by

Herman E. Krooss. New York: Chelsea House Publishers, 1969.

Hamilton, Earl J. "Prices and Wages at Paris under John Law's System." *Quarterly Journal of Economics* 51 (November 1936): 42–70.

Harberger, Arnold C. "Chile's Devaluation Crisis of 1982," unpublished English version of "La crisis cambiaria chilena de 1982" in *Cuadernos de Economía* 21, no. 63 (August 1984): 123–36.

Hetzel, Robert. "A Better Way to Fight Inflation." *Wall Street Journal,* April 25, 1991, p. A14.

Hofstadter, Richard. *The American Political Tradition and the Men Who Made It.* New York: Alfred A. Knopf, 1948.

———. "William Jennings Bryan: 'Cross of Gold' Speech, 1896." In *An American Primer,* vol. 2, edited by Daniel Boorstin. Chicago: University of Chicago Press, 1966.

Hoover, Ethel D. "Retail Prices after 1850." In *Trends in the American Economy in the Nineteenth Century.* National Bureau of Economic Research Studies in Income and Wealth, vol. 24. Princeton: Princeton University Press, 1960.

Huang, Andrew Chung. "The Inflation in China." *Quarterly Journal of Economics* 62 (August 1948): 562–75.

Hughes, Jonathan. *American Economic History.* 2d ed. Glenview, Ill.: Scott, Foresman & Co., 1987.

Hume, David. "Of Interest" (1742). In *Essays, Moral, Political and Literary,* vol. 1 of *Essays and Treatises.* A new ed. Edinburgh: Bell & Bradfute, Cadell & Davies, 1804. (a)

———. "Of Money" (1742). In *Essays, Moral, Political and Literary,* vol. 1 of *Essays and Treatises.* A new ed. Edinburgh: Bell & Bradfute, Cadell & Davies, 1804. (b)

Jastram, Roy W. *Silver: The Restless Metal.* New York: John Wiley, 1981.

Jevons, William Stanley. *The Coal Question.* London: Macmillan, 1865.

———. *Money and the Mechanism of Exchange.* London: H. S. King & Co., 1875. 9th ed. London: Kegan Paul, Trench, Trübner & Co., Ltd., 1890.

———. *Investigations in Currency and Finance,* edited by H. S. Foxwell and published posthumously. London: Macmillan, 1884.

Keynes, John Maynard. *The Economic Consequences of the Peace.* New York: Harcourt, Brace & Howe, 1920.

———. *A Tract on Monetary Reform* (1923). In *The Collected Writings of J. M. Keynes,* vol. 4, edited by E. Johnson and D. E. Moggridge. London: Macmillan, 1971.

Kreps, T. J. "The Price of Silver and Chinese Purchasing Power." *Quarterly Journal of Economics* 48 (February 1934): 245–85.

Laughlin, James Laurence. *The History of Bimetallism in the United States.* 1886. 2d ed. New York: D. Appleton & Co., 1895.

Leavens, Dickson H. *Silver Money.* Bloomington, Ind.: Principia Press, 1939.

Lerner, Eugene M. "Inflation in the Confederacy, 1861–65." In *Studies in the Quantity Theory of Money,* edited by Milton Friedman. Chicago: University of Chicago Press, 1956.

Linderman, Henry R. *Money and Legal Tender in the United States.* New York: Putnam's, 1877.

Marshall, Alfred. *Official Papers.* London: Macmillan, 1926.

Martin, David A. "The Impact of Mid-Nineteenth Century Gold Depreciation upon Western Monetary Standards." *Journal of European Economic History* 6 (Winter 1977): 641–58.

Mises, Ludwig von. *The Theory of Money and Credit.* Translated by H. E. Batson. New Haven: Yale University Press, 1953.

National Executive Silver Committee. *Silver in the Fifty-first Congress.* Washington: Gray, 1890.

The New Palgrave: A Dictionary of Economics, vol. 4, edited by John Eatwell, Murray Milgate, and Peter Newman. New York: Stockton Press, and London: Macmillan, 1987. S.v. "Walker, Francis Amasa."

Newcomb, Simon. "Has the Standard Gold Dollar Appreciated?" *Journal of Political Economy* 1 (September 1893): 503–512.

Nicholson, J. Shield. *A Treatise on Money.* Edinburgh and London: W. Blackwood & Sons, 1888. 3d ed. London: Adam and Charles Black, 1895.

Nugent, Walter T. K. *Money and American Society, 1865–1880.* New York: Free Press, 1968.

O'Leary, Paul M. "The Coinage Legislation of 1834." *Journal of Political Economy* 45 (February 1937): 80–94.

———. "The Scene of the Crime of 1873 Revisited: A Note." *Journal of Political Economy* 68 (August 1960): 388–92.

Paris, James D. *Monetary Policies of the United States, 1932–1938.* New York: Columbia University Press, 1938.

Rawski, Thomas G. *Economic Growth in Prewar China.* Berkeley: University of California Press, 1989.

Reagan, John H. In U.S., Congress, Senate, *Congressional Record,* 51st Cong., 1st sess., 1890, 21, pt. 3:2830.

Redish, Angela. "The Evolution of the Gold Standard in England." *Journal of Economic History* 50 (December 1990): 789–805.

Ricardo, David. *The High Price of Bullion.* 4th ed., corrected. London: John Murray, 1811. Reprinted in *The Works and Correspondence of David Ricardo,* vol. 3: *Pamphlets and Papers, 1809–1811,* edited by Piero Sraffa. Cambridge: University Press (for the Royal Economic Society), 1951.

———. *Proposals for an Economical and Secure Currency.* 2d ed. London: John Murray, 1816. Reprinted in *The Works and Correspondence of David Ricardo,* vol. 4: *Pamphlets and Papers, 1815–1823,* edited by Piero Sraffa. Cambridge: University Press (for the Royal Economic Society), 1951.

———. Minutes of Evidence Taken before the Secret Committee on the Expediency of the Bank Resuming Cash Payments, March 4, 1819. (a) Reprinted in *The Works and Correspondence of David Ricardo,* vol. 5: *Speeches and Evidence,* edited by Piero Sraffa. Cambridge: University Press (for the Royal Economic Society), 1952.

———. Minutes of Evidence Taken before the Lords Committee Appointed a Secret Committee to Enquire into the State of the Bank of England, with Reference to the Expediency of the Resumption of Cash Payments at the Period Now Fixed by Law, March 24, 1819. (b) Reprinted in *The Works and Correspondence of David Ricardo,* vol. 5: *Speeches and Evidence,* edited by Piero Sraffa. Cambridge: University Press (for the Royal Economic Society), 1952.

Roccas, Massimo. "International Bimetallism Revisited." Paper presented at the Second Annual Congress of the European Economic Association, Copenhagen, Denmark, August 1987.

Rockoff, Hugh. "The 'Wizard of Oz' as a Monetary Allegory." *Journal of Political Economy* 98 (August 1990): 739–60.

Rolnick, Arthur J., and Weber, Warren E. "Gresham's Law or Gresham's Fallacy?" *Journal of Political Economy* 94 (February 1986): 185–99.

Saint Marc, Michèle. *Histoire Monétaire de la France, 1800–1980.* Paris: Presses Universitaires de France, 1983.

Salter, Sir Arthur. *China and Silver.* New York: Economic Forum Inc., 1934.

Schuettinger, Robert L., and Butler, Eamon F. *Forty Centuries of Wage and Price Controls.* Washington: Heritage Foundation, 1979.

Schumpeter, Joseph A. *History of Economic Analysis,* edited by Elizabeth Boody Schumpeter. New York: Oxford University Press, 1954.

Stewart, William M. "Silver the Money of the People." In *Papers and Addresses before the First National Silver Convention Held at St. Louis, November 26, 27 and 28, 1889,* edited and compiled by E. A. Elliott. St. Louis: Buxton & Skinner Stationery Co., 1889.

T'ang, Leang-Li. *China's New Currency System.* Shanghai: China United Press, 1936.

Timberlake, Richard H., Jr. "Repeal of Silver Monetization in the Late Nineteenth Century." *Journal of Money, Credit, and Banking* 10 (February 1978): 27–45.

U.S. Bureau of the Census. *Historical Statistics of the United States, Colonial Times to 1970.* Bicentennial ed. Washington: Government Printing Office, 1975.

U.S. Commission on the Role of Gold in the Domestic and International Monetary Systems. *Report to the Congress.* Vol. 1. Washington: Government Printing Office, March 1982.

U.S. Secretary of the Treasury. *Annual Report of the State of the Finances for the Fiscal Year Ended June 30, 1899*. Washington: Government Printing Office, 1899.

———. *Annual Report for 1928*. Washington: Government Printing Office, 1928.

Walker, Francis A. "The Free Coinage of Silver." *Journal of Political Economy* 1 (March 1893): 163–78.

———. "Address on International Bimetallism," Schoolmasters' Club of Massachusetts, Boston, November 7, 1896. (a) In *Discussions in Economics and Statistics,* vol. 1, edited by Davis R. Dewey. New York: Holt, 1899.

———. *International Bimetallism*. New York: Holt, 1896. (b)

Walras, Léon. *Elements of Pure Economics*. Translated by William Jaffé. Homewood, Ill.: Irwin, 1954.

Warren, George F., and Pearson, Frank A. *Prices*. New York: Wiley, 1933.

——— and ———. *Gold and Prices*. New York: Wiley, 1935.

White, Andrew Dickson. *Fiat Money and Inflation in France*. New York: Appleton & Co., 1896.

Wignall, Christian. "The Fall of Silver: Part 1. China and the Silver Standard." *Asian Monetary Monitor* 2, no. 4 (July–August 1978): 33–43. (a)

———. "The Fall of Silver: Part 2. The Last Years (1914–1935)." *Asian Monetary Monitor* 2, no. 5 (September–October 1978): 28–39. (b)

Yang, Lien-sheng. *Money and Credit in China*. Cambridge: Harvard University Press, 1952.

Yang, Peixin. *Inflation in Old China* (in Chinese). Beijing: People's Publishing Co., 1985.

Yeh, K. C. "Capital Formation in Mainland China, 1931–1936 and 1952–1957." Ph.D. dissertation. Columbia University, 1964.

Young, Arthur N. *China's Wartime Finance and Inflation, 1937–1945*. Cambridge: Harvard University Press, 1965.

———. *China's Nation-Building Effort, 1927–1937*. Stanford, Calif.: Hoover Institution Press, 1971.